for Dad
Christmas 1990
Joyce.

THE CAPE OF GOOD HOPE

A MARITIME HISTORY

Also by Robin Knox-Johnston

A WORLD OF MY OWN
SAILING
LAST BUT NOT LEAST
THE TWILIGHT OF SAIL
SEAMANSHIP
THE BOC CHALLENGE 1986–87
(with Barry Pickthall)

THE CAPE OF GOOD HOPE

A MARITIME HISTORY

ROBIN
KNOX-JOHNSTON

Hodder & Stoughton

LONDON SYDNEY AUCKLAND TORONTO

British Library Cataloguing in Publication Data

Knox-Johnston, Robin
The Cape of Good Hope: a maritime history.
1. South Africa. Cape Province. Exploration, history
I. Title
916.87'04

ISBN 0-340-41528-2

First published in Great Britain 1989

Published by Hodder and Stoughton, a division of Hodder and Stoughton Ltd, Mill Road, Dunton Green, Sevenoaks, Kent TN13 2YA
Editorial Office: 47 Bedford Square, London WC1B 3DP

Photoset by Rowland Phototypesetting Ltd, Bury St Edmunds, Suffolk
Printed in Great Britain by St Edmundsbury Press Ltd, Bury St Edmunds, Suffolk

Contents

Acknowledgments

Much of the enjoyment that came with writing this book has been due to the immense support and enthusiasm from the many people who have assisted me with the research in Britain, South Africa and the Netherlands. I apologise where I have not used all the information that was passed on to me, but if I had, the book would have been three times as long. Sources in South Africa have been particularly helpful, and in no order of precedence these include Dr B. R. Stuckenberg of the Natal Museum, The South African Transport Services and in particular Captain R. S. Schooling at Cape Town and Captain B. Swemmer at Mossel Bay, the South African Navy Hydrographic Department, Mr P. V. Mills of Clarke's Bookshop in Cape Town, Dr David Smith and Mr Kenneth Payne. Not least of all those who gave time was Professor E. Axelson, who very kindly read through the draft and made a number of useful suggestions based upon his enormous experience of the history of the Cape coast.

In England the staff at the British Library, the Royal Navy Historical Library, the Westminster Library, and the South African Embassy Library, gave me valuable assistance, as did Rear-Admiral R. Morris and the Hydrographic Department of the Royal Navy at Taunton who allowed me to peruse their fascinating collection of original charts of the area. Miss June Foster of the British and Commonwealth Company was most trusting with the history of the company. Margaret Body and Claire Trocmé at Hodder and Stoughton encouraged me throughout the two years spent researching and writing.

My grateful thanks are also due to Rear-Admiral F. J. Haver Droeze and Captain Quare of the Royal Netherlands Navy, who helped me with translations and definitions, and to the Amsterdam Museum.

To all these, and my wife, who helped to type and correct the draft, I proffer my apologies for being such a persistent nuisance, and my grateful thanks for their interest and encouragement.

Maps and Line Drawings

CREDITS

1 The Cape Archives

2 Crown copyright. Reproduced from Admiralty charts with the permission of HM Stationery Office.

Illustrations

Credits

1 The Cape Archives
2 The Cape *Argus*
3 Rex Reynolds
4 National Maritime Museum, Greenwich
5 Africana Museum, Johannesburg
6 Science Museum, London
7 Robin Knox-Johnston

Part I

1

Introduction

Watching the waves of the Southern Ocean beat against the hard, impassive rocks at Cape Point, it is hard not to believe that these rocks have withstood the ceaseless onslaught for ever. In terms of human lifespans they have, but when measured against the Earth's five billion years, the sea and the Cape are new neighbours. Only 200 million years ago Africa, South America, India, Antarctica and Australia were all part of one enormous land mass called Gondwanaland. Then the lithospheric plates, on which this mass floated on the liquid centre of the Earth, started to move apart. One hundred and thirty million years ago a split began to appear between what we now know as southern Africa and southern America, which slowly spread up the continent until by 100 million years ago the Atlantic ocean separated them completely. At the same time, Antarctica commenced its southward movement, Australia began to move east, India shifted north-east and Africa appeared in very much the shape we are familiar with today.

At the time Gondwanaland began to break apart, life consisted of small mammals and large reptiles, the prehistoric monsters, who would have been as unaware of the enormous continental movements going on about them as we are today, when no one notices that Europe and North America are drifting apart by five centimetres a year. Species died out, and new ones evolved in their place. The fossils of one such species, *Mesosaurus tumidus*, are only found in identical Permian rock formations in Brazil and southern Africa, which match exactly if the two continents are swivelled together.

As the sea swirled into the gap between Africa and America, huge submarine plateaux formed, between two and three miles deep, which should have extended evenly between the diverging continents. But as the tectonic plates moved apart, the Earth's crust beneath the sea was stretched and weakened until it cracked. Molten rock from the Earth's centre found these cracks and other weak points, and poured through. The first outpourings occurred off Africa's south-east coast about 115 million years ago. The quantity was sufficient to create a continent the size of Argentina, which drifted slowly to a point midway between South Africa and

Australia. This continent once supported forests and dinosaurs before it sank beneath the waves. All that remains of it is a large underwater plateau half a mile deep, apart from a few surviving high points, the most obvious being the French-owned Kerguelen Islands after which the plateau is named. Lava poured out into the Atlantic basin about seventy million years ago, and thirty-five million years later southern Africa was surrounded by a submarine ridge of mountains, varying in height, between 500 and 1,200 miles from its coast.

Elsewhere, isolated mounts mark the sites of other crust weaknesses, and many of these are still growing today. Sea mounts, large underwater mountains that stand on the ocean floor between Africa and Antarctica, South America and Australia, are underwater volcanoes, many of which are active. Some have already broken through to the surface, creating small, desolate islands, whose peaks, whilst only a few hundred feet above the surface of the sea, tower 20,000 feet from the ocean plateau of the seabed. The nearest islands to the Cape are the Prince Edward and Marion islands, twin extinct volcanoes, which lie over 1,000 miles south-east of Cape Town. The most recent lava on these islands flowed about 15,000 years ago, but the main mass of the islands appears to be about 300,000 years old. Three other islands, or small groups, are slightly further from the Cape. Bouvetøya is some 1,400 miles south-south-west, Gough Island about 1,400 miles to the south-west, and Tristan da Cunha a little over 1,500 miles just south of west. On all these islands, the volcanoes were considered extinct, but quite recently that on Tristan da Cunha erupted unexpectedly, causing the small population to be evacuated for a number of years.

The exact number of volcanic seamounts in the vicinity is still uncertain, although recent improvements in surveying techniques have probably identified most. Apart from the small population on Tristan da Cunha, and research parties on some of the other islands, this whole vast area of ocean is visited only by the occasional research ship and yachts, and so evidence of underwater volcanic activity is not likely to be noticed. The lava pouring from active underwater volcanoes hardens quickly, helping to increase the size of the seamount, and hasten its progress towards the surface. The soundings over some have noticeably decreased since the earliest surveys, and although they may not appear in our lifetimes, new islands in the southern Atlantic and Southern Ocean are on their way.

The only other major change to the coastline of southern Africa occurred during the last Ice Age, between 20,000 and 25,000 years ago, when so much water was stored in the enormous ice caps at the two poles that the sea level fell by as much as 300 feet. This exposed a large area, particularly on the Agulhas Bank, of what is now a part of the continental shelf. During this period, the Agulhas Bank was a coastal plain covered with grasslands. Deposits in caves near Plettenberg left by the early human inhabitants, a type that was replaced by the yellowish-brown-skinned, small-statured Bushmen or San people, about 12,000 years ago, have indicated the change in diet from meat to fish and shell fish that occurred as the ice melted and the water level rose again.

The Hottentots or Khoikhoi, who followed the Bushmen, were herders rather than hunter gatherers, and they confined their maritime interests to obtaining fish and shell fish on the littoral. The Bantu-speaking peoples started to arrive in southern Africa from the north at about the time of Christ, and reached the Transkei shortly afterwards. They had a more settled society, and grew most of their food. Their lifestyle and skills were little different from those of the people in many parts of Europe at the time, and they were making iron in the Transvaal by about AD 250. However, whilst the Europeans in coastal areas were already undertaking quite long voyages by sea, the people of southern Africa were content to limit themselves to the land, and conditions for the development of a sea-going trade did not exist. The agricultural economy was able to sustain itself by barter between villages, so there was no need for trade with areas further afield. The protected water with access to the sea necessary for men to develop boats only existed in Delagoa Bay and possibly Natal Bay. Also in the south the rivers are fairly swift running, and their entrances frequently made dangerous from the swell.

The south coast is exposed to the largest stretch of unbroken water on earth, the Southern Ocean, which extends unbroken around the world between America, Africa and Australia and the ice-covered continent of Antarctica. Nowhere else does the sea roll uninterrupted around the world, nor the winds have such a range free of obstacles. No one can state with certainty how long the existing wind and weather patterns have existed. A series of oceanic high pressure systems are to be found around the world at roughly the latitude of the Cape, and the wind circulates in an anti-clockwise direction around them. On the eastern seaboard this pattern creates a north to easterly prevailing wind, whilst on the west coast the wind is largely south-easterly. To the south is the largest westerly wind formation in the world between roughly 35 and 55° southerly latitude, the zone known as the Roaring Forties. The movement of this huge mass of air is disturbed physically only by the southern extremity of South America, and meteorologically by a series of depressions. In the southern hemispheric summer, between September and March, the wind belt moves south, forcing the depressions further from the Cape and giving more moderate winds, but in winter they can sweep right across the whole Cape area, bringing wind strengths far greater than are found at a similar latitude in the northern hemisphere.

The most noticeable effect of this band of westerly winds in the Southern

Ocean is to be seen on the current and waves. The flow of air across the surface of the ocean starts to drive the surface water in the same direction and where there is no wind from the opposite direction to counter this movement, the current becomes continuous, constantly powered by the westerly winds. Waves, which are created initially by small disturbances in the surface waters, develop with the strength and consistency of the wind. In an area where the wind largely flows in the same direction, as in the Southern Ocean, the frequency of the wave-generating winds is such that the waves almost never dissipate completely, and there is always a long, low swell moving eastwards. Although high winds can be frightening, they possess only a fraction of the power of a wave, which can develop pressures in excess of one ton per square foot. The wind, on the other hand, even in extreme conditions, rarely exceeds fifteen pounds pressure on a square foot of surface. When a new gale or storm arrives in an area of ocean which already has a large swell, the swell and new wind-generated wave can combine to create a very large wave, extending well over a mile in length, and achieving a vertical frontal face just before it breaks. Whilst a wave of forty feet is considered very large in the north Atlantic, sizes of sixty feet are found in the Southern Ocean, and on very rare occasions there have been freak waves of a considerably greater height.

Waves of this magnitude are usually found only deep in the Southern Ocean, but a unique coincidence has caused them to appear quite close to the south-east coast of the Cape. Only recently have the studies of J. K. Mallory produced modern confirmation of the origin of the old sailor's fear of the Cape and highlighted its dangers. Its probable cause is a classic example of the wind-against-tide effect known to any sailor who is used to operating in a tidal river but on a gigantic scale. Where the wind and tide are running in the same direction, the waves tend to be longer and lower, but where the wind is running in the opposite direction to the tide, the waves are slightly checked and become higher and steeper.

Running south-westwards along the south-east coast of Africa is the Agulhas Current, which originates from the southern equatorial current of the Indian Ocean. As this current sweeps anti-clockwise around the ocean south of the equator, it is divided by Madagascar, so that two streams are formed, one between the island and the African mainland, and the other to the east of the island. South of Madagascar, about the same latitude as Durnford Point, the two streams are joined into one, which flows south-westwards as far as the Agulhas Bank, where it swings round in a great arc and joins the Southern Ocean current. It flows at great strength, between four and five knots, parallel to the coast from Durnford Point as far as Cape Recife. Since the continental shelf in this area is very narrow, and slopes down to 1,000 fathoms quite steeply, the strongest part of the current is just outside the continental shelf, but close to the coast.

An interesting drawing showing the fate of Pedro Cabral's fleet on the way to the East in 1500. Bartolomeu Dias's vessel appears at the bottom right hand.

The replica caravel which sailed to the Cape in 1988, to celebrate Bartolomeu Dias's voyage in 1488.

Jan van Riebeeck, the founder of the Cape station for the Dutch East India Company (left).

The replica of Bartolomeu Dias's furthest *padrão* at Kwaaihoek, 8 km west of the mouth of the Bushman's River (right).

Recent research has shown that when a depression with a centre of lower than average pressure develops between 900 and 1,200 miles to the south-west of the Cape, and then moves in onto the south-east coast, it will bring very strong south-westerly winds over the Agulhas Current, creating the conditions for an abnormally large wave. This wave is built up from a combination of the large swell waves developed hundreds of miles away in the Southern Ocean, the waves generated locally by the gale to storm force winds in the depression, and the steepness added because there is a strong current carrying the surface water in the opposite direction. The waves have different lengths and heights, the locally created ones being the smaller, but just occasionally the two wave crests are in conjunction. When this occurs a giant wave is formed which will last until they move out of conjunction again. A notable feature of these giant waves is an extremely long and low trough that develops immediately in front of the wave crest.

A wave reaches its theoretical maximum height and length if it has a fetch, or clear stretch of water, of about 1,200 miles. In the case of a wave generated as far away as possible downwind in the Southern Ocean, this distance is reached about level with Port Elizabeth. From here northwards along the coast, an abnormal wave can be created whilst the winds and current are strong, and in practice this means to a point somewhere north of Durnford Point, and it is in this area that these waves have been encountered.

The strength of the waves can be imagined when considering the case of the 14,600-ton cargo ship *Bencruachan*, which was proceeding southwards about fifty miles off the coast in typical abnormal wave conditions in May 1973. The bow of the ship fell into the trough, and then the wave broke over the forward part of the ship, bending the whole bow section downwards. The ship was lucky to survive and limped into Durban for major repairs. Other ships were less fortunate. In June 1968 the tanker *World Glory* of 46,400 tons split in two to the north of Durban in similar conditions. An even larger ship, the 258,000-ton and 1,109-feet-long *Svealand* on her maiden voyage in September 1973, ran into another huge wave. The master reported that whilst just outside the 100-fathom line in the vicinity of East London, and proceeding south at about three knots, a long deep trough appeared ahead of the ship. The bow plunged into the trough, and before it could rise, the wave came over and crashed down onto the first two hatches. The bow section was set down about two feet, the hatches smashed open, and two of the crew were injured. It was a miracle that the ship did not sink. The *Neptune Sapphire* of 15,501 tons had lost 200 feet off her bow through the same cause a month before off Port St. Johns. Although all these ships were on a south-westerly course, the wave can also affect a ship steering north-east, as the liner *Southern Cross* discovered in October 1969.

The significant factor is that everyone who has experienced the abnormal wave has been outside the 100-fathom line where the Agulhas Current runs strongly. Ships that keep between this line and the coast, where it is almost non-existent (there is even a north-east running counter-current), have not met the wave, even though they have been in similar weather patterns. The wave is a freak, since it only occurs in certain conditions, and these conditions are not repeated anywhere else in the world. Its identification and the discovery of its probable cause have been of inestimable benefit to all sailors using this area, but we shall probably never know how many ships it was responsible for destroying in the past.

2

Discovery

Probably the earliest maritime visit to the Cape of Good Hope occurred more than 2,500 years ago. Herodotus, the Greek historian, in his records compiled during the fifth century BC, writes of a Phoenician expedition that it was claimed had circumnavigated Africa. Since much of the information gleaned by Herodotus was by word of mouth, he is not always accurate, either in his facts or in his comments. It is, however, his rather dismissive remarks in this particular story which give it its credibility.

> But Libya [the name given to the whole of Africa at that time] is on this second promontory, for Libya comes next to Egypt. The Egyptian part of this promontory is narrow; far from our sea to the Red Sea it is a distance of an hundred thousand fathoms, that is, a thousand furlongs; but after this narrow part the promontory that is called Libya is very broad.
>
> I wonder then, at those who have mapped out and divided the world into Libya, Asia and Europe; for the difference between them is great, seeing that in length Europe stretches along both the others together, and it appears to me to be beyond all comparison broader. For Libya shows clearly that it is encompassed by the sea, save only where it borders on Asia: and this was proved first, as far as we know, by Necho II, King of Egypt. He, when he had made an end of digging the canal which leads from the Nile to the Arabian Gulf [Red Sea] sent Phoenicians in ships, charging them to sail on their return voyage past the Pillars of Heracles, till they should come into the northern sea and so to Egypt. So the Phoenicians set out from the Red Sea and sailed the southern sea; whenever Autumn came they would put in and sow the land, to whatever part of Libya they might come, and there await the harvest, then, having gathered the crop, they sailed on, so that after two years had passed, it was in the third that they rounded the Pillars of Heracles and came to Egypt. There they said what some may believe, though I do not, that in sailing round Libya they had the sun on their right hand.

To Herodotus, who lived all his life in the Mediterranean area in the northern hemisphere, the idea that by sailing around Africa the sun would always be on the right hand side of the boat, seemed to prove that the story was fiction. He was unable to visualise that in a spherical world, as a boat sailed south, the sun would slowly rise higher in the sky until, as the boat passed beneath the sun, its bearing would become northerly. Whenever Herodotus saw the sun, it was bearing south of him. But of course, today we know that if a boat left the Red Sea and sailed clockwise around Africa, the sun would have to be on the right hand side during the day when sailing around the southern part of Africa from east to west, and this one fact makes the whole story credible.

Necho II ruled Egypt from 609 to 594 BC. After his attempts to re-establish an Asian Empire had been thwarted by the Emperor Nebuchadrezzar at the battle of Carchemish in 605 BC, he turned his attention to making Egypt a great trading power. One of his difficulties was that Egypt had two coasts, divided by the isthmus of Suez, which forced him to keep two separate fleets, one in the Mediterranean, and the other in the Red Sea. When faced with maritime threat, he could not combine his fleets. A further disadvantage was that trade between the two seas had to be offloaded on one coast, and carried across the land by camel train and reloaded aboard ships on the other side. To attempt to solve this problem, his first move was to try and connect the Mediterranean and Red seas by digging a canal between the Nile and the northern end of the Red Sea through the Wadi Tumilat. This enormous civil engineering project, using no machinery, and dependent solely upon the muscle power of slaves and captives, was tackled with the confidence that the Egyptians had always shown in their building works. It proved too ambitious for its time, however, and after some 120,000 labourers had died, Necho was forced to accept that the Egyptian Empire could not provide sufficient manpower for a work of this magnitude. It is equally possible that Necho was persuaded to stop the work because of an augury that the canal would only benefit the Barbarians, as the threat from Mesopotamia was very real at the time.

Necho was obviously a determined and imaginative king, because he next turned to trying to discover whether there was a route around Africa that might provide an acceptable alternative to his abandoned canal. To undertake this exploratory voyage, he quite naturally looked to the Phoenicians.

The use of the Phoenicians by an Egyptian king in the year 601 BC is totally believable. The Phoenicians were the most experienced and boldest navigators, and greatest explorers of ancient times. They had built up a merchant empire based entirely on the sea, which, at its height, had over forty trading factories spread throughout the known world, with one of the most famous being Carthage. Their knowledge of the sea was unrivalled.

Their ships travelled regularly as far as Britain for tin, and there is evidence that they went to the Canary Islands in the Atlantic, and the mouth of the Indus in India on trading expeditions. There had been for some centuries a routine trade with the land of Punt, modern Somalia, and it is easy to imagine that they might well have advanced further south down the coast of Africa in search of commerce.

As the sea trade in the Mediterranean Sea was almost totally in their hands, no ruler at that time could contemplate a war which required shipping, without first coming to an arrangement with the Phoenicians, who had the ships and the expertise. Their interest was entirely mercenary, they fought on land only to protect their homeland, in what is now the Lebanon. Furthermore they had for centuries been a subservient ally to the Egyptian kings.

Unfortunately, no details survive of the voyage around Africa, nor how many ships and men were involved. The Phoenicians probably stayed close inshore all the way using their decked double-ender trading ships of fifty to eighty feet in length rather than galleys. As these ships depended upon a large and simple square sail for their main propulsion, which limited them to sailing well off the wind, they were equipped with oars, and the whole crew would row in calm or contrary wind conditions, apart from the helmsman who steered by means of an oar over the stern, a system of steering still in use for emergencies today. The slow progress they made was because of their habit of pulling into the shore each evening to camp rather than chance sailing on during the dark and risk running into unseen dangers. If they camped in the Cape area, the only people they would have been likely to encounter were the Strandlopers, people who lived by scavenging along the sea shore, or possibly the Bushmen, who passed down no verbal records of any encounter. Some beads found near Port St. Johns have been attributed to the Phoenicians, but these could easily have been brought there by land, or by later explorers.

In the nineteenth century, there were rumours of the remains of a Phoenician ship being found just above the Cape Flats near Tygerberg. The reports started after an attempt by the British to find coal in the area in 1797, and their boring rods brought up lignite with iron pyrites. The story spread slowly that this was the remnant of a Phoenician ship, and the site was investigated again in 1852 by Charles Bell, the Surveyor General of the Cape Colony. His initial report to the Governor was very positive, and he gave it as his opinion that what he had found was the remains of a seventy-foot-long open vessel which had been wrecked centuries before when the sea level in the area was higher. He found the fragments embedded in clay on the bank of the Elsjieskraal River. Locals claimed they had used parts of the boat for firewood, and that they had found traces of iron bolts in the timber. Bell managed to obtain a grant of money to undertake further excavations, but no account exists of the result, and, unfortunately, none of the supposed timbers survived. About five years later a mining engineer, Andrew Bains, was asked to inspect the wreck, and he definitely identified the wood he examined as a part of a bed of lignite.

Another legend surrounds the remains of an ancient ship, thought to be a Phoenician, which is said to appear occasionally in the sand dunes inland from Sandwich Harbour, about twenty-seven miles south of Walvis Bay on the south-west African coast. The whole coast in this vicinity is a long range of sand hills which are shifting continually, and the harbour itself has closed completely since it was surveyed in 1880. The supporters of the Phoenician wreck theory suggest that the boat could have landed on what was the beach in those times, since the beach has moved considerably seaward in the intervening years.

Unless further evidence is uncovered, it is impossible to show actual proof of a Phoenician visit to the Cape area, but the account by Herodotus is compelling and does suggest that the Phoenicians did circumnavigate Africa and, as such, were the first sailors to visit the Cape.

One hundred and forty years after the Phoenician voyage around the Cape, Hanno, a Carthaginian, sailed from the Mediterranean and down the west African coast on what appears to have been a colonising voyage. This voyage is recorded in remnants of Hanno's logs which he deposited in the Temple to Saturn on his return. He is said to have taken a fleet of fifty to sixty ships, with fifty oars each, and 30,000 men and women. Trading cities were established along the coast, mostly north of Cape Bojador, but one further south at a place named Cerne (Arguin). Hanno's explorations went as far as what he called the 'Southern Horn' of Africa, which was most probably in Sierra Leone. There is no evidence of the voyage reaching the Cape; they turned back when they came to a 'country of fire', which has been explained subsequently by the custom of the inhabitants of central west Africa burning their grass each year. However, it is obvious from the confidence with which the Carthaginians established towns, not only on the coast but in Madeira and the Canary Islands, that they had some knowledge of these parts already and were aware of the existence of potentially profitable trading conditions. Like the canny traders they were, the Phoenicians would have tried to keep any information that would benefit their trade to themselves, and this secrecy has deprived us of knowing for sure the full extent of their explorations.

Although Herodotus does not believe the story of the Phoenician circumnavigation, he does recount the story of another expedition which attempted the same voyage. Also in the fifth century BC, a nobleman called Satespes, who had been sentenced to death by Xerxes, was told that he could earn a reprieve if he took a boat and sailed around the continent of Africa. He departed from the Mediterranean, and travelled down the west

African coast, but lost heart when in 'a country of little men, who wore palm leaf raiment'. On his return home, Satespes naturally reported his trip in glowing terms, and told of how his boat had been restrained from going further by supernatural forces. His account was no doubt embellished in an attempt to gain favour and win his pardon. It was to no avail: Xerxes was obviously unconvinced by his tale, and had him put to death anyway. Quite how far Satespes sailed is difficult to establish. The little men could have been Bushmen, in which case Satespes possibly reached the Cape, but we shall never know.

Pliny records a man named Eudoxus, who made a voyage to India from Egypt on the orders of Ptolemy VII, some time between 170 and 160 BC. During his return he was driven southwards by adverse winds along the coast of east Africa, where he landed and traded with the natives for food. On the beach he discovered a portion of the prow of a ship in the shape of a horse which he took home. Egyptian pilots recognised it as having come from a ship that had sailed from Gades (Cadiz in Spain), down the west African coast beyond the river Lixus (Al Arish in Morocco) and not come back. Strabo, the Greek geographer writing just before Christ, poured scorn on this story, but since his books on geography were largely written in the library at Alexandria, his criticism must be treated as theoretical rather than practical. This unknown Spaniard may have been the first sailor to round the Cape from west to east.

Apart from the Bushmen and Hottentots, the Cape was left to itself after the Phoenician visit until the early part of the Christian period. Probably the next people to explore this far south by sea were the Arabs. By the first century AD they had progressed down the African east coast as far as Rhapta, near Dar-es-Salaam in Tanzania, and they were certainly at Sofala, near Beira in Mozambique, by the eighth century. Evidence is now appearing of trade between the Bantu people in the vicinity of the Mzimkulu River, about 120 miles south of Durban, and coastal traders from the north during the fourth century AD, and if they had advanced this far, it is not stretching the imagination to assume that they would have advanced further southwards.

Writing in AD 1000, the Arab geographer Al Biruni says, 'But this [land] does not prevent the Southern Sea [South Indian Ocean] from communicating with the Ocean [South Atlantic] through a gap in the mountains along the south coast of Africa. One has certain proofs of this communication although no one has been able to confirm it by sight.' An Arab chart produced about 1154 shows Africa coming to a point south of Sofala, and there are symbols for mountains just about where the Drakensberg is situated. This chart even names the local people in the south as the 'Wak-Waks', a description that would fit the Bushmen in view of their clicking language. Bushmen paintings of ships exist in caves in the south-west Cape, but whether these refer to the Arabs or later visitors remains to be shown. All this data points strongly to the Arabs having reached the Cape, and certainly they had the experience and expertise to make journeys of this length. There is even an Arab legend about islands beyond the Cape in the Atlantic. But they made no settlements of a permanent nature south of Sofala; presumably there was no trade worth pursuing.

The Arabs' knowledge of the Cape probably forms the basis of information for the charts of the Genoese cartographer Petrus Vesconte in about 1320. Another chart produced by Fra Mauro in 1457 clearly shows a channel between the Atlantic and the Indian Oceans through southern Africa as described by Al Biruni, which tends to support the theory that the Europeans had, by that time, access to the Arabs' charts.

A second group of sailors who could well have reached the Cape were the Javanese, from modern Indonesia. These Javanese people were from the same stock that had started to explore and colonise the Polynesian Islands of the Pacific from about 600 BC. They colonised Madagascar during the early centuries after Christ, and had trading ties with the African coast as far north as modern Kenya, where they are thought to have introduced the Asian banana. Since they sailed along a large part of the east African coastline, it is reasonable to suppose that they would have explored the southern African coast. No evidence has been found as yet, but there is a theory that the spread of non-African food crops to the western coast could have been due to them, in which case they must have sailed around the Cape of Good Hope, perhaps in the fourth or fifth century AD.

The Chinese, however, possess records which would indicate that they guessed the existence of a sea connection to another ocean south of Africa, even if they did not sail it themselves. The Chinese had regular trading ties with India from quite early on, and there are some slight indications that they may have sailed as far as the west coast of America. The Chinese junk is a remarkably seaworthy vessel, and quite capable of sailing in very boisterous conditions, so that long-distance voyages were well within its capabilities. Coins, dating from the time of the T'ang Emperors (AD 618–907) have been found in east Africa, which may not prove that the Chinese themselves had reached those shores, but does demonstrate that they were in regular contact with people who did trade there. On their annual voyages to India the Chinese would have met the Arabs who had been sailing those waters from before the time of Mohammed, and have learned of the country and trade further to the west. By the eleventh century the Chinese had definitely sailed to Africa and Sung period coins (AD 960–1279) have been found there. The people of Malindi even sent a giraffe to the Emperor of China at the beginning of the fifteenth century. Apparently it arrived alive, despite the difficulties that must have been experienced in transporting such a tall animal in a ship of those times.

The Europeans may have found the route in 1291 when two Genoese brothers set out for the Indies around Africa. There are no details of the craft used by the Vivaldis and the last report puts them at Cape Nun in Morocco on their way down the west African coast. There was no further news from them, so whether they did reach India or died on the way will never be known. Another Italian, Marco Polo, who returned to Europe by sea, sailed with a Chinese fleet to Hormuz at the entrance to the Persian Gulf in 1292. During this two-year voyage he had an opportunity to talk to the sailors and has left a report of what reliable sources told him of the seas and islands on the southern coast of Africa.

> You must know that this island [Madagascar] lies so far to the south that ships cannot go further south or visit other Islands in that direction, except this one, and that other of which we have to tell you, called Zanghibar [Zanzibar]. This is because the sea current runs so strong towards the south that the ships which should attempt it never would get back again.

The sea current running strongly to the south is an obvious reference to the Mozambique Current which continues south to become the Agulhas Current. He goes on to report that on islands further to the south is found an enormous bird, known locally as the ruc, capable of lifting an elephant into the air. The Emperor of China had received a ruc's feather as a gift, which measured ninety hand spans in length! Except that the bird was said to resemble an eagle, it might well have been the dodo or the extinct giant ostrich of Madagascar, but the tale had probably become well exaggerated by the time Marco Polo came to hear it.

The earliest Chinese chart was produced by Chu Ssu-pen in about 1320, and copied in the sixteenth century. A later chart, made about AD 1400 by Ch'uan Chin shows the shape of southern Africa fairly accurately, with mountains and rivers roughly where they are known to lie. It marks a river flowing westwards at about the position of the Orange River, which demonstrates that someone had a detailed knowledge of what lay to the west of the Cape at that time; whether it was the Chinese or Arabs or both, and if they arrived by sea or by land is not known. Another Chinese chart, produced in the sixteenth century, almost confirms the connection with the Arabs as it refers to the people of the Congo as the Sang-Ku, which is very close to the Arabic 'Zangue', meaning 'black people'. There is another similarity with the Arabs who referred to the Drakensberg Mountains as Jebal Ma, Jebal being the Arabic for a mountain. On the Chinese chart the same mountains are called the Che-pu Lu Ma, and Che-pu Lu could be taken to be a phonetic version of Jebal.

For a time there was a delightful theory that the yellow colour and slanted eyes of the Bushmen were due to a Chinese expedition that was blown off course and rounded the Cape before being wrecked somewhere on the south-west coast. One of their ships may well have been lost at the Cape, but no evidence has ever been found, and the Bushmen were in the area many centuries before the Chinese could have arrived by sea.

The arrival of the Portuguese, about sixty years after the last presumed voyage by the Arabs, marks the real beginning of the modern era, since their voyages led to the use of the Cape as a route, and not an obstacle to explore beyond. The rise of the Portuguese as a maritime nation owes as much to the Moors as it does to Portugal's position on Europe's west coast. The Portuguese had expelled the Moors from their country by 1249, but had continued to fight them in Spain and in north Africa. These wars had gained for Portugal Ceuta and, later, Tangier, both important trading stations for north Africa, providing regular communication with the countries to the south and west of the Sahara desert, via the camel trains from Timbuktu. These contacts gave the Portuguese valuable knowledge of the intricate trans-Saharian camel routes, and, in particular, the lucrative trade in gold dust from the upper reaches of the Senegal, Niger and Volta Rivers, in what was then the large and powerful African state of Ghana. It was in an attempt to intercept this trade, which would strike a blow for Christianity against the Moorish heathens and, of course, enrich their own country, that the Portuguese started to sail down the African west coast at the beginning of the fifteenth century, and establish trading forts.

It was a fortunate coincidence that at the same time the country produced a patron who could provide royal sponsorship and the inspiration for navigation and voyages of exploration. Prince Henry, known as the Navigator, was born in 1394, the third son of King John I, and his English queen, Philippa, daughter of John of Gaunt, Duke of Lancaster. His early life was spent as a soldier fighting against the Moors, but his interest in geography led him to invite foreign mathematicians to Portugal to instruct sailors in navigation and astronomy. He built a naval base at Sagres, at Cape St. Vincent, where he frequently resided after 1438.

Prince Henry studied the world as far as it was known, and its trade, surrounded by experts, many of whom he had attracted by granting them sanctuary, when they had been expelled from other countries. A particular example, the Jewish cartographer Jehuda Cresques, son of Cresques le Juif, or Abraham Cresques, was the man responsible for the Catalan Atlas of the known world in 1375. He was exiled from Aragon when that country's attitude towards Jews turned from toleration to persecution. He would have known that the Arabs had a well-established trade in and around the Indian Ocean, and thus controlled the movement of spices from the Indies to Arabia. In order to participate it was necessary for Portugal to find a sea

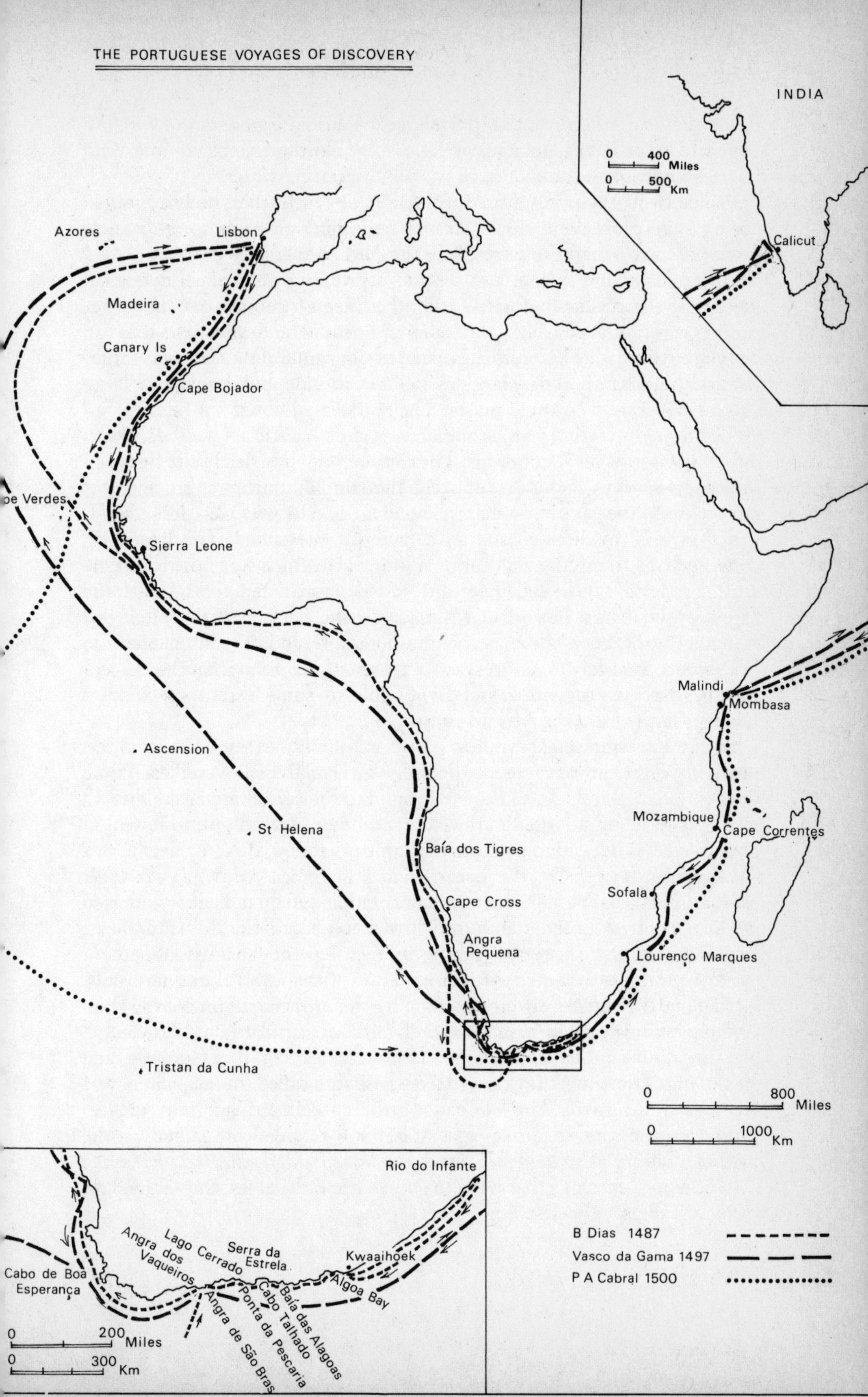
THE PORTUGUESE VOYAGES OF DISCOVERY
INDIA
0 400 Miles
0 500 Km
Calicut
Azores
Lisbon
Madeira
Canary Is
Cape Bojador
pe Verdes
Sierra Leone
Ascension
St Helena
Malindi
Mombasa
Mozambique
Cape Correntes
Baía dos Tigres
Sofala
Cape Cross
Angra Pequena
Lourenço Marques
Tristan da Cunha
0 800 Miles
0 1000 Km
Rio do Infante
Lago Cerrado
Angra dos Vaqueiros
Serra da Estrela
Kwaaihoek
Cabo de Boa Esperança
Algoa Bay
Baía das Alagoas
Cabo Talhado
Ponta da Pescaria
Angra de São Bras
0 200 Miles
0 300 Km
B Dias 1487
Vasco da Gama 1497
P A Cabral 1500

route from the Atlantic to the Indian Ocean. With this vision, and with the support Prince Henry gave to his sailors, the Portuguese began to extend their explorations southwards, down the African coast.

Prince Henry not only urged his sailors to sail further, he encouraged them to develop their ships. At the beginning of their long-distance voyages, the Portuguese were using the *barca*, a small vessel, not unlike a Viking galley, and in many ways more primitive than the Phoenician galleys of 2,000 years before. During the fifteenth century AD, the larger caravel was developed along very similar lines to the Arab dhows that can be seen to this day. The usual European trading craft of the time was rather cumbersome, hampered by large castles fore and aft, and rigged with large square sails on up to three masts. The square sail could not be trimmed efficiently to the wind, which meant that any voyage to windward was difficult, lengthy, and dangerous. The caravel, which varied in size between fifty and 100 tons, had a curved stem and simple transom stern, and was built without the castles, so that the windage and leeway were lessened. It had from one to three masts, all carrying a lateen sail. The lateen rig consisted of a triangular sail, set on a long yard which was hoisted up the mast in order to set the sail. The yard extended fore and aft of the mast, the forward end being hauled down close to the deck, and the after end extended well above the mast height. This fore and aft sail enabled the Portuguese caravels to sail relatively closer to the wind than the current European square-rigged vessels, and thus to some extent speed their voyages home from the African coast.

As the Portuguese exploration advanced, the lateen rig was found too unwieldy on ocean voyages, as the long yard had to be lowered each time the boat wished to tack, and carried round to the other side of the mast, a task that required a large fit crew. On a modern Arab dhow a crew of at least twenty is needed to perform the same operation. As a replacement, a square sail was rigged on the fore mast, and the rig was known as a *caravela redonda*. This was the type of craft mainly employed by the 1480s and used by Dias, but he found it had too low a freeboard for the Cape seas. Experience with the lateen sail on the *caravelas redondas* had no doubt taught the Portuguese seamen how to improve the efficiency of the square sails, by hauling the square yard round more to the fore and aft line of the ship, and improving its performance to windward. As a result of this knowledge, and no doubt influenced by the large carracks of the Genoese and Venetians of the time, they developed a new ship called the *nao*, which was larger than a caravel. The *nao* had a greater freeboard, and was square-rigged on the fore and main masts, but still retained the lateen on the mizzen. This was the vessel used by Vasco da Gama, and was the forerunner of the ships that were to stay in use right to the end of the days of sailing ships.

In 1419 the southern limit of the Portuguese voyages was Cape Bojador. The north-east trade winds made the journey south a relatively simple one, but the passage home, which required a long battle against head winds, was far more difficult and entailed a lengthy tack out into the Atlantic. It was on one of these return voyages that Madeira was rediscovered in 1419. These islands, known to Pliny as the Purple Isles, and explored by the Phoenicians and Genoese seafarers, had disappeared from the charts. Prince Henry sent colonists to the islands almost immediately, and imported grapes from Cyprus to start wine cultivation. The significance of this colonisation lies in the confidence of the Portuguese sailors in their navigation. By 1419 they already felt capable of being able to find a small group of islands in the middle of the wastes of the Atlantic.

In each of the following years, until 1434, Prince Henry sent expeditions south to attempt to round Cape Bojador. We do not know if Henry was aware of the Herodotus account of the Phoenician or Hanno's voyage, but it is quite likely, and one can imagine his frustration when each year his captains returned having failed. Perhaps it was the currents around the Cape, or the fog, or a growing knowledge of the Atlantic weather systems which discouraged them. The sailors knew that the further south they went with the north-east trade winds behind them, the longer and harder their return voyage would be against these same winds. Finally, however, in 1434 an expedition under Captain Gil Eannes passed the Cape and psychologically unlocked the route to the south. Even then progress was not rapid, only some 1,500 miles of coast, down as far as Sierra Leone, being explored and opened up for trading when Prince Henry died in 1460. During this period, however, the Azores were discovered (1420s–1450s) and the Cape Verde Islands (1456) and both were colonised. The Prince also made strenuous and unsuccessful efforts to wrest the Canary Islands from the Spanish.

He was responsible for training a whole generation of Portuguese seafarers, and making them into Europe's foremost navigators. The country's eyes had been turned firmly towards the sea, to the trade on the west coast of Africa, and the search for a route to the Indies. Shortly before his death, a further impetus had been given to this search by the fall of Constantinople to the Muslims in 1453, which both threatened Christian Europe and greatly restricted the flow of spices.

The lucrative monopoly of bringing spice from Arabia to Europe had been in the hands of the Venetians. These spices, such as pepper, nutmeg, cinnamon and cloves, were essential ingredients for improving the flavour of the rather poor quality meat, and were brought by sea from India and south-east Asia to Arabia, and then overland by camel train to the Mediterranean, and in particular to Constantinople. There they were collected by the Venetian merchants and transhipped to Europe. Because it was a monopoly, enormous profits were made and it was on these that the greatness of Venice was built. The fall of Constantinople gave complete control of the trade to the Arabs, and supplies were much reduced. Inevitably the prices rose in Europe because the demand remained and any nation that could find an alternative route to the spice islands was guaranteed riches. This acted as a spur to both of the leading Atlantic maritime powers, Portugal and Spain. The Portuguese continued their search via Africa, and the Spanish tried an alternative by sailing west and discovered America by accident on the way.

An extra incentive for a Christian monarch to find another access to the East was to try and locate Prester John. A huge mythology had arisen around this legendary Christian leader, who may, in fact, have been king of a small Tartar tribe destroyed by Genghis Khan, but was variously reported as ruling a kingdom somewhere in Asia or Africa. We now know that such a kingdom did exist in the middle and upper Nile, and although Christian Nubia was destroyed by the Muslims in the thirteenth century, the religion has lasted in Ethiopia right down to the present day. Travellers in the Middle East would have undoubtedly heard rumours of the wars with this kingdom from Muslim soldiers, and brought the information back to Europe. At a time when Europe felt under constant threat from the Muslims, and was still trying to expel them from Spain, a potential ally to the south of their enemy must have seemed like the answer to their prayers and so the Popes promoted endeavours to search for him by land and sea.

It is difficult for us in modern times to appreciate the enormous political power exerted by the Papacy in the late Middle Ages. The Pope in Rome could and did dictate to kings, who went to enormous lengths to keep in his favour. When an argument developed between Spain and Portugal over the boundaries that should exist between their newly discovered territories after Columbus returned claiming to have found a route to the Indies, the Pope was automatically consulted. His suggestion, that the boundary should be drawn on a north–south line 270 leagues west of the Cape Verde Islands, was extended to 370 leagues, about 60° west longitude, and accepted by both parties, in the Treaty of Tordesillas, signed on 7th June 1494. It is this treaty that is responsible for modern Brazil being Portuguese-speaking whereas the rest of Latin America uses Spanish. For King Dom João II of Portugal, finding Prester John and the kingdom he was reputed to have created would establish him as a champion of Christianity, and therefore enhance his position with the Pope. No doubt he hoped also to organise a flourishing trade with Prester John's kingdom. So the twin driving forces for Portuguese exploration were the search for trade, in particular gold, spices and later slaves, and the hunt for heathens to convert to Christianity.

In 1469, a monopoly for all African trade was granted by the Crown to a

Lisbon merchant, Fernão Gomes. During the six years that he held this, Gomes sent his ships to explore a further 2,000 miles of the African coast. Then in 1475, Prince Dom João took back the monopoly on behalf of the Crown, and continued the development of exploration and trade on his accession, as King João II, in 1481.

About this time the Portuguese would have become the first Europeans to have sailed south of the equator. This fact would have become apparent to the navigators who used the Pole Star for calculating their latitude. As they sailed south the star would have slipped down nearer to the horizon, until just before the equator it would have disappeared completely. They would also have noted that when on the equator, the sun bore north for half the year and south for the other half, but that once they passed the tropic of Capricorn on their way south, the sun always had a northerly bearing – further confirmation of the sun's movements in the celestial sphere. One can imagine the excitement caused when it was realised that they had probably crossed the halfway point on the world's surface, and perhaps they expected to see an Antarctic pole star slowly rising above the horizon as they sailed south. If so they were disappointed, but what else lay ahead? Did the land reflect the land masses of the northern hemisphere, and might they perhaps find other white people? One thing that they would have quickly discovered was that the seasons were reversed, and that mid-summer south of the equator coincided with mid-winter in the northern hemisphere. They would also have realised that the wind circulation seemed to reverse itself south of the equator, so that the clockwise circulation of the winds in the northern Atlantic was replaced by an anti-clockwise circulation in the south.

King João II inherited his Uncle Henry's desire to find the route to the East, and his ability to spur his sailors towards this goal. In 1487 he prepared a small expedition, and dispatched it with express instructions to find the southern limit of Africa. The fleet of three caravels, two of fifty tons, and a smaller one used as a store ship, were placed under the command of an experienced captain, Bartolomeu Dias, born about 1455. The Dias name appears frequently in the records of Portuguese navigation. João Dias was one of the first captains to round Cape Bojador in 1434, and a Diniz Dias discovered the Cape Verde Islands. It is probable that both were kinsmen of Bartolomeu. The expedition sailed from Lisbon in August of that year. Dias followed the normal route down the west African coast as far as Baía dos Tigres, where he left his supply ship with nine men aboard. Continuing southwards, he passed Cape Cross, in latitude 20° 30′ south, so called because Diogo Cão had placed a *padrão*, or stone cross, there in 1485–86, to mark the furthest point reached by the Portuguese at that time, and pushed on exploring new coastline. At about 26° south, he paused long enough to erect one of his *padrões* in a place the

Portuguese subsequently called Angra Pequena, in modern Namibia, which was re-christened Lüderitz some 400 years later by the Germans. When he sailed again he was forced south by winds which continued for thirteen days and forced him well out of sight of land. As soon as the conditions allowed, he turned eastwards to find land again, but after some days on this course, and no sighting being made, he turned his ships north. When the coast was re-sighted it was close to the mouth of the Gouritz River, which they named Angra dos Vaqueiros (Anchorage of the Cowherds), due to the many cattle they found ashore. Not surprisingly, the herdsmen drove their cattle away the moment they sighted the Portuguese, so Dias was unable to report back in detail about the first European sighting of the natives in the country except to say that 'they were blacks, with woolly hair like those of Guinea'. No effort was made to land here, and the ships sailed on to a more sheltered bay at what they called Angra de São Bras, known as Mossel Bay today.

After leaving Mossel Bay, Dias found that the coast tended to the east, which greatly encouraged his expedition. As he sailed along he gave names to various easily identifiable features such as Ponta da Pescaria (Fish Point), which is Gericke Point, no doubt because he found an abundance of fish in the area, and a Lago Cerrado (Hidden Lake), which may be Swartvlei or possibly Knysna. Later he passed Cape Seal, or Robberg, which he called Cabo Talhado (Steep Cape), and Plettenberg Bay which Dias named Baía das Alagoas (Bay of the Lagoons), behind which he noted the Outeniqua Mountains which he called the Serra da Estrela (Mountains of the Stars). When Dias reached Algoa Bay his crew demanded that they should turn round and return home, but after a conference, he managed to persuade them to continue for a few more days. Just beyond Algoa Bay, at Kwaaihoek, he erected a final *padrão* on 12th March 1488, and managed to persuade the reluctant sailors to press on a little further. However when they reached a river which they named 'Infante', after Captain João Infante of the *São Pantaleão*, who discovered it, the men refused to go further and Dias regretfully turned for home. Fifteen leagues, or forty-eight miles, from the *padrão* is a point two miles to the south of the Keiskamma River. However, this would have meant that he averaged only thirteen miles a day for four days. Subsequent Portuguese descriptions of the coast indicate that there was confusion as to which river was in fact the Infante, and the Keiskamma is the least likely. The Great Fish River would fit João de Lisboa's report in 1514, and the Msikaba that of Perestrelo, but the Buffalo River, twenty-five leagues from Kwaaihoek, is the most likely. The confusion is caused by the lack of a log to measure distance accurately, and the varied adverse effects of the Agulhas Current.

Although it must have been frustrating for Dias to have to turn back when the coast was tending to the north-east and the route looked so

A painting by Kobell showing shipping in Table Bay in 1777 with Table Mountain in the background. This painting indicates how busy the Cape had become by the eighteenth century.

A contemporary cartoon by Cruikshank of life aboard an East Indiaman.

A graphic painting of the loss of the East Indiaman *Doddington* on Bird Island in Algoa Bay in 1755.

hopeful, one can sympathise with the seamen. They were exploring new territory and nothing resembling India had been sighted. There would be no rewards for the men when the ships reached home unless a good cargo were to be found, and the Cape coast showed no signs of providing anything of value. The longer the voyage continued the greater the risks from the unknown. It was by no means accepted at the time that the world was round, and no one knew the boundaries of sea. Given our shortage of knowledge even today on what still remains to be discovered beneath the sea, one can imagine the fears of the uneducated and superstitious seamen of those times. What monsters might be lurking for them? Did the world end in a sudden edge over which they might sail one stormy night? The voyage carried enough risks from bad food and disease, and the longer it lasted, the fewer their chances of returning home alive.

On the homeward voyage Dias sailed along the coast, sighting and naming Cape Agulhas and the Cape of Good Hope. He christened the Cape of Good Hope 'Tormentoso' initially, because of the stormy weather he encountered there. This was subsequently changed to 'Cabo de Boa Esperança', or Cape of Good Hope, as it held out hope for the long-searched-for route to India. He erected another *padrão* near Cape Tormentoso, which he named São Filipe and it is presumed that this was on the Cape Peninsula but no signs of it have ever been found. Then he continued homewards, returning to his supply ship on the way. He found that in the nine months since he had left her the ship had become rotten and only three of the nine men on board were still alive, and one of these died from the excitement of seeing Dias return. The little fleet sailed up the African coast, calling at Principe Island, where they found Duarte Pacheco Pereira, and the survivors of the crew of his ship, which had been wrecked whilst exploring in the vicinity of the Zaire River. He arrived back in Portugal in December 1488 after a voyage lasting sixteen months and seventeen days.

Whilst Dias was sailing around the Cape, another Portuguese, Pero de Covilhã, had travelled via Cairo to India, and then taken a ship to the east African coast, voyaging down as far as Sofala. He managed to get the news of his explorations back to his king, although he stayed in the east and eventually died there. Dias must have been most disappointed when he realised how small the gap was between his last position on the coast and the position of Sofala. The unknown area between the two was just over 1,000 miles, but the coast had been tending towards the north, and he would have received the credit for definitely discovering the route to the Indies had he persevered for another few weeks.

There are no records of any further expeditions during the remainder of King João II's reign until 1495, but even before his death he had claimed the right to overlordship of the Indian Ocean, and a Portuguese domination of its trade. Soon after Dias's return the king had ordered three special ships to be built to complete the exploration, but departure of the expedition was delayed, possibly whilst he awaited the report from Pero de Covilhã, or for the results from ships sent to study the wind systems of the western Atlantic. Under João's successor, King Manuel I, nicknamed The Fortunate, because it was during his reign that the grand Portuguese design came to fruition, little time was wasted in completing the ships and organising another expedition to consolidate these claims. As its leader he chose Vasco da Gama, who has become perhaps one of the most famous names in maritime exploration. Da Gama, son of a minor official, was born in Sines, a small seaport in the province of Alentejo, in 1460. In his early years he had fought and proved himself in the Portuguese wars against Castile, and afterwards developed an excellent reputation as a sailor.

The fleet of three ships and a store ship, equipped with three years of supplies, sailed from Restelo on 8th July 1497. It was accompanied by Bartolomeu Dias in his caravel, possibly called *São Cristovão*, as far as St. Jago Island in the Cape Verde group, but the pilot from Dias's voyage around the Cape, Pero de Alenquer, continued with da Gama. Da Gama's flagship *São Gabriel* and her sister ship the *São Rafael* were *naos*, and it is estimated that they were 84 feet overall in length, with a waterline of 64 feet. The keel length was 56 feet, the beam 28 feet, and depth of hold 17 feet. They drew 5 feet 6 inches forward and 7 feet aft, and displaced 178 tons. Da Gama sailed a different course to Dias, taking a wide sweep through the south Atlantic to avoid the head winds Dias had experienced as he sailed down the coast. He sighted land on 4th November, having run into large patches of kelp weed which are such a feature of the south-western coast, and then tacked out to sea, finding land again on the 7th in a large bay he called St. Helena. During this stay contact was made with the natives, some of whom he took aboard. Unfortunately, as was so often to be the case with the local inhabitants in the Cape area, these initial good relations deteriorated rapidly when one of da Gama's crew, Fernão Veloso, probably became overfamiliar and was attacked whilst returning from a visit to the Hottentots' village, and three men were injured in the fray.

On 16th November 1497 the fleet sailed on, and sighted the Cape on the 18th. Here the wind turned against them and they put in a tack out to sea and rounded the Cape on the 20th. Da Gama noticed a large bay immediately after Cape Point which he described as being about six leagues (eighteen miles) across its entrance and six leagues deep. On the 24th they anchored in Mossel Bay, which they called Aguada de São Bras (The Watering Place of St. Blaize). They soon met the local herdsmen, and the initial encounter was cautious – hardly surprising after the previous experience. Da Gama's boats, well armed, rowed towards shore. When close, bells were thrown onto the beach, and once these had been accepted, friendly contact was made with almost ninety men. The following day, nearly 200 natives arrived bringing cattle and sheep. The Portuguese rowed ashore, and were greeted by dancing and well-harmonised flute music, to which they responded with trumpets and dancing of their own. The day ended with the seamen buying a fat ox for three bracelets, the first record of a trade for fresh provisions.

After a pause of thirteen days in São Bras, the fleet moved on, and nine days later passed Dias's last *padrão*, which they estimated to be sixty-five leagues (205 miles) from São Bras. They reported strong currents in this area. The ships kept near the shore, enabling the sailors to observe the country, which they found 'very pleasing, with many cattle wandering around'. Shortly after passing Rio do Infante, the fleet may have headed offshore, as it was driven back sixty leagues to the south-west by a strong current. Da Gama probably recognised that he was in an adverse current, the one that came to be called the Agulhas Current, but it is doubtful if he realised its extent because he certainly headed offshore again which would have put him right back where its flow is strongest. He nevertheless made progress north-east and his next landfall was further up the coast although no one knows its exact location. Since he sighted land on this occasion on 25th December 1498, he christened the land Terra de Natal, the name that is still used today. Da Gama's precise position on 25th December is subject to much debate. He had re-passed Dias's *padrão* on the 20th, and estimated that they had sailed seventy leagues, about 220 miles, which would have put them close to Port St. Johns. But there is no way of knowing whether this figure was the distance sailed along the coast or the distance sailed by the ships. In the latter case they would not have travelled so far because of the effects of the Agulhas Current.

Da Gama reports losing an anchor off a point along the coast where he stopped to fish. This is probably the Bluff at Durban, which was known for its good fishing, and given the name Point Pescaria by the Portuguese. A few days later he anchored off a small river and made contact with the natives. Here da Gama traded for ivory and provisions and left behind two malefactors to explore the territory. This seems to have been a common occurrence at the time. Condemned prisoners would be given the opportunity to avoid their punishment by being taken on a voyage and put ashore in a newly discovered land to explore and report. If they lived they regained their freedom. However, there is no record that da Gama called in on his return voyage to see how the men had fared. Along the coast da Gama landed again on 11th January 1499, where he met some black people of 'large stature'. Four days later he sailed past Cape Correntes, and fifty leagues beyond he went ashore and met people who spoke Arabic, which was the first concrete proof that they were in the Indian Ocean.

They called at the Arab ports of Mozambique, Mombasa and finally Malindi, in modern Kenya, and were amazed at the size and prosperity of these trading towns. They found a well-organised trade which connected all the countries around the Indian Ocean and beyond as far as China, using ships that were larger than their own. Eager to pursue his voyage, Vasco da Gama took on board a pilot in Malindi who knew the Indian Ocean trade, and then headed out across the ocean. This pilot was none other than the most famous Arab navigator of the time, Ibn Majid, and it is one of the great historical ironies that the most eminent Arab navigator should have been responsible for introducing the Portuguese to India and thereby sowing the seeds for the destruction of Arab domination of the Indian Ocean trade. Later Arab historians have tried to justify this by saying that Ibn Majid must have been drunk at the time!

Eventually da Gama's fleet reached Calicut in India, where some members of his crew were accosted by surprised Spanish-speaking Tunisians who asked them what they were doing there. The reply, 'We have come to seek spices and Christians,' demonstrates clearly that the twin incentives of the Trade and the Cross were uppermost in their minds. Although they found no Christian kingdom, they did discover a far more wealthy country than they had dared to expect, and having filled their ships with produce, they set out on the homeward journey.

Da Gama called again at São Bras, and rounded the Cape of Good Hope on 20th March 1499, arriving home in Portugal on 28th August the same year. It is interesting to note the time it took from the Cape to Portugal, 161 days, to cover a distance of 5,400 miles. This is an average speed of 1.4 knots, about five times slower than a moderate-sized sailing yacht, which explains why so many of the crew died on the voyage through illness and malnutrition, their only food being dried or salted, and their water, except what they could catch in rain showers, quickly going bad in barrels.

Despite the loss of life, da Gama's voyage was an immense triumph for the Portuguese. The route to the Indies had been discovered, and the trade potential was enormous, proof of which lay in the 600 per cent profit made by the voyage. Da Gama was rewarded and made two further visits to the East, the first as Admiral of a fleet of ten ships in 1502 and the second when he went out as an old man aged sixty-four, to be the Viceroy of India in 1524. He died in the Indies in 1524, and his remains were returned to Portugal and reburied in the church of Nossa Senhora das Reliquias in Vidigueira in 1539. In 1880 what were thought to be his bones were reinterred in Santa Maria de Belem in Jerónimos.

Da Gama had provided Portugal with the key to the riches of the East, and another expedition was quickly prepared to take advantage of this bonanza. The following year, in 1500, a fleet of thirteen ships left Portugal under the command of Pedro Alvares Cabral. Cabral took a course which had been recommended by da Gama. Instead of sailing slowly down the African coast, south of the equator against the winds, he set a course west of south from the Cape Verde Islands. The significance of this route is that it made best use of the trade winds, which, on the western side of the southern Atlantic, become easterly and then north-easterly, finally coming through north round to the west as the Southern Ocean is approached. This is interesting as it shows how quickly the Portuguese had mastered the wind circulation of the South Atlantic.

Cabral sighted Brazil and landed well south of Recife and claimed all that territory for Portugal. He sailed from Brazil on 2nd May taking a southerly course at first and then altering to the east towards the Cape of Good Hope. It is recounted that ten days after leaving, a comet was sighted in the east which became so bright over the next ten days that it was visible day and night. On the twenty-fifth day a waterspout appeared to the north-east which for some reason they took to indicate that the wind was going to moderate. No sooner had the fleet set full sail than a furious wind sprang up with such violence that the ships were blown onto their beam ends. Those whose sails were shredded quickly righted themselves, but four, including the one commanded by Bartolomeu Dias, were held by the wind's pressure so that they filled with water and sank with all hands. The wind then veered south-west and continued to blow at storm force for two days, during which time it was so dark that the ships could not see each other. Surprisingly, when the wind eased, the remaining ships soon re-formed, but only in time to be struck by an even more violent wind from the east and north-east. The waves are described as being 'as high as mountains, so that one moment the ships seemed to be tossed above the clouds, and the next to be plunged to the bottom of the deep.' Anyone who has ridden out a storm in the Southern Ocean will find that an apt and vivid description. This adverse wind lasted for twenty days, and when it eased, the Portuguese found that they had rounded the Cape of Good Hope, but four more ships had disappeared. Eventually two of these made their way home independently. One of them, captained by Pedro d'Ataide, made shelter at São Bras. Not knowing what had happened to the others, Pedro d'Ataide continued his voyage to the east. On his homeward voyage he again called at São Bras and left a message for any other ship in a shoe suspended from a tree. In all, the fleet had been halved by the storm, and from the fact that they found themselves east of the Cape after twenty days of easterly winds, it is more than probable that the other two ships were lost in the vicinity of the Agulhas Bank.

During Cabral's voyage, one of his captains, Diogo Dias, discovered Madagascar and called it the Isle of St. Lawrence, while others were busy exploring further in the Atlantic. João da Nova found Ascension Island in 1501, on his way to the East, and also came upon the message at São Bras left by Pedro d'Ataide. On his way home in 1502 he discovered the island of St. Helena. Within four years, in 1506, Tristão da Cunha found the islands of his name as he headed east on the by-now-established Portuguese route to India, thus completing the discovery of all the southern Atlantic islands.

The Portuguese moved very quickly to consolidate and protect their route. They first gained control of the Indian Ocean by means of their superior ships and guns, and by conquering the main trading towns. As the Indian Ocean trade had been controlled completely by the Arabs and the Muslims of India, their ships, because they had never faced a threat to their supremacy, were largely unarmed. The only opposition was a combined Egyptian and Indian fleet that was destroyed off Diu by Francisco de Almeida in 1509. The surprise appearance of two armed French corsairs under Captain Mondragon, who captured a Portuguese ship under the command of Job Queimado in the Mozambique Channel in 1507, led to a major search until Mondragon was apprehended by Pacheco Pereira off Cape Finisterre in 1509. Thereafter the Portuguese exercised more or less complete domination over the ocean and its trade, and became the major supplier of eastern imports to the rest of Europe. The most important Arab trading towns of Kilwa, Mombasa and Malindi were in their hands, and forts were either built or captured to hold them. This chain of forts extended to Muscat, and the then key to the Mediterranean trade, Hormuz, at the entrance to the Persian Gulf. They only just failed to take over the Red Sea when an attempt to storm Aden was narrowly defeated in 1513. For a while they even held Bahrain.

On the Indian sub-continent, one of Portugal's greatest generals and colonisers, Afonso d'Albuquerque, seized the island of Goa from the Sultan of Bijapur in 1510, built a fort and founded Portugal's eastern capital. In 1511, he took Malacca, which gave control of the Java Sea and the Indonesian spice industry.

Other conquests, or treaties, followed rapidly, and within a few decades a series of over forty forts or trading factories were spread from Sofala in modern Mozambique to Macao in China. A very lucrative trade had been established which was to make Portugal, with its population of not much more than one million people, one of the wealthier states in Europe. As a contemporary writer expressed it, 'The Portuguese Empire to the Eastward extends from the Cape of Good Hope in Africa to Cape Liampo [Ningpo] in China, 4,000 leagues along the sea coasts, without including the shores of the Red Sea and Persian Gulf, which make about 1,200 leagues more. Within this space lies half Africa and all Asia.'

This wealth, based upon a trade with far-flung outposts, was totally dependent on the sea, and ships being able to ply safely between Lisbon and the East via the Cape. The numbers of sailings are indicative of its importance, and the immense effort required by the Portuguese to keep it maintained. In the twenty years that followed Vasco da Gama's return to

Lisbon, 234 ships sailed to the Indian Ocean. In the next twenty years they decreased slightly to an average of seven sailings a year, and subsequently the average for the next 200 years was about five each year. The reason for the greater numbers in the early years was the demand for warships and soldiers whilst they were establishing themselves and creating their supremacy. The early fleets thus carried a far higher proportion of soldiers and sailors.

Apart from the Frenchman Mondragon, the Portuguese trade monopoly was only challenged twice in these early years, both times also by the French. In 1527 three ships sailed from Dieppe for India. One was lost on the way, and a second wrecked off Sumatra and all the crew murdered. The third reached Diu, where its crew were seized by the Portuguese and handed over to the local Mohammedan ruler, who forced them to change their religion and enter his service. Two years later a second expedition of two ships captained by the brothers Raoul and Jean Parmentier, reached Sumatra in October 1529. There their crews went down with sickness, and the ships turned for home, meeting severe weather off the Cape. The Portuguese only became aware of this voyage when they found one of the crew who had been left behind at Madagascar. The difficulties experienced by these two ventures discouraged the French from making further assaults for seventy years.

Although the early expeditions called into southern Africa as they passed to collect water or try to barter for fresh meat, efforts were not made to set up a permanent outpost. There were no signs of an organised society, such as the kingdoms in India, and the only items for trade were livestock and farm produce and then on a small scale. Quite understandably no one was enthusiastic about collecting hides or starting to farm, which could be done easily in a relatively unpopulated Portugal, when their ships could be filled with spices and other riches available in the Indies.

Slowly, however, a little knowledge of the coast and the people began to be acquired in pilotage instructions as each fleet noted down its observations. It seems surprising that Table Bay was not explored until 1503, and then only by accident. A small fleet under a Castilian knight, Antonio de Saldanha, who was working in the service of the Portuguese king, was separated by a storm and became lost. Saldanha entered Table Bay thinking he was already round the Cape. They anchored and went ashore to find water. Soon they were met by Hottentots with whom they bartered for a cow and two sheep. Apparently the Hottentots were dissatisfied with the deal, because the next day about 200 of them attacked Saldanha and his men, and the captain was wounded in the fight. Nevertheless, he stayed long enough to climb Table Mountain, from which he was able to see the Cape of Good Hope, and his men visited Robben Island, where they killed numerous penguins and sea-wolves. Having found his whereabouts,

Saldanha sailed for India, but he christened the bay Aguada de Saldanha, or The Watering Place of Saldanha, and the bay retained this name until changed to Table Bay by the Dutch in the seventeenth century.

Saldanha reported favourably on his watering place, but the Portuguese did not consider it to have any special significance or advantages over São Bras. In 1506, a small expedition was sent to explore the coast from the Cape of Good Hope to Sofala, near to the modern port of Beira, to see whether a better haven existed. It was also to search for signs of the ships and crews of some of the missing ships from d'Albuquerque's fleet in 1503, and Pedro de Mendoça's in 1505, which were thought to have been wrecked on the coast. The expedition was led by Cide Barbudo, but the *roteiro*, or pilot, was produced by Duarte Pacheco Pereira, who had been rescued by Dias on his homeward voyage from Principe Island in 1488. Pereira was one of Portugal's most experienced seamen, so well thought of that he had been chosen to represent his king at the signing of the Treaty of Tordesillas. Between 1506 and 1508 he composed a *roteiro* for the African coast from Ceuta to Rio do Infante which was called the *Esmeraldo de Situ Orbis*, but unfortunately the original has disappeared, and only an eighteenth-century copy exists. Pereira made short notes of the salient features on the coastline, but found no sign of the lost ships except for some burned timber. Any surviving crewmen had vanished. The significance of this *roteiro* is the accuracy of the latitudes given for the major headlands, even Mossel Bay's being only nineteen miles different from its true position, which, considering that his only instrument for calculating latitude was an astrolabe which measured to the nearest quarter of a degree, is truly remarkable.

Pacheco Pereira's *roteiro* marks the end of the period of discovery of the Cape. Little was known about the interior of the land beyond a mile or so from the coast. This remained to be explored, but the main features such as mountains, headlands and rivers were familiar. No detailed charts existed as yet, but the seamen had sufficient information to navigate around the Cape on their way to and from the Indies; the Cape's position and importance on the world's surface was established, and the Cape route was open.

3

The Cape Route – The Age of Sail

The rapid development of the Portuguese Eastern Empire called for regular sailings between the homeland and the East. This was known as the *Carreira da India*, which took about a year and a half and was by far the most dangerous and arduous of any route that had been sailed by man. It was therefore essential that the Portuguese quickly mastered the weather principles that governed the passage.

The dominant factor was the monsoon of the Arabian Sea and north Indian Ocean. Unlike the large oceans, where the trade winds blow steadily in one direction all the year round, in the Arabian Sea the trade winds reverse themselves twice a year. The south-west monsoon begins in May and blows from east Africa to India until September. The slightly less powerful north-east monsoon, which blows in the opposite direction, starts about October and fades in March or April. The strength of the south-west monsoon is such that trade on the west coast of India for sailing ships was limited to the period between September and March. In order to reach India and take advantage of the trading season, an outward-bound ship had to catch the south-west monsoon from the coast of Africa during the summer months. Similarly, it was essential that a homeward-bound ship leave India during the northern winter whilst the north-east monsoon was blowing, so that she could round the Cape of Good Hope before the winter season there began in May. The Portuguese developed a pattern of sailing from Lisbon before Easter, or, as one captain put it, 'the last day of February is time enough, the first day of March is late', and their homeward fleets would leave Goa around Christmas time. Usually ships that risked sailing late from Portugal failed to complete the voyage, and they either wintered in Brazil or returned home. It was too dangerous to try and round the Cape in the southern winter, and, in any case, they had missed the south-west monsoon for that year.

The route they chose showed their understanding of the world's ocean winds and currents. After leaving Lisbon they sailed down the west African coast before the north-east trade winds, and then altered course to the south-west at the Doldrums, that area of calms that separates the trade winds either side of the equator. In the South Atlantic they sailed close-hauled in the south-east trade winds, near to the coast of Brazil, and then followed the wind as it slowly backed round to the west and south-west about the same latitude as the Cape. The northern edge of the Roaring Forties blew them around the Cape, after which they turned north on the voyage up the south-east coast of Africa, usually taking the Mozambique Channel between Africa and Madagascar. If they passed the Cape after the middle of July, they frequently took a course east of Madagascar. Once they had crossed the equator they picked up the south-west monsoon to India. The Mozambique Channel route was banned by royal order after 1525 due to the unhealthiness of the climate at Mozambique, but ships continued to use it, and as a number of vessels using the eastern route disappeared without trace, the Viceroy in India officially authorised the use of the Channel again in 1597.

On the homeward run, if they sailed before the end of December, they took the north-east monsoon from Goa towards the Arabian coast, and then down the east African coast to the Cape. If they left Goa in January or sailed from Cochin or Malacca, they generally took a more direct route east of Madagascar. From the Cape they headed north-east to the equator, crossing between 20 and 30° west longitude, and then sailed close-hauled in the north-east trades until they came to the Azores, from where they sailed directly to Lisbon. Often the voyage both out and home was made without a stop, but if it was necessary to call in for supplies, Mozambique or St. Helena became more favoured than the Cape. St. Helena ceased to be used after the Dutch started their Eastern trade, as it became too dangerous for the Portuguese.

The average time for an outward or homeward voyage was seven or eight months, but some remarkably fast passages were made on occasions. The quickest outward run on record was by Captain João da Costa in 1645, who took three months and twenty-seven days from Lisbon to Goa. The fastest homeward passage of 156 days was made non-stop by Dom Francisco da Gama in 1600–1601. He boasted that the main-yard was not lowered once during the voyage.

The principal Portuguese trading vessel was still the *nao*, or big ship. The term *galeos* was also used, but the distinction between the two was not always obvious. The *nao* was a standard, rather cumbersome, trading ship of about 400 tons. The Portuguese developed the ship into a giant of up to 2,000 tons with three or four flush decks. *Naos* were built for their cargo-carrying capacity rather than speed, and were not considered good sailers. As experience with the *Carreira* developed, it was realised that the *naos*, although they represented the 'super' ship of the time, were not the most efficient and economical for the route, and an effort was made by royal decree in 1570 to reduce the size. However, despite the appalling loss of wealth each time one of these ships was lost, they continued to be built well into the seventeenth century.

The *naos* were lightly armed for ships of their size, carrying perhaps twenty 8-pounder guns, although they were, under Portuguese law, supposed to carry a minimum of twenty-eight and of a heavier type. The smaller galleons of between 400 and 600 tons were the main fighting ships and were both better armed and more manoeuvrable. The fleet, which averaged between five and seven vessels, would try to keep together for protection and security, but it was rare for all the ships to remain in contact on so long a voyage.

Ships of the period built in Europe were either of pine or oak, but the Portuguese quickly realised the value of teak as a shipbuilding material, and many of their largest *naos* were built in India, at the Royal Arsenal in Goa, or under contract at the shipyards in Cochin, Bassein or Damão. In 1585 a Royal Order was issued by the then Spanish King of Portugal, Philip II, that all ships should be built in India if possible because experience had shown that vessels constructed there lasted longer, and the cost was less. Materials for shipbuilding were also becoming increasingly hard to obtain in Spain and Portugal at the time, perhaps because of Philip's programme for his Great Armada against England. The superiority of the Indian ships shows in the records of the *Cinco Chagas*, built in Goa in 1560. She survived for twenty-five years and made at least eight round voyages, whereas the average for a European-built ship was only four.

The crew might number as many as 200, augmented by soldiers and passengers to bring the total to 700 or 800. Often half this number would die on the voyage because of the insanitary and crowded conditions. The Portuguese were not renowned for keeping their ships clean, there was no discipline about using the heads, and people defecated wherever convenient. Frequently rubbish from the decks ended up in the bilges, where it mixed with the stagnant water that was always caught beneath the stone ballast. This rancid smell, a combination of rotting meat and public lavatory, permeated the living accommodation, which was packed with people living on straw, if they were lucky. Packed unwashed humanity, no hygiene, and a filthy ship meant that disease was rife and spread rapidly. The miracle is that anyone survived a voyage to the East in these conditions.

The captains were usually landsmen of noble birth. They were appointed on the assumption that they could be trusted and would be used to taking command, but they did not necessarily have any knowledge of navigation or seamanship. The navigational control of the vessel was in the hands of the pilot and his assistants, who would decide the course to be taken. The success of any voyage depended totally upon the professionalism of the corps of pilots, and in general, considering their lack of detailed information, they maintained a very high standard throughout the 300 years that the *Carreira da India* was run. Writing 100 years later in 1622, Sir Richard Hawkins described the Spanish and Portuguese pilots as follows:

> In this point of Steeridge, the Spaniards and Portuguese do exceed all that I have seen, I mean for their care, which is chiefest in navigation. And I wish in this, and in all their works of discipline and reformation, we should follow their example . . . In every ship of moment, upon the halfdeck or quarterdeck, they have a chair or seat out of which, whilst they navigate, the pilot or his adjutants (which are the same officers which in our ships we term the master and his mates) never depart, day or night, from the sight of the compass; and have another before them; whereby they see what they do, and are ever witness of the good or bad steeridge of all men that do take the helm.

Cargoes outwards were scanty, mainly specie, and some trading goods. The passengers were soldiers or merchants. Women rarely accompanied their husbands, and few European women lived long in the East even if they survived the journey. On the homeward voyage, however, cargo occupied every available space including the deck. Wages were very low but the crew were allowed to bring back a chest of spices each which would have been sold for a great deal more than their wages on their return to Lisbon. The captain was allocated fifteen chests. The main items of homeward cargo were pepper and cinnamon, which were usually carried in bulk in the lower hold, but other spices, gold, diamonds, silks, hardwoods, indigo and saltpetre, were stowed in the tween decks.

The Portuguese rarely stopped at Table Bay on their round voyages, partly on account of the massacre of many of their men by the Hottentots seven years after Saldanha had given the bay his name. A small fleet, bringing home the Portuguese Viceroy in India, Dom Francisco d'Almeida, and many of his seasoned officers, called there in 1510 to obtain water. Barter commenced with the Hottentots, but when one of the shore party tried to take two of the natives back to the ship by force, he was severely beaten. A council of war was held, with the sailors wanting to continue the voyage, but d'Almeida and his veterans from the battles to create their Eastern Empire felt that they had lost face, and this must be revenged. A party of 150 men was landed at night and attacked the Hottentot village, burning it down and seizing cattle and children. The Hottentots, who initially had fled, rallied quickly, and started a running fight using stones and fire-hardened darts. The Portuguese, perhaps too confident, had brought no bows or firearms, and had to defend themselves with hand weapons only. The Hottentots got amongst their cattle and, using these for shelter, began to pick off their opponents. The retreat became a rout. D'Almeida was killed by a spear through the neck, and most of his senior officers died trying to protect his body. Sixty-five men were killed, as well as many wounded, the survivors having to fight their way through the surf to the ship's boats. After Saldanha's experience and the massacre of d'Almeida and his men, the Portuguese avoided the south African coast. When it was necessary to stop they landed mainly in São Bras Bay, and rarely ventured inland.

Covetous eyes were cast on Portugal's new wealth by neighbouring Spain, who had already tried to reach the Indies by sailing across the Atlantic with Columbus's famous expedition in 1492. The opportunity of discovering an alternative western route came when a disaffected Portuguese offered his services to take a fleet and find a way round America. Ferdinand de Magellan was by birth a Portuguese, and had served with merit under d'Albuquerque in the Indies, distinguishing himself in fighting at Malacca in 1510 and 1511. He had approached King Manuel of Portugal with his plans, but the King had refused his request for ships to attempt the voyage, as he felt that if another route were to be discovered, it would open the Indies trade to other nations. Accused of peculation in Lisbon, Magellan went to Spain, to the court of Charles V, and persuaded that monarch to back his scheme.

Magellan sailed with five ships and 236 men from San Lucar de Barrameda on 20th September 1519. Although he died during the voyage as a result of wounds received in a small local war in the Philippines, his flagship, the *Vittoria*, sailed on and rounded the Cape of Good Hope on 19th May 1522. The ship did not stop at the Cape: the crew was wary of meeting the Portuguese, who did not take kindly to this incursion into their area of influence and would have captured the vessel if possible. Eventually the *Vittoria* arrived back in Spain, with only eighteen of the original crew on board, having completed the first circumnavigation of the world, and proved that, although it might be longer and more arduous, there was an alternative route to the East by sea.

This voyage focused Spanish interest on the western route, and led to Spain colonising central America as a staging post for her trade with the Philippines and China. If Magellan had not made his voyage, it is likely that Spain, already an emerging sea power, but with far greater resources, would have competed with the Portuguese on the Cape route, and might well have placed fortifications and a colony in southern Africa. It is interesting to speculate on what the future history of Africa might have been had the Spanish settled, as they did in America, and indeed, whether the subsequent exploration and development of the southern part of the continent by the Dutch would have taken place.

Once the Spanish had found an alternative route to the Indies, transhipping their valuable cargoes across the Isthmus of Panama to avoid the dangers of Cape Horn, competition with the Portuguese seemed inevitable. However, by the Treaty of Saragossa, signed in 1529 between the two nations, it was agreed that everything west of a meridian 17° east of the Moluccas was to be Portuguese, and east of the line would belong to Spain. This treaty gave the Portuguese continued monopoly of the Cape of Good Hope route which was well developed by the middle of the sixteenth century.

The losses of Portuguese ships on the *Carreira da India* varied, but in the first eighty years of the sixteenth century thirty-one ships were lost for one reason or another. Between 1580 and 1610 the total was thirty-five, or just over one ship a year, and it has been estimated that the total between 1500 and 1650 was 130 vessels from all causes. From 1650 the loss rate diminished remarkably, and this was probably due to the royal frustration with the high rate of wrecks caused, as much as anything, by some owners and captains flouting the regulations covering the operation of the *Carreira*. Two captains, who had flagrantly disobeyed the rules, were hanged as an example, and standards improved. Most of the losses were caused by being wrecked on the east African coast, or by foundering in the Indian Ocean because of overloading or lack of maintenance. Fourteen wrecks are known to have taken place on the coast of southern Africa, but the total is probably higher, as some ships would have broken up completely, leaving no clue as to their whereabouts, and the survivors, if any, would have been either killed or absorbed into the local population.

The first recorded Portuguese wreck, apart from the loss at sea of Bartolomeu Dias and five other ships from Cabral's fleet in 1500 somewhere in the South Atlantic, was in 1504 or 1505, probably a short distance west of São Bras. The ship was in company, and the other saw her go aground but was unable to render any assistance, and no sign of her or the crew has ever been found. The authorities were always concerned because the loss of just one homeward-bound ship in a year could mean the forfeiture of twenty per cent of that year's trade, plus a valuable ship and crew. Part of the problem was that the lumbering carracks being used were cumbersome to control, and navigation was still very imprecise, a backstaff and astrolabe being the only instruments available. In this context it is interesting to note that the pilot of the *São Bento* thought the wreck occurred in latitude 32° 20′ south, whereas it appears to have happened at 31° 19′ south.

In 1575, Manuel de Mesquita Perestrelo, a captain with considerable experience of the African coast and who was one of the survivors of the *São Bento*, wrecked on the coast in 1554, was sent by King Sebastian to produce a better *roteiro* for the coastline between the Cape of Good Hope and Cape Correntes. One of his specific orders was to try and locate safe havens for ships to shelter from the winter storms off the Cape. The difficulty with

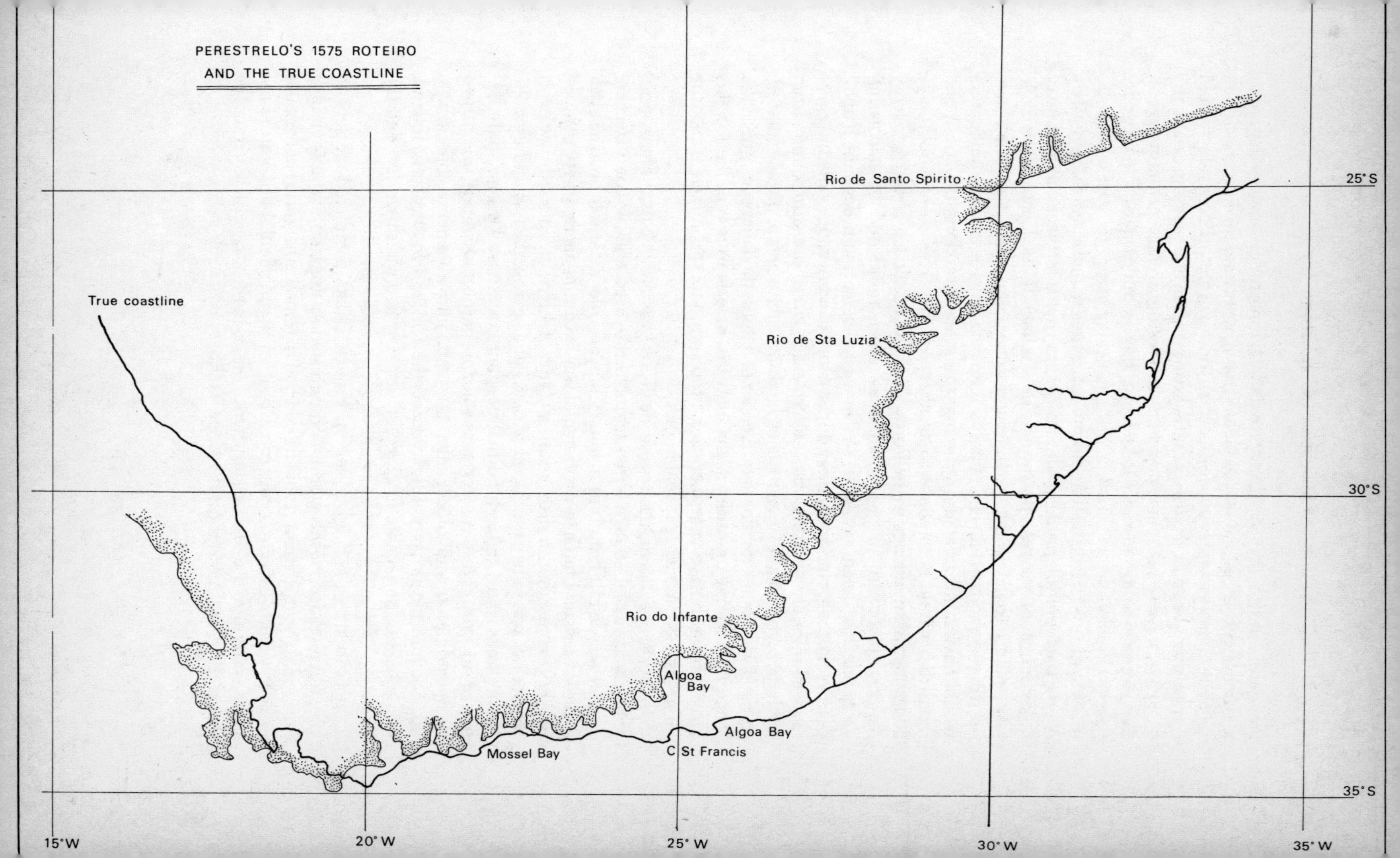
PERESTRELO'S 1575 ROTEIRO
AND THE TRUE COASTLINE
True coastline
Rio de Santo Spirito
Rio de Sta Luzia
Rio do Infante
Algoa Bay
Algoa Bay
C St Francis
Mossel Bay
25°S
30°S
35°S
15°W
20°W
25°W
30°W
35°W

navigation at the time was how to establish longitude with any degree of accuracy, a problem that was to bedevil navigators until the invention of an accurate chronometer by John Harrison in 1735. Perestrelo would obviously have started with a point whose position had been agreed by the other Portuguese navigators, and it is interesting to note just how far out they were in some instances. Delagoa Bay is put at about 30° east by Perestrelo whereas its actual position is nearer to 33° 30′ east, about 140 miles to the east. His coastline slowly converges with the real thing until by Algoa Bay, the longitude is almost correct, but it is placed almost sixty miles north of its real position. The outline of the coast bears little resemblance to the actual coastline, and some points, like Cape Natal, have been over-emphasised. This is perhaps not so surprising, as the navigators would have concentrated on the important features along the coast, and those that would be obvious to another seafarer. The *roteiro* would have added a little knowledge to the Portuguese, but would have been decidedly dangerous to use for a landfall if an efficient method of calculating longitude had been available. As it was, the mariners depended upon dead-reckoning, the calculation of the course and distance sailed, to give them a longitude, and this was not very exact. Even so, a ship coming from the Indies would have often reached land some days before it was expected. In the days when safe navigation depended upon the keen eyesight of the lookout, it is not extraordinary that they lost at least fourteen ships on this coast during the 150 years between 1500 and 1650; the miracle is that the numbers were not a great deal higher.

In 1578, the Portuguese were dealt a devastating blow. Their king, Sebastian, was killed on a Crusade in North Africa, and the country came under the rule of Philip II of Spain. Philip, an ardent Catholic, had a revolt in his Protestant Dutch territories, and was becoming increasingly irritated by the Protestant English seamen. One of his first edicts, by way of retaliation, was to ban the export of merchandise from the East Indies to the Netherlands and England, both Protestant countries. This not only deprived his Portuguese subjects of a valuable part of their trade, and turned their traditional and oldest ally, England, into an enemy, but it also provided an incentive to England and the United Provinces of Holland, two of the most capable maritime nations, to find their own route to the East.

In 1580 also, the Englishman Sir Francis Drake completed the second circumnavigation of the world, and returned to England with his ship so laden with Spanish booty, that he had had to remove the gravel ballast and replace it with silver in order to carry it all home. He did not stop at the Cape, although he did go aground on a flat rock, which, from the description, was not far off the Cape itself:

A contemporary painting by S. F. Holman showing Indiamen under construction at the Blackwall Yard on the River Thames.

A print of the auxiliary paddle-steamer *Enterprise,* the first steamer to sail via the Cape to India in 1824.

'Women and children first': the troopship *Birkenhead* sinking off Danger Point in 1852. The young soldiers stood firm on deck as the ship sank, to allow the women and children to be evacuated in the ship's lifeboats.

> From Java Major we sailed for the Cape of Good Hope, which was the first land we fell withal; neither did we touch with it, or any other land, until we came to Sierra Leone, upon the coast of Guinea; notwithstanding we ran hard aboard the cape, finding the report of the Portugals to be most false, who affirm that it is the most dangerous cape of the world, never without intolerable storms and present danger to travellers which come near the same. This cape is the most stately thing, and the fairest cape we saw in the whole circumference of the earth, and we passed it on the 18th of June [1580].

By throwing cannons and some cargo overside, he refloated the *Golden Hinde*, but the significance in this extract is the length of voyage without stopping and the confidence with which it was undertaken, despite the shortage of pilotage information. It is interesting that the English crews did not suffer from disease to the same extent as the Portuguese on their long passages. This was probably due to the habit of cleaning the decks regularly with a mixture of vinegar and water, and airing the accommodation whenever possible. When Drake arrived back in Plymouth on 3rd November 1580, Spanish wrath was mainly directed at Drake's freebooting, and they failed to appreciate the full implication of his circumnavigation. The way east was wide open to any nation that did not feel bound by the Pope's edicts, provided that they went with sufficient strength to protect themselves.

Drake's voyage had shown that the rounding of the Cape was much easier than the Portuguese had allowed others to believe, and shortly after his return, another Englishman arrived home from the East, having served on the Portuguese fleet of 1597, and was able to add to the English knowledge. Thomas Stephens gained invaluable experience from his voyage and made very useful notes. For example he reported that the Portuguese used the variation of the compass needle to give themselves an idea of longitude. He also reported that they had two routes to India from the Cape, one within and one without Madagascar. Of the two, the mariners preferred the inside route as they could stop at Mozambique for refreshments, whereas on the other route many more sailors died from the extra time at sea.

In 1588 Thomas Cavendish rounded the Cape during his circumnavigation, the second by an Englishman, in the *Desire* of 120 tons. Although, like Drake before him, he did not land, he has left a description of sailing past the Cape.

> The next day, being the 11th of May, in the morning one of the company went into the top, and espied land bearing north and north and by west of us, and about noon we espied land to bear west of us, which, as we did

> imagine, was the Cape of Buena Esperança, whereof, indeed, we were short some 40 or fifty leagues. [Unlikely, as this would have been 120–150 miles.] And by reason of the scantiness of the wind we stood along to the south east until midnight, at which time the wind came fair, and we haled along westward. The 12 and 13 days we were becalmed, and the sky was very hazy and thick until the 14 day at three of the clock in the afternoon, at which time the sky cleared, and we espied the land again which was the land called Cabo Falso [Hangklip], which is short of the Cape de Buena Esperança 40 or 50 leagues. [In fact 18 miles.] This cape is very easy to be known; for there are right over it three very high hills standing but a small way one off another, and the highest standeth in the midst, and the ground is much lower by the seaside. The Cape of Good Hope beareth west and by south from this said Cabo Falso. The 16 day of May, about four of the clock in the afternoon, the wind came up at east a very stiff gale, which held until it was Saturday, with as much wind as ever the ship could go before; at which time, by six of the clock in the morning, we espied the promontory or headland called the Cape de Buena Esperança, which is a reasonable high land, and at the westermost point, a little off the main, do shew two hummocks, the one upon the other, and three other hummocks lying further off into the sea, yet low land between and adjoining unto the sea. The Cape of Buena Esperança is set down and accounted 2000 leagues from the island of Java in the Portugal sea-chart; but it is not so much almost by 150 leagues, as we found by the running of our ship. We were in running of these 1850 leagues just nine weeks.

Cavendish's voyage, finishing as it did just as England defeated the invincible Spanish Armada, emphasised for the English their abilities at sea, and the weakness of the enemy. Within less than two years, the first English expedition to the Indies sailed from Plymouth on 10th May 1591. The small fleet of three ships, the *Penelope*, *Merchant Royal* and *Edward Bonaventure*, departed under the command of Captain Raymond, with James Lancaster in charge of one of them. The fleet took seventy-nine days to reach the Cape of Good Hope where contrary winds and sick crews forced them back into Table Bay.

> The 28 of July we had sight of the forsayd Cape of Buona Esperenza. Until the 31 wee lay off and on, with the wind contrary to double the Cape, hoping to double it and so to have gone seventie leagues further, to a place called Agoada de S. Bras. But our men being weake and sicke in all our ships, we bare up the land to the northward of the Cape; and going along the shore we espied a goodly baie with an island lying to seaward of it [Robben Island]; into which we did beare, and founde it

> very commodious for our ships to ride in. This baie is called the Agoada de Saldanha [Table Bay], lying 15 leagues [48 miles] on the hither side of the Cape. The first of August we came to anker in the baie, sending our men on land: and there came unto them certaine blacke savages, very brutish, which would not stay, but retired from them. For the space of fifteen or twenty dayes we could find no reliefe, but only foules which we killed with our pieces, which were cranes and geese. There was no fish but muskles and other shellfish, which we gathered on the rockes. After 15 or 20 dayes being here, our admirall went with his pinasse unto the iland which lieth off the baie, where he found great store of penguines and seales; whereof he brought good plenty with him. And twise after that we sent certaine of our men, which at both times brought their bots lading unto our ship. After we had bene here sometime we got here a negro, whom we compelled to march into the country with us, making signs to bring us some cattell; but at this time we could come to the sight of none; so we let the negro go; with some trifles. Within 8 dayes after, he, with 30 or 40 other negros brought us downe some 40 bullocks and oxen, with as many sheepe; at which time we bought but few of them. But within 8 days after, they came downe with as many more, and then we bought some 24 oxen, with as many sheepe. We bought an ox for two knives, a sterk [calf] for a knife, and a sheepe for a knife; and some we bought for less value than a knife.

The *Merchant Royal* was sent home with fifty men sick with the scurvy and the remaining two ships sailed on six days later, heading for Nicobar and Ceylon. Between 12th and 14th August, the accounts vary, when either four or six days' sailing from Table Bay, and so probably in the vicinity of Algoa Bay, they were struck by very strong winds. According to the crew of the *Edward Bonaventure*, 'this evening we saw a great sea break over our Admirall, the *Penelope*, and their light strooke out; and, after that we never saw them anymore.' Although they waited a good time in the Comoroes for their Admiral, the *Penelope* was never seen again, and she may have been the first witnessed victim of the freak wave phenomenon, recently identified in this vicinity. The *Edward Bonaventure* was captured by the Spanish in the West Indies on the return voyage, but her master, James Lancaster, escaped and returned home by a French ship in 1594.

The first Dutch account of the route to the Indies came from Jan Huygen van Linschoten, who sailed there on a Portuguese ship in 1583, as an employee of Vicente da Fonesca, who had been appointed primate of India. Upon his return to the Netherlands he wrote a book about his travels, which was published in 1595. The book gave a detailed account of the Portuguese sailing directions, and, in particular, how to find the Cape of Good Hope by watching for seabirds and kelp, and the sort of bottom to be found in the vicinity from the taking of soundings with a lead armed with tallow, one of the sailors' most trusted means of finding their position. Nevertheless, these methods in the days of indifferent surveys still could be fifty or more miles out, and Linschoten included a detailed description of the obvious land features, which would enable a seafarer to fix his landfall. The following year he published another book describing the Indies, in which he mentioned the wealth of the Portuguese trade, and how the Governor of Mozambique expected to collect nine tons of gold in the course of a three-year tour of duty. As with the English, his report showed that the route was easier than the Portuguese would have everyone believe, and could be made by experienced captains, even if they did not have pilots with local knowledge. He also demonstrated the value of the rewards that could await those bold enough to take the risks.

The rise of the Dutch Republic and its rapid emergence as Europe's largest maritime power were due to two factors. The first was geographical. The Dutch people had been brought up fighting the sea for survival. The most effective means of transportation in a country criss-crossed by canals was by boat, and it was natural as time passed for these boats to sail further and grow larger. The other reason they held in common with the Portuguese of more than a century before: the emergence of the new nation from a war of independence, and the search for an outlet for the energy no longer required for that fight. Even during the war for independence from Spain in the late sixteenth century, Dutch ships were a common sight in European ports, and were taking an increasing proportion of the carrying trade. By the end of that century, with the Netherlands now an independent republic, the Dutch fleet was the largest in Europe, and the merchants of Amsterdam and Rotterdam dominated European seaborne trade and were moving further afield. They were taking over the trade between Portuguese Brazil and Portugal itself, and it was therefore a natural extension to follow the Portuguese to the Indies.

The Dutch expedition which sailed under Cornelius de Houtman in 1594 was not a success. It was followed by three attempts to find an alternative route round the north of Russia. Barents, the leader of one of these expeditions, died in the sea that now bears his name. The combination of the failure to find the north-east passage and the publication of Linschoten's account of his voyages with the Portuguese focused attention once again on the Cape route, and in the excitement of the thought of the large profits to be made, a company was formed named the 'Company of Far Lands', to trade with the Indies. A fleet of four ships was collected and sent to the East. In 1597, three of the ships returned to Texel with a quarter of the original crew. The ships were not heavily laden, but the cargo of pepper was more than enough to provide a handsome profit on the adventure. The next year, in 1598, five companies sent a total of twenty-two ships to the East. Four of the fleets took the route round Africa. The fifth, commanded by Olivier van Noort, went around Cape Horn and across the Pacific, thereby becoming the first Dutch ships to circumnavigate the world. The most successful of the fleets was that of the Company of Far Lands, under Jacob van Neck, which returned home in July 1599 with the richest cargo ever seen in Holland.

Although eight ships were lost from the 1598 expeditions, the returns on investments were so good that in 1601 no less than fourteen fleets totalling sixty-five ships were dispatched. This proliferation of companies for the Indies trade created unnecessary competition between Dutch nationals, and in 1602, after lengthy negotiations, most were amalgamated into the Vereenigde Oostindische Compagnie (The United Netherlands Chartered East India Company), known as the VOC. The company was given a monopoly for twenty-one years for all trade east of the Cape of Good Hope and west of the Straits of Magellan.

The English were more cautious. James Lancaster had seen the wealth in the Indies and realised the potential, but for a number of years he could not find the financial backing he needed to mount another expedition. However, the success of the early Dutch voyages and the threat that this posed to the English access to the spice trade forced the London merchants to take action, and in 1600 a charter was granted by Queen Elizabeth I to a group of merchants giving them the exclusive privilege of trading between the Cape of Good Hope and the Straits of Magellan for fifteen years. Lancaster was appointed Admiral of the fleet of three ships which sailed in 1601. This time all three returned home safely, after a profitable trading voyage. The British East India Company was off to a good start, with James Lancaster, now Sir James, as one of its directors.

In the early days of the British East India Company the number of ships sent out to India was small, and, because of a shortage of investment, these voyages were each a separate stock venture and their success depended to a very large extent upon the character and determination of the 'General' in each fleet. From 1615, when there had been a few good expeditions with returns of over 250 per cent, and it was possible to organise joint stock voyages, the importance of the 'General' in charge of a fleet declined as merchants were installed ashore. The Dutch moved more quickly, setting up their own factories where trade could be developed. Their centre of operations at Batavia (Djakarta) in Java soon rivalled Malacca, the main Portuguese city on the strategically important Malacca Strait. The usual Dutch East India Company practice was to sail three fleets a year from the East back to Holland. Two went at Christmas, and the other in late spring. The ships sailed in company whenever possible to avoid pirates, or enemies, and provide mutual assistance. The British, meanwhile, organised themselves in India, and traded with Batavia, Malacca, Persia and

Japan when the absence of war allowed. They had sailed a total of 166 ships by the end of the seventeenth century, when the average sailings had risen to twelve ships a year.

In the first decade of the seventeenth century, traffic around the Cape of Good Hope increased dramatically as the Portuguese struggled to retain their Eastern Empire, and Britain and the Netherlands strove to establish themselves, often at the expense of the Portuguese. The appearance of the English and Dutch as rivals for the trade with the Indies created a hazard for the Portuguese, who were considered fair game by both since they were ruled by Spain. In 1613 a British fleet defeated a Portuguese fleet at the Battle of Swally Hole, near Surat, where the British were trying to establish a trading factory. Portuguese ships at sea anywhere on the route east were equally at risk. In March 1622, the Goanese-built *nao São João Batista* sailed on her maiden voyage from Goa in company with the *Nossa Senhora do Paraiso*. Fifteen days out the hold was found to have fourteen hand spans of water, but because the pump fitted to the ship was for a smaller galleon, they had to lower barrels into the hold, which were filled by the crew, and then hoisted on deck and emptied. On 17th July the ships became separated during the night, and two days later the *São João Batista* sighted two Dutch ships coming towards her when in a latitude of about 35° 30′ south. They cleared the ship for the action they knew was coming, although this was made more difficult by the large quantity of private cargo stowed on deck. This cargo was to come in useful later. The Dutch ships, the *Mauritius* and the *Wapen van Rotterdam*, had left the Cape on 13th June bound for Batavia. They closed with the Portuguese and a battle commenced. The rate of fire cannot have been fast, as the Portuguese managed to loose off only two broadsides before night brought an end to the action.

The next morning the fight was resumed. During this day the Dutch received a fright as they sighted the Portuguese outward fleet of five ships. However, the fleet did not see the *São João Batista*, and sailed on towards the Mozambique Channel where four of its ships were destroyed by a combined English and Dutch fleet a few days later. These losses misrepresent the fighting abilities of the Portuguese which were well respected by their adversaries. On one occasion, two of their ships had beaten four Dutchmen at St. Helena.

Meanwhile the running battle between the solitary *nao* and the two Dutchmen continued for a total of nineteen days, during which the ships sailed as far as 42° south.

> We made bulwarks of the liberty-goods, which proved to be a great help, since thereafter they killed very few of our people, whereas they killed twenty men in the first two days before we adopted this device. During nine of these days they fought with us from sunrise to sunset,

> and they finally reduced us to the most miserable condition that can be imagined; for they shot away our bowsprit close to the gammoning and the mainmast a yard and a half above the partners, and the foresail, and the rudder which was an old one, having belonged to a great ship that had been broken up in Goa and been left lying on the beach for two years, and so was rotten, for this is the usual way in which they fit out ships in this country. I say this because the want of a rudder caused our destruction, for it was in such a state that two shots sufficed to shatter it to pieces. Nor was this the only deficiency with which this ship left Goa, for she did not carry a sufficient armament for fighting, mounting only eighteen guns of very small calibre; but withal we fought on until we had only two barrels of powder and twenty-eight cartridges left. Seeing that the ship was completely dismasted, and that the spare spars were so riddled with shot that the least damaged had nine holes in it, and that the ship was foundering through shot which struck us a fathom under water, while the rudder in breaking wrenched away two of the gudgeons, leaving open their bolt holes, so that we were slowly sinking without being able to overcome the leak or apply any remedy, and although every soul on board worked night and day at the pumps and scoops [. . .]

At this point part of the crew wanted to negotiate with the Dutch, but two emissaries who went to the *Mauritius* did not return owing to bad weather, and were made prisoner. The *Mauritius* disappeared at this stage, but the other ship continued to follow, even asking the Portuguese if they had seen the *Mauritius*. By this time they were sufficiently far south for it to snow, and the cold killed some of the slaves, but despite the weather they moved the mizzen-mast forward, and rigged a jury-bowsprit so that the ship was able to sail downwind, and they headed towards land. They managed to shake off their pursuer by lowering their sails one dark night, and thus stopping their boat. The Dutchman following at what had been their speed, overshot them and was not seen again. However, if they had got rid of their enemies, they were still in a pitiful condition. They tried to rig a jury-rudder, but after fifteen days awaiting better weather, it broke loose and started to damage the stern so they were glad when it came adrift altogether. Thereafter they steered the ship with two sweeps made from pieces of spars.

Eventually on 29th September they sighted land, and anchored off what they thought was a sandy beach on the 30th, and sent ashore a party of armed men to reconnoitre. Later the entire crew were landed, eighteen being drowned when the small anchor used to steady the boat in the surf broke loose, but in all 279 people reached the beach. The site of the landing is not known, it may be just east of Algoa Bay, where cannons have been found, but the account of the march would indicate a site further west. The ship was burned before the party set off overland for Sofala, but only thirty-one survived the march. The Dutch suffered severely as well, only seventy-five of the *Mauritius*'s crew of 317 reached Batavia, and on the *Wapen van Rotterdam* ninety-four out of an original company of 371.

From the earliest days an uneasy alliance existed between the British and the Dutch, sometimes they teamed up to fight the Portuguese, but on other occasions they fought each other on sight. A peace signed in 1619 between the two companies in Europe was celebrated, when the news arrived eight months later, by a one-hour lull between two fleets battling in the Indies. The Dutch were much the greater power at the time, and an idea of the strength of their merchant fleet can be gauged by the rough figures for tonnages of the main European maritime nations engaged in overseas trade about 1660. The Dutch are estimated to have had 900,000 tons, the British 500,000. The French, Portuguese and Spanish had about 250,000 each. Although the wars between the Dutch and the British were slowly whittling down Dutch strength, as the Dutch had to pass the British Isles either by the more dangerous northern route or through the English Channel where they were exposed to British privateers – in the war of 1652, for example, the Dutch lost some 1,700 ships whilst the British lost only 400 – the Dutch East India fleets were much the larger during the seventeenth century. Between 1610 and 1700 the Dutch sent 1,730 ships to the East, almost ten times the British figure, and this gave them a dominance of eastern trade. By the middle of the seventeenth century, no Portuguese possession was safe from Dutch attack, and the Portuguese had been pushed down the trading table to fourth behind the Dutch, British and French.

This concentration of shipping on the Indies trade could make the Cape area extremely dangerous for individual ships, particularly when there was a war between any of the nations concerned, and most were sent out and home in fleets for their own protection. However, actions in the Cape waters themselves were infrequent, probably because of the poor weather conditions, which meant that even if a ship won the fight and was only slightly damaged, she would be ill-prepared to face the next gale. A rare example occurred on 3rd February 1692 when a British Indiaman, the *Samuel*, met a French frigate, *L'Escueist*, off the Cape and was captured after losing her masts. After seeing his ship looted, the captain had to pay a ransom of £200 before he was released and sailed for shelter with his damaged ship.

Although all Indiamen were armed, they could not usually expect to defeat a warship of frigate size and above, neither would they be likely to outsail her. The Indiaman, although of a similar size to a frigate, was heavier, had smaller guns, and about a quarter of the crew. The best they could hope for was for a lucky shot at the warship's rigging to bring a mast

The *Batavia*, a typical Dutch East Indiaman, 1628.

down, and if that did not happen, surrender was inevitable. Throughout the history of the East India Company, the Indiamen relied upon being sufficiently well armed that, when in company with other Indiamen, they could between them keep their enemy at bay. An example of this occurred on 9th March 1757 when two French frigates attacked three British Indiamen in Cape waters. The British ships rounded on the frigates which hauled off in the face of a determined defence.

Indiamen would attack each other if their countries were at war and the odds looked attractive, but in peace they would assist a foreigner if it was in distress. In any case there must have been enough dangers for them to handle without fighting each other. Pirates had been quick to appear on the scene of so much valuable cargo, and they had established a major base for their operations at the island of St. Mary's near Madagascar as early as 1685. For a time the island rivalled Jamaica as a pirate lair, and one of the leaders, John Plantain, grew so powerful that he declared himself King of Madagascar in 1720. Thomas Tew, of Newport, Rhode Island, used St. Mary's on his very successful foray to the Indian Ocean in 1694, and each of his crew 'earned' £1,200 a man, a fortune in those days. Henry Every caused even more damage. With five other pirate ships he captured the Grand Mogul's treasure ship on its way from the Red Sea to India, with the result that the British East India Company's trading posts at Surat, Broach, Agra and Ahmedabad were closed down for a while.

Captain Kidd, however, famed as one of the most notorious of pirates, and one of the few to be caught and executed at Wapping Steps in London, did very little damage during his brief career from 1696 until 1700. He was commissioned originally to put down piracy, and take his share of their plunder as a reward. Somewhere on his voyage to the Indian Ocean he seems to have changed his mind, and decided to take up piracy himself. He was not very successful, and was arrested on his return to his native New York, from whence he was sent to London for trial and subsequent execution. Shortly afterwards, the Royal Navy sent a squadron of four ships to deal with the lair at St. Mary's, and piracy in the Indian Ocean declined for nearly twenty years, until the pirates were forced to return after Woodes Rogers had made the Caribbean too dangerous for them.

The Indiamen began to dread seeing the black flag of pirates on their long voyage from India to the Cape, but some would put up a good fight if attacked. In 1720 the British East Indiaman *Cassandra* was assaulted by two pirate ships, the *Fancy* and the *Victory*, off Madagascar. Another Indiaman, the *Greenwich*, was with the *Cassandra* at the time, but sailed clear and then hove-to to watch the proceedings. Captain Macrae of the *Cassandra* fought alone for four hours, and then, realising that he could not win, and in order to save his men from being butchered, he ran his ship ashore and escaped. The pirates were so furious that they offered a £2,000 reward for Macrae's head. None the less, this brave captain returned ten days later, and managed to bargain with the pirates for their badly damaged ship *Fancy* and half his cargo!

The captain of the *Victory*, John Taylor, took over the *Cassandra* and in April the next year sailed the two ships into Mauritius and attacked the Portuguese Indiaman *Nossa Senhora do Cabo*, which, hopelessly outgunned, surrendered; with her went a cargo of diamonds valued at about half a million pounds. This was one of the last real successes for the pirates, as once again the Royal Navy was dispatched to deal with the menace and they dispersed to other waters rather than face the warships. Piracy continued spasmodically, which is not surprising at a time when seamen were treated little better than gaolbirds, with hard labour and a good chance of being drowned. The last recorded case on the Cape route came as late as February 1832, when the British barque *Morning Star* was intercepted in the south Atlantic on her way home from Ceylon, by the Portuguese pirate Benito de Soto. Having injured the captain and raped the women passengers, de Soto holed the ship and abandoned her to sink and her crew to drown. Fortunately the crew managed to stop the leaks, and de Soto was subsequently caught and, on their evidence, executed at Cadiz.

But if the risks from piracy had declined, the normal dangers of a long ocean voyage were still as great. Ships continued to be lost or disabled by bad weather, and considered themselves lucky if they could find assistance. When the Dutch Indiaman *Naarstigheid* was badly damaged in a storm south of Mauritius, her two consorts lost sight of her, and she was left to jury-rig masts and head for shelter to undertake proper repairs. The hull was shaken so severely that ropes had to be passed round to hold it together and nearly all the cannons were flung overside to reduce weight. The crew was fortunate, as no one was lost: although three men were washed overside whilst hacking away the wreckage of the mizzen-mast, the next wave washed them back on board again. In this pitiable condition the ship headed for the African coast. On Tuesday 17th May 1757, another ship came into sight and was attracted by firing a cannon. She proved to be the British Indiaman *Delewar*, whose log for the day reads as follows:

> Light airs, calm and Fair weather.
>
> At half past 3 p.m. sent the pinnace on board a Dutch ship in distress and at half past 8 she returned. The ship is the *De Naarstegheyt* from Bengal which in a gale of wind on the 9th April was dismasted to her mainmast.
>
> At 11 sent the pinnace aboard the Dutch ship.
>
> Wednesday 18th May 1757.
>
> At 1 p.m. the pinnace returned and brought with her an half worn

> mainsail and a steering sail, for which in return we sent her a small spar and mizzen topsail yard.

The latitude is given as 33° 18′ south, and the longitude as 48° 44′ west of the *Delewar*'s departure point of Point Palmiras, which would put the position at about 300 miles south-east of Durban.

The *Naarstigheid* had hoped to reach Mossel Bay, but north-westerly winds prevented this so she headed for Mozambique, and anchored in Delagoa Bay in June 1757. Three parties were sent to try and reach Dutch outposts in the Cape, but all were forced back. A ship's boat was sent for help in May 1758, but it was never heard of again. Finally they were released from their enforced imprisonment by the arrival of the *Hector*, which had been dispatched to search for them after a message had been received by the Company in Holland from the *Delewar*. The Company provided another ship to remove the precious cargo, and the *Naarstigheid* was put ashore and burned.

Almost twenty years earlier the abandonment of the East Indiaman *Sussex* by her officers and most of her crew ended in a celebrated case in the London Law Courts. The story begins when two ships, the *Sussex* and *Winchester*, were sailing home in company from Java Head towards London and had reached a position about 500 miles east of Durban. The log of the *Winchester* states:

> 11th March 1738
>
> At 1 p.m. the Sussex makes a signal of distress, made sail and spoke her, she is very leaky and cannot keep free, had got 9 foot water in her hold when they cutt the masts away. Desired us to keep him company. At break of day the Sussex made a signal of distress and fired three guns. Made sail and ran under her stern and spoke to Captain Goslin. Desired for Gods sake to send our boats on board. Sent my Chief Mate on board with the yawl, he returned with Mr. Climsworth supercargo. Hoisted out their pinnace and little yawl and kept all these boats employed to save their people, their ship having three foot above the ceiling, the Captain, Supercargo and Officers having in consultation resolved to quit their ship. At noon had all their officers and sailors on board except about 15 who resolved to stay in their ship and accordingly as soon as my boats put off they set their foresail and steered away about north. I have 84 people aboard.

The immediate question is why did fifteen seamen decide to stay on board a ship that all the officers had given up as lost? The answer lies in the system of paying seamen at the time, by which if the ship failed to return home they received no pay for the voyage. If a ship were wrecked or abandoned the seamen lost everything, so it is not surprising that there are so many records of the men getting hopelessly drunk when a ship went ashore. The men who remained aboard the *Sussex* apparently felt that it was worth an effort to save the ship and her cargo so that they could claim all their pay since the voyage started, probably nearly two years' wages at this point. However, they took the precaution of asking the mate for a letter stating that the rest of the crew had left the *Sussex* voluntarily, so that they could, if necessary, prove that they were not pirates.

When the *Winchester* sailed away, the seamen, none of whom knew how to navigate, set course to the north for Madagascar, and pumped out the hold. Four days later they sailed into St. Augustine's Bay. For four weeks they worked at repairing the ship, and then decided to sail to Mozambique. It was on this voyage that their lack of navigational knowledge brought them to grief, and they piled up on the Bassas de India. Only five of the men managed to reach the shore, and of these just one, John Deane, survived to be rescued by another outward-bound British ship the following July. The story has a happy ending for Deane, who dictated an account of his adventures on the voyage to Bombay. When the East India Company read the report it sued Captain Goslin for £30,000, the value of the ship, and made Deane an award of £100 a year for life, a large sum in those days. It is salutary to note that the Company refused to employ anyone who had been in the crews of either the *Sussex* or *Winchester* again, to make an example for others.

One of the most famous Indiamen wrecks on the south African coast took place in 1782. The wreck itself did not cause the greatest loss of life, and the ship was a standard Indiaman of the time, but the fame of the *Grosvenor* is due largely to the rumour, which started towards the end of the nineteenth century, that she was carrying a fortune in treasure. The *Grosvenor* was the second of the name to serve with the East India Company, it being the practice at that time for the Company to charter vessels over a long period from selected owners who could replace one vessel with a new one and keep the charters running, a practice known as building on the bottom of an existing ship. The average life of an Indiaman was four voyages, which would mean between eight and twelve years in total. The first *Grosvenor* was built in 1762 and the second in 1770. The second, built by Joseph and William Wells at Rotherhithe, was of 729 tons, fifty tons heavier than her predecessor, but both were chartered officially at under 500 tons, for if a ship was greater than 500 tons a chaplain had to be carried. Oak was the material used in her construction and the ship measured 138′ 10″ overall in length, 35′ 3½″ beam, 14′ depth of hold, and 5′ 10″ between decks. She was three-masted and rigged as a ship. The Wells shipyard was highly regarded, as it built 108 Indiamen between 1757 and 1827 for various owners. The armament of East Indiamen was laid down by Act of Parliament, and thus the *Grosvenor* carried twenty 9-pounders and six 6-pounder cannons, making her not dissimilar to a 4th Rate of the Navy.

On her fourth and last voyage from India in 1782, the *Grosvenor* was delayed on the Indian coast carrying supplies for the army fighting against Hyder-Ali, and later by the need for ships to sail in convoy because of the war with France. She left Madras on 31st March, and took part in the action against Admiral Suffren between 12th and 19th April, before arriving at Trincomalee, where she remained until 13th June. Captain Coxon, who had served as mate of the ship on her first two voyages, and was about to complete his second voyage as master, must have found the delays vexatious, as apart from the loss of a year, which meant that his own anticipated profit on his private trading, perhaps worth as much as £10,000, would be spread over three instead of two years, he had missed the best time to round the Cape.

The *Grosvenor* followed the usual route for Indiamen, south through the Indian Ocean to roughly the latitude of Cape Sainte Marie, the southern end of Madagascar, and then south-west for the Cape. Bad weather and a sprung mainmast slowed her progress as she approached the African coast, and the overcast weather prevented the captain taking any observations, so he was dependent upon dead-reckoning. On the evening of Saturday 4th August 1782, when the captain thought he was some 300 miles from land, the ship was at last experiencing a favourable wind and the course was west-norwest. At one o'clock the next morning a cold front passed and the wind veered to the south-west and increased. Sail was reduced to the foresail and mizzen staysail and whilst aloft, one of the seamen reported that he could see two large lofty spreading lights. The mate decided to wear ship and come round to an easterly course, but the captain, who had just come on deck, countermanded the order. At the change of watch at four in the morning, the lookout reported that he could plainly see land on the starboard bow. Other members of the crew began to pick out the land, but the third officer refused to believe them, and so the crew awoke the captain, who came on deck and immediately gave the order to wear ship. The ship was in the process of coming round when, according to the survivors' accounts, the port bow struck the rocks. The fact that it was the port bow that struck indicates just how near the ship was to getting clear. Efforts were made to sail her off when the wind came offshore at daybreak, but the rocks tore a hole in the bottom and the ship filled rapidly with water. Some of the crew managed to get a hawser ashore in an attempt to help the others to safety, but shortly after midday the ship broke in two. The two halves were swept inshore by the waves, and most of those left on board were able to reach land. In all fifteen men were lost, and 123 of the crew, including some women passengers, reached the beach. Their march to the south is an horrendous tale, most dying of exhaustion or from injuries received from natives, and only seventeen survived. In 1790 an expedition found three old women, apparently British, living in a mixed community of non-Africans, near the Mngazi River south of Port St. Johns, and these may have been from the *Grosvenor*.

The position of the wreck has been established as Tezani Bay a few miles north of Port St. Johns. *Tezani* in the local language means 'gather firewood', and the survivors said that the natives collected timber from the wreck and burned it for the iron it contained. However, it is possible that the Dutch Indiaman *Bennebroek* went ashore in the same spot, or close by, in 1713, and the cannon and pig-iron ballast that have been found in this vicinity could therefore have come from either ship.

The *Grosvenor*'s loss has to be blamed on her master, Captain Coxon, because although the charts available at the time were wildly inaccurate and put land 100 miles west of its actual position, he had been unable to obtain a check on his latitude for some time, and should have been more cautious since the last accurate longitude was Ceylon. Still, this does not excuse the lack of response by the third officer, who should have informed his captain of the crew's subsequent sightings, and it is certain that if the ship had started to wear even a few minutes before, she might have been saved. For many years it was believed that the *Grosvenor* was carrying a part of Sir Robert Clive's fortune as well as a cargo of bullion, and strenuous efforts have been made to recover this treasure, the most energetic being in the early 1950s. However, Professor P. Kirby, who has made a detailed study of the ship, states quite categorically that although she carried a valuable cargo, most of this was cloth and timber, with the usual spices, and the value of the gold, silver and diamonds on board at the time of the wreck, although considerable, does not warrant the description treasure ship.

A year later the Company apparently lost another of its Indiamen, the *Nicobar*, just east of Cape Agulhas, from which only eleven of the crew succeeded in getting ashore. However, although the wreck of the *Nicobar* is recorded, the name does not appear in the list of Company ships, so she may have been on a one-voyage charter. Another vessel chartered for one voyage with a cargo of rice was the American-registered *Hercules* which was deliberately beached to save the crew on 8th June 1796, after she had lost her rudder and smashed her stern frame in severe seas off the coast, and was in danger of foundering. All the crew survived.

Just before the *Hercules* was lost, the Dutch surrendered control of the Cape to the British in 1795. The Dutch East India Company had been in decline for some time; it had become less enterprising and its power had begun to wane. The confidence with which the early Dutch merchants had gone to the East and carved out a trading empire was slowly sapped. The early energy was dissipated by the lifestyle of its merchants, and the demands for profit above everything else created an attitude which discouraged long-term investment. The dominance of the Dutch in the East was being challenged by the rising ambitions of the British and French, both of whom had greater populations and resources, and eventually this forced the VOC to provide expensive warships to escort its ships in waters it had formerly dominated. In part, the Dutch East India Company's decline was just a reflection of a general collapse of Dutch maritime leadership. At the end of the century, the Company still employed close to 30,000 seamen, but the standards of both the seamen and their shipping had fallen behind those of their rivals. The Company was no longer making the enormous profits that had given it power in the seventeenth and early eighteenth centuries, and when France invaded and occupied the Netherlands in 1792, the Company was almost bankrupt, although it continued to operate independently from Batavia.

During the Napoleonic Wars the number of British East Indiamen sailing increased greatly, although their losses from enemy action were slight. A number of ships disappeared, however, between Mauritius and the Cape, and there is no record of exactly where they were lost. In 1802 the *Prince of Wales* vanished in a gale in June, and in 1806 the *Skelton Castle* parted from her consort, the *Union*, on 21st December and disappeared. In 1807 the *Ganges* foundered in position 39° 22′ south, 19° 50′ east. The following year no fewer than three ships, the *Lord Nelson*, the *Glory* and the *Experiment*, all parted company from the return fleet in a gale on 28th October and were never seen again.

One of the heaviest losses in the Company's history occurred on 15th February 1809, to a convoy of Indiamen assembled south of Ceylon for the voyage home under the escort of Captain Sir Edward Pellew on HMS *Culloden*. On 14th April, when south of Mauritius, the convoy met a very strong gale which lasted for three days and separated the ships. Once the storm had blown past, Sir Edward set about collecting the fleet, but five of the Indiamen were missing. Assuming that they had managed to go on ahead, the rest of the ships headed towards Cape Town for repairs. Whilst in Table Bay, they saw one of the missing ships, the *Sir William Bentley*, sail past. In May the fleet reached St. Helena, a normal convoy collecting-point for homeward-bound vessels, but the other four missing ships had not yet arrived. Sir Edward continued to England, but a short time later, when another ship arrived from St. Helena, it was realised that four large Indiamen, the *Calcutta*, *Bengal*, *Lady Jane Dundas*, *Jane Duchess of Gordon*, and their valuable cargoes, had vanished completely. No clue has yet been unearthed to show what happened to them. The wreck of the *William Pitt* on 16th December 1814 with all her crew east of Algoa Bay is one of the last known East India Company losses in Cape waters, but to put matters

A view of Simon's Town in the mid-nineteenth century, showing Admiralty House and the Wesleyan Chapel.

The entrance to Knysna Harbour, bearing north-north-east, showing the prominent cliffs on either side.

The clipper ship *Cutty Sark* by C. D. Cobb, one of Britain's finest tea clippers, now at Greenwich, London.

J. Rogers' painting of the SS *Great Britain,* built in 1843 and for many years the world's largest iron-built steamer. It is now preserved at Bristol in England.

into perspective, forty-four ships sailed from England for India and China that year.

At the end of the Napoleonic Wars in 1815, Britain had gained full control of the trade in the Indies, and had captured or destroyed all her rivals' trading bases, apart from a few small enclaves. The Cape had been seized from the Dutch again in 1806, and the Seychelles and Mauritius taken from France in 1810. Java was captured from the Dutch in 1811. Ceylon was now a British territory, and the Mogul Emperors of India were under East India Company protection. To the south-east, Australia was being developed as a British colony, and New Zealand was to follow shortly. The Chinese and Japanese trades were still open, but control of the seas meant that the British were dominant in these areas as well. Shipping using the Cape route was about to experience its greatest increase since the Dutch and British first came onto the scene.

4

The Cape Route – The Age of Steam

Within ten years of the end of the Napoleonic Wars, and whilst the East India Company was still building slow and cumbersome sailing ships for its trade, the first of a new kind of ship arrived at the Cape, which was to lead to the greatest transformation in shipping since men first made boats. This was the 464-ton auxiliary paddle-steamer *Enterprise*, which called at Cape Town to replenish her coal bunkers on 13th October 1825, whilst on passage to Calcutta from Falmouth. She was attempting to win a prize of 100,000 rupees being offered for the first ship to complete a round voyage from Britain to India in 140 days. The *Enterprise* was powered by two sixty-horsepower engines, one for each of the fifteen-foot diameter paddles, and so much space was required for the machinery and coal that there was room left for only a few passengers. She took fifty-eight days on her voyage from England to the Cape, during which she steamed for only thirty-five, relying on her barque rig for the remainder, and reached Calcutta after 113 days, which included ten days for re-bunkering. Although the *Enterprise* had not achieved the passage time stipulated, her performance was considered impressive enough to warrant her owners receiving half the prize money. She was subsequently bought by the Bengal Government for £40,000, just £3,000 less than she had cost, and remained in service until 1838.

Another steam-assisted vessel made the same voyage shortly after the *Enterprise*. This was Lord Yarborough's yacht *Falcon* of 170 tons. Although these voyages attracted a great deal of interest – over 4,000 people visited the *Enterprise* in one afternoon whilst she was in Cape Town – they also showed that the early steamships were as yet too expensive on a long run. In 1831 a small steamship, the *Sophia Jane*, was brought from England and offered for sale for the coasting trade, which gives an indication as to how this trade had grown. Unfortunately no one bought her, and she continued to Australia, the first steamer to arrive there, and was employed as a coaster for many years.

The transmission of dispatches and mail from India to Britain had been safely entrusted to vessels sailing via the Cape, but, in emergencies and when conditions allowed, it was quicker to send them on what became known as the overland route. In 1830, the East India Company sent a Bombay-built steam packet, the *Hugh Lindsay*, to Suez which resulted in mails arriving in London in fifty-nine days, then an incredibly short time. This route (by ship to Suez, then overland to Cairo, where the mail and passengers took a Nile boat downriver to Alexandria, and from there were transhipped onto a packet vessel for Marseilles or England) proved, on average, marginally quicker than the route from Calcutta to England via the Cape. It was championed by the Bombay Merchants because it gave them a slightly speedier access to their mails, which otherwise had to be transhipped from the Calcutta ships. However, the voyage from Bombay to Suez was often slow in a sailing ship, and difficult for steamships because they had to have coal sent in advance by sailing ships to strategically placed depots along their route, and so the favoured mail run remained via the Cape for the present.

In 1828 Thomas Waghorn, a retired Naval Officer, had attempted to start a service to India via the Cape using small 250-ton packet ships, which would carry mails and passengers only, but provide a faster and more reliable service to both places. Unfortunately the rates for Indian postage were reduced at the same time, and finding no commercial support for his project, he concentrated on developing the overland route instead.

Although a regular steamer service was not established, Cape Town saw a succession of steam-assisted vessels pass through on their way for service in the East from 1837 onwards, particularly after the East India Company decided to adopt steamships for its whole fleet in 1836. The first of these was the 617-ton *Atlanta*, which called in February 1837, and she was soon followed by many others. From being a rare sight in 1837, steam no longer attracted particular attention by 1840, although in that year one ship equipped with steam did create interest. This was the East India Company's frigate *Nemesis* of 700 tons, the first iron-built ship to round the Cape.

The overland way for mails from India became the prime route in 1844, when the Peninsular and Oriental Steam Navigation Company, which had started services from England to India with the *Hindostan* in 1842, was given a contract for a monthly service to take Indian mails to and from Suez for £160,000 a year. The *Hindostan* and the *Bentinck* were new steamers built especially for this run, but they had to make their way out via the Cape, and, as usual, coal had to be sent on in advance to Cape Town. From this time the bulk of mail and passengers took the overland route, but heavier cargoes still had to be carried around the Cape until the opening of the Suez Canal, which reduced the distance from England to Bombay by 4,500 miles.

Even as steam was slowly gaining a reputation for speed and reliability over the heavy and slow-sailing vessels of the time, a development in the United States provided sail with an advance that was to make it competitive on most routes until the opening of the Suez Canal. The new vessel, the apogee of commercial sail, was the clipper ship. The first of the true clippers was the *Rainbow*, of 750 tons, built in 1845. A great deal of controversy surrounded her building, many people saying that her sharp ends and concave bow would make her unmanageable. However, she soon disposed of all criticism by sailing from New York to Canton and back in six months and fourteen days, considerably faster than normal. Others followed, and in 1850 the *Oriental* was chartered by British tea shippers to take a cargo back to London. Her time of ninety-seven days from Hong Kong to the West India Docks via the Cape was almost a month faster than the best British ships could make and caused a sensation in London.

British ships had been hindered by the tonnage laws of 1773, which measured a ship on length and breadth but ignored depth. These requirements resulted in heavy, safe but very sluggish sailers. The practice of the East India Company in automatically renewing charters for ships had not encouraged innovation as no syndicate or owner was going to spend extra money on a fast ship when the charter was guaranteed. Towards the end of the East India Company's reign as a trading company (from 1834 it became the administrative ruler of India), the arrival of the famous Blackwall frigates of about 1,000 tons was some improvement on the previous sailing boxes, but in no way compared with the new American ships. The arrival of the *Oriental* in a record time was greeted with dismay, and caused long editorials about the decline of the British merchant fleet in the London papers.

However, the British response was not long in coming and the incentive was, as usual, commercial. In those days a premium of £1 or £2 per ton could be gained for the first tea landed in England, and when the freight rates were in the region of £5 a ton, a premium of forty per cent was not to be lightly ignored. The ships nearest in appearance to the American clippers were Alexander Hall's Aberdeen clippers, which had introduced a sharper bow in 1841. After the *Oriental*'s success, two new ships were ordered from Hall's, the *Stornoway* and the *Chrysolite*. They were narrower than the American ships, which made them less powerful in heavy weather, but they were faster in moderate breezes. In 1851 the *Chrysolite* completed her maiden round voyage of 29,837 miles in 206 days, a time that was not beaten by an American that season. The following year the *Chrysolite* and the *Stornoway* left Whampoa together and raced for home. For forty-five days of their passage across the Indian Ocean and round the Cape of Good Hope to the Atlantic they were in sight of each other, but *Chrysolite*, despite being slightly the smaller of the two, reached Liverpool three days before her rival arrived in London.

The racing became intense between the two nations, and each year saw new ships especially commissioned to compete in the most coveted and best publicised commercial contest of the time. Designers, captains and shipyards all vied to produce faster ships, knowing that in one year success could make a reputation. Usually the American ships went out from New York via Cape Horn to California, where in the early 1850s the gold rush created a huge demand for passages. From there they sailed across the Pacific to China to load. The return route was normally via the Cape of Good Hope, which the British ships used both ways. In general the American ships were the larger, but they were built of softwood and were less rigid in their construction. Although this made them cheaper to build, they did not last as long as the British hardwood and composite wood-and-iron ships. Four years was a good average racing life for a tea clipper, after which she would be put onto another, less demanding, run, but even there she could easily outsail the traditional heavy ships. The competition forced all shipowners who were not dabbling in steam to adopt the clipper ship model on every route.

The heyday of the China tea run was during the 1850s and 60s, when the fastest ships and finest crews took part in races that rivalled the Derby in public interest. From 1860 onwards it was an almost entirely British affair, as by then the Americans had withdrawn from the scene, and the battle for supremacy in ship design and building was waged between the Clyde and Aberdeen.

The greatest race took place in 1866, when no less than fourteen clippers loaded together at Foochow. *Ariel* was the first to depart, but accidents during her tow downriver delayed her so that *Fiery Cross* took the lead, and *Taeping* and *Serica* caught up. The first part of the race was to Anjer in the Sunda Strait, which *Fiery Cross* reached on 18th June two days ahead of *Ariel* and *Taeping*, and she increased her lead by a day at the longitude of Mauritius. *Fiery Cross* closed the Natal coast to obtain the best of the Agulhas Current, but the other ships went further south and obtained a better wind. From the Cape, *Taeping* took a course close to the African coast, and when she passed St. Helena on 27th July was a day ahead. *Fiery Cross* and *Serica* passed on the 28th, and *Ariel* on the 29th. At the equator *Fiery Cross*, *Ariel* and *Taeping* were once again level, and although *Ariel* took a lead of a day by the Azores, she and the *Taeping* entered the English Channel together with every inch of canvas set. Both passed the Lizard at 8 a.m. on 5th September, and took their pilots at the South Foreland at 6 a.m. the next day. *Ariel* had a slight advantage at this point, but was picked up by a slower tug in the Downs, and arrived at Gravesend fifty-five minutes behind *Taeping*. The race was not over yet though, as both vessels had to be towed up river, the competition being over only when the ships docked. *Ariel* had the shorter distance to travel to the East India Docks, but, because of her extra draught in the water, she was unable to enter, and *Taeping* managed to get inside the London Docks twenty minutes ahead. So *Taeping* won the extra 10s. a ton freight, but it had been agreed between the owners that the money would be shared, as they suspected that if the ships docked simultaneously the tea merchants might claim that there was no winner. *Serica* arrived at the West India Docks on the same tide, so all three ships shared a homeward passage time of ninety-nine days.

None of the ensuing tea races was to be as close as that of 1866, but in 1872 a contest between *Thermopylae* and *Cutty Sark* aroused great interest because each was considered to be the fastest ship afloat by her supporters. Both left Shanghai at the same time, and *Cutty Sark* had a useful lead when she lost her rudder south of the Cape. For six days she was hove-to whilst the crew made and fitted a jury-rudder, and just as it was rigged, another strong westerly gale delayed her further. By this time *Thermopylae* had taken the lead, which she held to the finish, arriving six days ahead of her rival. Although *Thermopylae* was the winner, it was held generally that had *Cutty Sark* not lost her rudder she would have been home first, so the argument as to which of these beautiful clippers was the fastest was never resolved.

The opening of the Suez Canal in 1869 brought an end to the China tea races, and the last proper sailing race took place in 1873. Thereafter the fast steamers were able to cut fifteen to twenty days off the clipper times by going through Suez, and guaranteeing to reach the London market first. The clippers continued to trade for the next few years, but gradually the numbers diminished as they were transferred to other trades, in particular the Australian run.

Even as public interest was excited by the record performances of the clipper ships in the 1850s and 1860s, a quieter revolution was taking place on another of the Cape sea routes, between Britain and Australia. Australia had been colonised initially with convicts in 1788, but the first free immigrants arrived in 1793, and thereafter the colony expanded rapidly. Trade between Britain and Australia grew steadily throughout the nineteenth century as the population was increased by more immigrants who, having settled, began producing for the British and Indian markets. This expansion, and the commerce it developed, was almost totally dependent upon shipping from Britain.

The traditional route for sailing ships to Australia was out via the Cape of Good Hope and home via Cape Horn, taking advantage of the prevailing westerly winds of the Roaring Forties which are to be found in a consistent stream between latitudes 40 and 50° south. Some services avoided Cape Horn by returning via the Cape, picking up the southern edge of the ocean wind circulation in the Indian Ocean, which is easterly at about 35° south. This route was preferred by the steamships. Most of these ships called in at Cape Town on their way to take on supplies and give their passengers a chance to stretch their legs.

Then gold was discovered in Australia about 1849 and there was an immediate rush of prospectors anxious to try and achieve wealth overnight. The requirement for berths to Australia from Britain, and also the desire for a speedy passage, brought a sudden influx of steamships onto this longest of all the ocean runs. Sailing ships and steamers alike were taken off other runs to supply the demand. In 1852 the first regular steamship mail-run to Australia was commenced by the Australian Royal Mail Navigation Company. The *Australian*, of 1,500 tons, sailed in 1852, and was followed by two others, the *Sydney* and *Melbourne*. However, the ships proved unreliable and the company lost the contract in 1853. The gold rush was also the cause of the largest ship in the world visiting the Cape. The *Great Britain*, of 3,448 tons, built of iron in a special dock in Bristol in 1843, made an appearance at Cape Town on 10th October 1852. An advertisement placed in the Cape Town papers by her agents ran:

> The magnificent and celebrated screw steamship Great Britain, 3,500 tons register, 500 horse-power, may be expected in Table Bay on the 20th September. Her sailing qualities and those of a powerful steamship combined have been found far to exceed anything yet accomplished. Her cabin accommodations are of extreme splendour, fitted up quite regardless of expense. Descriptions having been so fully set forth in the English newspapers, accompanied with the highest eulogiums, further comment is now needless. Passengers may be conditionally engaged in the fore and aft saloon, or second cabin.

The cost of a saloon passage to Cape Town was fifty guineas, and although the ship was expected to arrive on 20th September, thus making a passage of twenty-six days' duration, she suffered the not unusual fate of steamships at that time and had to return to St. Helena on the voyage out in order to replenish her bunkers. The *Great Britain* only called at the Cape twice again during her long life. The first time was on the return voyage from Australia, the second when carrying troops out to India to help quell the mutiny in 1857. She is now preserved in dry dock in Bristol.

The numbers travelling out for the Australian gold rush peaked during 1852, when it was estimated that at one time as many as 5,000 people were sailing from Britain every week. Shipping home was seriously affected for a time as entire ships' crews deserted to seek their fortunes, once they reached Australia, and the men to crew the ships for the return voyages could not be found.

The increased traffic generated by the gold rush had scarcely subsided, when the Indian Mutiny broke out in 1857. A huge uprising of this kind could not be quelled by the relatively small detachments of British troops in the Indian Ocean area, and the British Government set about requisitioning ships on a scale only slightly less than that required for the Crimean War which had just finished. Some regiments were sent directly from the Crimea to India and it was over twenty years before these soldiers saw their homeland again. Detachments of troops in southern Africa were rapidly dispatched, and as other troopships arrived in the Cape, they were diverted to India. Vast numbers of reinforcements were sent out, most of which were still in transit when the mutiny was crushed in November 1857. In December 1857, there were 68 India-bound troopers and supply ships anchored in Table Bay, amongst them the two largest steamships in the world, the *Great Britain* and the *Himalaya*, the ex-P & O liner purchased by the Government as a trooper. Of this great fleet, only five ships were in fact steamers, the remainder were sailing ships, which shows that even after steam seemed to be well established, the bulk of the world's maritime trade was still carried in sail.

The situation began to change rapidly once the Suez Canal was opened in 1869, and the Cape route to the East and Australasia became less important. Although the saving on distance between England and Sydney over the Cape route was quite small, sailing ships came under increasing economic pressure. They were soon forced to cut down their crews, which in many cases meant re-rigging the fully rigged ships as barques, and accepting the less urgent or cheaper freighted cargoes. The Indian trade transferred immediately to the Suez route, which was considerably shorter, and most of the steamship trade to Australasia chose the new route for both their outward and homeward passages because they could guarantee a faster time. Cargoes from the Cape to India and Australasia were small, and hardly justified the additional time and distance that had to be covered for them, and the Cape route began to lose its passing steamer traffic, although, at the same time, it had been developing its own direct run to and from Britain.

A company that had regularly made use of the Cape route for its voyages to Australia was the Orient Line, founded in the middle of the nineteenth century. It continued to use this route until 1883, when, as a part of the conditions of obtaining the New South Wales mail contract, it was obliged to move its ships onto the Suez route. Money, Wigram and Company, Alfred Holt's Blue Funnel Line, and the Commonwealth and Dominion Line, all of whose ships had called habitually at the Cape, also found at about the same time that the Suez route was more economic for their steamships, and although some ships continued to sail out via Table Bay, these Companies' house flags were seen less and less in Cape waters. However, sailing ships used the Cape route until their virtual disappearance from the maritime scene at the end of the First World War because of the high cost of taking tugs through Suez, and the need to time the voyage to coincide with a favourable monsoon in the Indian Ocean. They rarely stopped on their lonely run down the Atlantic and across the Indian Ocean in the Roaring Forties, unless they had a cargo to load or discharge.

Ships to New Zealand took the same course as those to Australia, using the Cape route until the Suez Canal was available. Later, in 1914 when the Panama Canal was opened, much of the traffic transferred to the western route from Britain across the Atlantic and Pacific Oceans. The distance from Britain to New Zealand via Suez was 13,000 miles, but by taking the Panama Canal, this was reduced to 11,000 miles. Sail had just been able to compete with steam, mainly on the long-distance trades, until 1914, but the opening of the Panama Canal that year dealt it the final economic blow. From Sydney, Australia, to Britain via Cape Horn was 16,000 miles, but via Panama it was only about 12,200 miles. Perhaps more importantly, the distance between New York and San Francisco was drastically cut by avoiding the long passage around both sides of South America, and this, the Chilean nitrate trade, and the Australian wool trade were the last routes on which sail had been able to compete.

One of the most famous of the shipping companies to ply the Cape route to China and Australia after the opening of the Suez Canal was the Aberdeen Line (George Thompson and Company) later known as the Aberdeen White Star Line, which started services in 1846. Its ships, renowned for their fine appearance, were regular callers at Table Bay unless compelled to crack on as happened in the tea races. Until 1881 its fleet consisted entirely of sailing vessels, including *Thermopylae*, the premier ship of the China tea run and the fastest sailing ship on record in the British merchant marine. On one occasion she managed to cover 425 miles in a twenty-four-hour period. However, in 1881, Thompson's took delivery of the 3,600-ton steamer *Aberdeen*, the first ocean-going ship to be fitted with the more efficient triple expansion engines, and began the gradual replacement of the sailing vessels with steamers. Most of these still went out to Australia via the Cape, some returning by the same route, but others via Suez. Amongst these was a new *Thermopylae* which, on a return voyage in 1899, went ashore off Green Point as it entered Table Bay. All the passengers and crew, as well as two valuable racehorses, were recovered, but the ship broke up, covering the shore with frozen meat which had been her principal cargo. The Company continued to operate this run until 1928, when it became amalgamated with Lord Kylsant's shipping empire, and from then on remnants of the fleet, but in the Shaw Savill livery, made only occasional stops in Table Bay.

Another company that used the Cape route was the Blue Anchor Line, which served Australia with sailing vessels until 1880, when its first steamer, the 1,807-ton *Delcomyn*, was commissioned. In its early days it concentrated on cargo, and one of these vessels, the *Wallarah*, was wrecked on Dassen Island in 1891. In 1896 accommodation for passengers was introduced, and a rivalry developed between the Blue Anchor and Aberdeen White Star lines. When in 1908 the Aberdeen Line brought out the *Pericles*, which was a considerable improvement on any existing via Cape liners, the Blue Anchor Line responded by building the twin-screw 9,339-ton liner *Waratah*, an imposing vessel for the time, but one which was to disappear without trace, providing yet another sea mystery in Cape waters.

The *Waratah* was on the homeward part of her second round voyage in July 1909, when she put into Durban for coal bunkers. She sailed on 26th July, and the next morning exchanged visual signals with the *Clan MacIntyre* about twelve miles off the coast in the vicinity of Mbashe Point. This was the last time the *Waratah* was seen. The day after the *Waratah* had overtaken her, the *Clan MacIntyre* ran into hurricane-force winds and mountainous seas, which were also experienced by other vessels in the area. The Rennie ship *Ilovo*, which had left Durban two days before the *Waratah*, eventually reached Cape Town a day overdue, having encountered very heavy seas near Danger Point on 27th July. A Norwegian steamer, the *Solveig*, had had the same experience, but off Algoa Bay. The *Waratah* was expected in Cape Town on Thursday 29th July, and when she did not arrive it was supposed that she might have been held up by the bad weather. Few ships carried radios in those days, and if they were delayed there was no way to inform the authorities ashore. By the weekend she had not appeared and other ships were dispatched to look for her, and the coast lookout stations alerted, in case she had suffered a mechanical breakdown. No trace of the ship, or of her seventeen lifeboats was ever found.

Two operations to find the *Waratah* were launched, one by the Government which chartered the Union–Castle's *Sabine*, to search the area from the south African coast to the Crozet Islands, and another from Melbourne, which sent the *Wakefield* to investigate in the Southern Ocean as far as the Marion Islands. Although these expeditions overlapped, nothing was sighted. A speedy response was essential in case the ship had gone ashore on one of the Southern Ocean islands. An emigrant ship bound from England to New Zealand in 1849, the *Richard Dart*, was wrecked on Marion Island, losing all but eleven of her crew, who existed on sea birds and eggs for seventy-two days until rescued by a visiting sealer. Eight years later the same sealer, the *Maria*, stranded on Prince Edward Island, and her crew had to wait seven months before they were collected. Even assuming that the *Waratah* had gone ashore, it was very doubtful whether the large numbers on board, including many less fitted to the survival existence than the seamen of the other two ships, could have endured for long.

Apart from a rash of eye-witness accounts of sightings of the vessel between East London and the Mbashe River, the only possible evidence from the ship was the sighting of four clothed bodies in the water off Mbashe Point by the steamer *Insizwa* in early August. Because of the heavy seas, she was unable to recover any of them, so it will never be known for sure whether these were from the luckless ship. At a subsequent enquiry the stability of the vessel was questioned, but any conclusions were pure conjecture. Possibly she lost her engines, and swung beam onto the seas which might have rolled her over, but it is equally possible that she was another victim of the freak waves in that area.

For some time after her disappearance, it was believed that the *Waratah* might have suffered the same fate as the 4,700-ton steamer *Waikato* which experienced an engine breakdown 150 miles south of Cape Agulhas on 6th June 1899, when bound for New Zealand. She was next sighted and taken in tow by another steamer, the *Asloun*, on 15th September the same year, when in position 39° 20′ south latitude, and 65° east longitude. During 101 days in the Southern Ocean the ship had drifted 2,076 miles almost due east, at an average speed of just under one knot.

The loss of the *Waratah* was a blow from which the Blue Anchor Line could not recover, and in 1910 it was taken over by P & O. New tonnage was added for the Australia-via-Cape service, which continued until 1929, when the decline in trade due to the depression made the Cape Town stop unprofitable and the ships were re-routed via Suez.

In the meantime, in 1904, the Cape inadvertently had become involved in the war between Russia and Japan. Two Russian auxiliary cruisers slipped out of the Dardanelles, and one, the *Smolensk*, made her way down to the Cape where she stopped the Harrison liner *Comedian*, bound for Durban, some eighty miles from East London. After looking for further ships which she believed might be carrying goods for Japan, the *Smolensk* joined her consort in Zanzibar. A much larger effort was put into the Russian attempts to destroy the Japanese fleet. The Russian Baltic fleet was dispatched under Admiral Rozhdesvensky to sail round the Cape and relieve the blockade of Port Arthur on the Manchurian coast. The fleet of obsolete ships sailed in October and almost immediately drew attention to itself by firing on British fishing vessels working on the Dogger Bank in the North Sea, which it suspected might be hiding Japanese torpedo boats. Despite British public outcry, they were allowed to continue, and in December re-bunkered at Lüderitz. There was considerable alarm lest Cape fishing vessels might also be mistaken for the Japanese, but no incidents occurred, and the fleet, accompanied by a train of colliers and store ships, sailed safely past Cape Town on 19th December. The Russians eventually reached Japanese waters in May 1905 after an epic voyage, and were attacked by the Japanese fleet in the Tsushima Strait on 27th May. For a while the resulting battle was indecisive, but after Admiral

Rozhdesvensky was wounded, the Japanese began to gain the upper hand, and by the next morning, after night attacks by Japanese torpedo boats, the entire Russian fleet was either captured or sunk. The battle aroused great interest in naval circles as it was the first engagement between armoured battle fleets at sea.

As the South African economy developed with the discovery of diamonds and then gold, a number of direct South African shipping services were established in the years prior to the First World War. The British India Steam Navigation Company extended their Zanzibar mail service from India down to Durban and Cape Ports in 1902, and Andrew Weir's commenced one to India from Durban in 1906 which was later extended to the Far East. Apart from the direct New Zealand service sponsored by the New Zealand Government, and operated by Federal, Shire and Houlders, another was inaugurated in 1902 between Canada and South Africa by Furness Withy and Elder Dempsters. For a short period between 1901 and 1908 there was even an irregular service operated between South American ports and South Africa by the Nelson Line.

The uninterrupted peaceful traffic around the Cape came to an end when the First World War began in August 1914. Just before war broke out, the small German gunboat *Eber* had been on a visit to Cape Town, but no warships were available to apprehend her, and she escaped, to transfer her crew and armament to the auxiliary cruiser *Cap Trafalgar*. On 14th September, the *Cap Trafalgar* met the ex-Cunard liner and now auxiliary cruiser *Carmania*, and in a long, hard-fought engagement, the *Cap Trafalgar* was sunk. As in the Napoleonic Wars 100 years before, the Cape route at once became of vital importance to the Allied Forces of Britain and France, particularly when Turkey entered the war on the side of Germany.

At the start of hostilities the greatest menace to Cape shipping came from the German cruisers that were at large all over the world. Considerable numbers of British warships had to be diverted to deal with this danger. The most powerful enemy force at sea was the cruiser squadron of Vice-Admiral Graf von Spee, which met and defeated an inferior British squadron off Coronel, in Chile, on 1st November. Immediate steps were taken to reinforce the small Cape squadron, as it was felt that von Spee might well decide to strike at this important centre for British shipping, but, just over a month after Coronel, a superior British Squadron caught and sank four out of the five German warships off the Falkland Islands. Only the *Dresden* escaped, and she was destroyed three months later by British cruisers in Chilean waters, having sunk only one sailing ship in the interim. The light cruiser *Emden* had played havoc with Indian Ocean shipping and almost brought it to a halt, before she was found and destroyed at the Cocos Islands by the cruiser HMAS *Australia* on 9th November 1914, after sinking twenty-three ships.

The German cruiser *Königsberg* was in east African waters at the beginning of the war, and the Cape Squadron of three old cruisers under Rear-Admiral King-Hall was sent to deal with her. Before she could be found, the *Königsberg* came across the light cruiser HMS *Pegasus* in Zanzibar cleaning boilers and destroyed her. With Dar-es-Salaam closed by a block ship, the *Königsberg* now made for the Rufiji delta where she was blockaded. Her disposal was another matter, however, as the British ships could not see their quarry because of the thick mangrove swamps. Eventually, a converted passenger ship, HMS *Kinfauns Castle*, arrived with a spotting aircraft – the first aircraft to be used for this purpose – and on 13th July 1915, the *Königsberg* was sunk. The actual damage caused by the *Königsberg* was limited to the *Pegasus* and the SS *City of Winchester*, but whilst her whereabouts were unknown, she caused severe disruption to the east African route to the Cape. With her destruction, there were no German warships left outside Germany, apart from the U-boats, but at that time they did not have the range to extend their campaign to the Cape waters.

German merchant shipping was quickly removed from the scene. Ships that could not get home or to a neutral port were soon captured and put to use in the Allied cause. Four were taken around the Cape. The first, the *Hamm*, sailed into Cape Town a week after war started, assuming that all was normal because she did not have a radio on board. Two others followed, and were arrested, and a fourth, the *Birkenfels*, was apprehended off Cape Point by a small torpedo boat and taken to Simon's Town as a prize.

In March 1916, German submarine attacks in the Mediterranean had become so serious that shipping using the Suez Canal was re-routed around the Cape, and large convoys of ships, bound from Australia and New Zealand with troops for the European theatre, and from Britain for Mesopotamia, became a regular sight in Table Bay. Ships from countries not directly involved in the war also diverted via the Cape, and these added a touch of colour to the port which was otherwise filled with ships painted in sombre grey. For about a year after the destruction of all German warships at large outside Germany, merchant shipping was able to proceed much as it had in peacetime, but then, in 1916, the Germans came back with a new weapon. These were converted merchant ships, armed and disguised, which made their appearance on the world's shipping routes, when it was realised by the Germans that their warships had little chance of evading the British blockade of the North Sea. The *Moewe* had a successful cruise in 1916 which accounted for thirty-four Allied merchant ships, and the *Wolf* laid mines off Dassen Island and Cape Agulhas on 16th January 1917, whilst on her way with ammunition to Tanganyika, and sank twelve ships in the Indian Ocean. The *Wolf*'s mines probably accounted for the *Matheran* close to Dassen Island on 17th January 1917, and the *Cilicia* and

City of Athens in the same area in February and August the same year. The Spanish ship *Cabo de Elizaguirre* sank after hitting a mine near Robben Island in May, and two other ships, including the troopship *Tyndareus*, carrying soldiers to Hong Kong, were damaged off Danger Point and the Cape Peninsula. The most romantic of the commerce raiders was the *Seeadler*, a captured American sailing ship commanded by Graf von Luckner. She sailed from Germany on 21st December 1916, and operated briefly in the south Atlantic before sailing on to the Pacific. She accounted for ten Allied ships before being wrecked at Fiji in August 1917. She was the last square-rigged ship to see service as a warship.

The immediate post-war years saw the Cape route revert to its usual peacetime traffic as world maritime trade was re-established. But there were obvious changes. Apart from the rapid disappearance of sailing ships, the New Zealand steamers now used the Panama Canal, which also gave United States shipping an alternative route to the East. The post-war depression, which began just as companies had rebuilt their fleets in the mid-1920s, further depleted the via Cape shipping, as shipowners cut out any diversions or routes that would not make a profit. Most of the UK to Australasia shipping companies, which had made stops in Cape Town, now found it no longer profitable, and transferred their ships to the Suez route.

The few sailing ships which had survived this long found cargoes even harder to come by, but a few were operating until the Second World War, after which they ceased to trade, being used solely as training ships. One training ship, the Danish *Kubehaven*, disappeared on a voyage from the River Plate to Australia via the Cape in 1929. A search was made, which included the Southern Ocean islands, but no trace of the ship or her crew of ninety was ever found.

Some of the old via Cape services survived the great depression, but on a very limited basis. George Thompson's Aberdeen steamers had changed their livery to that of Shaw Savill, but the 11,231-ton *Themistocles* continued to call on her way to Australasia, operating the vestiges of a joint service with the Blue Funnel Line. But the story is not all that of a general running down of services. A Norwegian company, Wh. Wilhelmsen Line, started a fast service with motor ships between the Cape and Australia, and a new trade, that of the cruise liner, taking passengers to visit other countries, which had started in 1911, began again after the First World War. Although it received a knock during the depression, it picked up again in the late 1930s, bringing many large ships to South African ports.

An innovation almost as epochal as the change from sail to steam was the change from coal to oil for firing the ship's boilers. The new shipping tonnage produced at the end of the First World War to replace wartime losses and the ships that had worn out or reached retirement age during the war were almost entirely mechanically propelled, and used oil instead of coal for their fuel. Oil had major advantages for ships. It was more efficient as a fuel, was easier to load, and could be stowed in areas such as double-bottom tanks beneath the cargo holds, and other awkward and unusable gaps, instead of taking valuable cargo space. South Africa, which had plenty of coal, did not have any natural oil, and this meant that oil for bunkering shipping had to be imported. The difference in the cost of oil bunkers was not great, mainly the additional cost of shipping it to the Cape, but it was marginally more expensive than, say, at Aden on the Suez route, and was another saving that shipowners could make.

The only via Cape shipping to continue through the 1930s were those services where the route offered obvious savings to the shipowners, or sufficient freight or passengers could be relied upon *en route* to make the passage there viable. The Portuguese still used the route to Mozambique because the distance from Lisbon to Delagoa Bay is fractionally less round the Cape than through the Suez Canal. In any case most Portuguese services to Mozambique also included stops in Angola, on the west side of the continent. A modest amount of passing traffic was created by the export of oil products from the Persian Gulf region to South America, but this was as yet small, and did not compensate for the loss of traffic to the Suez route. The Japanese Nippon Yusen Kaisha started sending ships to South America via the Cape in 1904 on an irregular basis, but a six-week service was inaugurated in 1916. A year later the Osaka Shoshen Kaisha also appeared on the same route, but returning via the Panama Canal, and a fierce rivalry ensued. The two services called at South African ports with cargo and passengers, and later the OSK launched a separate service from Japan to Durban via east Africa. By agreement between the companies, the OSK took over the South America service in 1931.

The outbreak of the Second World War in September 1939 brought the Cape route back into prominence again. At the start of hostilities between Britain and France against Germany, Italy was sympathetic to Germany, and their entry with their large modern fleet of warships on the enemy side would effectively close the Mediterranean/Red Sea route to India and Australasia. In the first few weeks, the Mediterranean services were halted whilst Italy's position was clarified, but reopened when Italy declared herself neutral. However, this provided just a short breathing space before the Italians finally committed themselves on the German side.

The pattern of the war at sea was largely similar to the First World War, but with the additional threat of enemy submarines, which developed the range to reach the Cape during the war. Once again, at the outset the greatest threat to shipping came from a number of powerful warships that had slipped out of Germany in the weeks before war was declared. Their purpose was to prey on British and Allied shipping, and draw large forces away from Europe to search for them. The German pocket battleship *Admiral Graf Spee*, a ship of 10,000 tons but carrying six powerful 11-inch guns, had been sent to cruise in the Indian Ocean. The pocket battleships were given a speed of twenty-seven knots, and were capable of out-gunning the cruisers whose normal purpose was to protect the sea routes. The *Admiral Graf Spee* sank three merchant ships on her way to her hunting ground, and then reappeared on 15th November in the Mozambique Channel, where she destroyed a small tanker, the *Africa Shell*. As was her practice she now disappeared again, doubled round the Cape well south of the searching British warships, and back into the Atlantic. Enormous forces had to be deployed to search the south Atlantic and Indian Oceans. Two 8-inch gun cruisers, the *Sussex* and the *Shropshire*, were dispatched to the Cape, and Force I, consisting of the aircraft carrier *Eagle* and two more 8-inch cruisers, was sent to the Indian Ocean. For a month nothing was heard, and then the *Graf Spee* pounced on the Cape to Freetown route, sinking two ships on 2nd December and another on the 7th. This time the net was drawn in. The story of what followed is well known. As the German ship approached the River Plate in South America, another rich source of Allied shipping, she found an inferior force of one 8-inch cruiser, the *Exeter*, and two light 6-inch cruisers waiting for her. The *Graf Spee*'s best plan would have been to run and pick off her pursuers with her longer-range guns. Instead she headed straight for the *Exeter* which moved apart from the lighter ships to split the Germans' gunfire. The *Exeter* was soon out of action, but the *Graf Spee* had been damaged as well, and found herself relentlessly harried by the two light cruisers as she made her way to Montevideo. The problem for the Germans was that under the neutrality laws, they could go into a neutral country for repairs for forty-eight hours only, and they needed longer. They also knew that large units of the British fleet were on their way, and were deceived into believing that they were already off Montevideo. Faced with overwhelming force, the captain took his ship to sea and scuttled her.

The threat to Cape shipping from German surface units had been removed for a few months, but plans were already being made by the German High Command to send six disguised heavily armed merchant ships to disrupt worldwide shipping movements. Early in 1940 these ships began slipping past the blockade and out to sea, one of them going straight to the Pacific Ocean via the North-East Passage, her path through the ice being cleared by a Russian icebreaker. These ships reached the high seas to threaten Allied shipping just as Europe erupted with the German invasion of France, and Italy declared on the side of Germany thus closing the Mediterranean route to the East. The shortage of escorts to protect shipping convoys against the German raiders and the U-boats was dealt a further blow by the capitulation of France. The immediate effect of the

The clipper ship *Thermopylae* by F. I. Sorenson, owned by Thompson Lines and reputed to be the fastest commercial sailing ship ever built for the British flag.

The wreck of the *Thermopylae* at Mouille Point.

Thompson Lines' SS *Aberdeen,* of 3,600 tons, built in 1881, the first ocean-going liner to be fitted with triple-expansion engines.

A painting by H. Clifford of the *Great Eastern,* the nineteenth century's most famous steamship, built in 1858 on the Thames for the Australian run. At 18,914 tons, she was the largest ship in the world for nearly forty years. She visited the Cape in 1869.

French surrender was the loss of most of the French fleet and bases to the Allied cause just as the need for ships had increased. Steps were taken to prevent this loss benefiting the Germans, and Dakar in West Africa was attacked by a combined Free French and British force, to try to prevent it becoming a base for U-boats and allowing them to extend their range to the Cape.

The first of the German commerce raiders to reach Cape waters was the *Atlantis*, which sank the *Scientist* in May and then laid mines off Cape Agulhas. In June she was joined by the *Pinguin*, and between them these two ships accounted for nineteen Allied ships before the *Pinguin* was destroyed by the cruiser HMS *Cornwall* in May 1941 in the Indian Ocean, and HMS *Devonshire* caught up with the *Atlantis* on 22nd November 1941. In the meantime the *Coberg* was sunk by the cruisers *Canberra* and *Leander* in the Indian Ocean in May, the *Elbe* was sunk by aircraft from HMS *Eagle* in the south Atlantic in June, and the *Kormoran* sank after an engagement with HMAS *Sydney* in the Indian Ocean in November, during which the *Sydney* was destroyed. The *Thor*, which had returned to Germany after being damaged in an engagement with the armed merchant cruiser HMS *Carnarvon Castle*, returned to prey on the Cape route in March 1942, and added seven more ships to her tally. The *Michel* accounted for a further nine ships, including the *Gloucester Castle* whose unfortunate survivors were interned in Japan. Although nearly all these raiders were eventually dealt with they created a disproportionate amount of damage and disruption to the Cape route for their own cost and effort.

The *Atlantis* is known to have laid ninety-two moored mines on the Agulhas Bank between 9th and 10th May 1940. The minefield was discovered quickly, and sweeping operations cleared eleven of them. However, some broke loose and these were probably responsible for the damage caused to three ships in 1942. An unknown number of mines laid off Green Point by another raider, the *Doggerbank*, during March 1942 are thought to have been answerable for the British ship *Soudan* and the Dutch ship *Alcyone*. Although some of these mines have been washed ashore or destroyed, as recently as July 1986 a fishing boat caught one on the Agulhas Bank. It was suspected that more mines were laid off Cape Columbine, but none have been found in the area.

With the arrival of Japan in the war on 7th December 1941, the situation in the East became extremely serious as the Japanese Forces overran most of South-East Asia and threatened India. America was in the war at last, but her contribution was small to start with while she geared her economy to the war. Apart from the threat to India and Ceylon, the loss of Singapore and two British battleships off Malaya had left the Indian Ocean defenceless, and there was considerable apprehension that the Japanese might try and invade Madagascar. Their objective was thought to be the Vichy

French base at Diego Suarez, which could be used by their submarines attempting to cut the supply route to Africa and India. A force was gathered in Durban, consisting of the battleship *Ramillies*, the aircraft carriers *Indomitable* and *Illustrious*, two cruisers and eleven destroyers, and a force of assault ships. The operation was a complete success, and Diego Suarez surrendered on 7th May 1941. Subsequently it became necessary to capture the whole island, and this was achieved, using some South African troops, on 29th October 1942.

The Japanese submarine offensive in Cape waters started in June 1942, with the destruction of fifteen ships, and five more followed in July, but then the assault fizzled out as the submarines were required elsewhere, and only one more vessel was lost to the Japanese close to the Cape waters during the rest of the war: the Greek ship *Faneromeni* in October 1943. But as the Japanese pulled out, the Germans moved in with longer-range submarines supplied from specially adapted U-boats and supply ships. For the German U-boats, 1942 had started out well, but as it progressed the Allies slowly took the offensive in the north Atlantic. Seeking safer waters, they went further afield to the south Atlantic and Indian Oceans where the convoy system was not in full operation, and single merchant ships presented an easy target. The first loss occurred in September 1942 when the *U-68* sank the Dutch *Breedijk* just south of the equator. By October the U-boats were operating in Cape waters, and were to destroy twenty-four merchant ships before the month was out for the loss of *U-179*, sunk off Dassen Island by HMS *Active*. In November, twenty-five ships were sunk for no loss, but in December the figure fell to four as the Germans were reviewing their tactics after huge losses in the north Atlantic. The following year, 1943, saw the loss of fifty-six merchant ships to U-boats, and a further five were destroyed by one Italian submarine, all for the loss of only three U-boats in Cape waters. But this was the year that the tide turned at last. During 1943 the Allies managed to build a greater tonnage of merchant shipping than the enemy could sink, and they sank more U-boats than the enemy built. In the first two months of 1944 there were no losses to submarines, but two vital German supply ships were sunk south-east of Mauritius, and during the rest of the year four U-boats sank and two were damaged for the loss of sixteen ships. Before the war ended, just one more ship was to be torpedoed by a U-boat, the *Point Pleasant Park* in February 1945. In addition to these heavy losses, a further three ships were sunk and three damaged by mines laid on the Agulhas Bank between March and May 1942. The total number of Allied merchant ships sunk in the south Atlantic and Cape waters in the war was 252, of which Britain had the greatest number, 132. The United States lost forty-one and South Africa five.

These stark figures hide the human misery that each sinking caused. To be torpedoed at sea by a submarine that probably didn't even show itself, left the crew of a ship in a desperate plight. Whilst their ship still floated they had to collect the injured and as many stores as they could, and then climb into small open lifeboats and attempt to reach land. The chances of being rescued by another ship were small in the vastness of the oceans, and it was only on rare occasions that a distress message could be transmitted. In the case of the *City of Cairo*, sunk in the south Atlantic in November 1942, one overcrowded lifeboat tried to sail towards St. Helena island, but after thirty-six days, the three remaining survivors did not have the strength to control the sails and were lucky to be found by a German ship, the *Rhakotis*. The casualties were not all one way, but usually German shipping was captured, as the Allies had the ports available, whereas the Germans had to run a blockade if they were to get their prizes home. Early on in the war most German merchant shipping worldwide was captured or interned, and turned to Allied use. Later the same fate befell the Italians. Some of this shipping was handed over to the South African Railways and Harbours to operate, the most interesting being the Finnish four-masted barque *Lawhill*, which was used on the trade with Argentina: South African maize out, and Argentine wheat home.

Even before the war had finished, once the Italians had been removed as an effective fighting force, and the Germans pushed back, the Mediterranean became sufficiently safe for the Suez route to be reopened, and the traffic via the Cape began to diminish. By the time of Japan's surrender the Cape had become a backwater in the maritime war, and world trade, as it picked up again, followed the same trends as pre-war, with very little shipping passing around the Cape. The situation was changed dramatically in 1956 when the Suez Canal was closed during the short war between Egypt on the one hand, and Britain, France and Israel on the other. By this time the Suez Canal was handling anything between 100 and 150 ships a day, and for over a year all this trade between Europe and the American east coast with Arabia, Asia and Australia had to use the Cape again, providing a welcome stimulus to South African shipping services. A second closure during the Egypt/Israeli war of 1967 once again focused attention on the Cape route, which could not be closed by man-made political or physical barriers. This time the Canal was closed for eight years, until 1975, and the Cape welcomed its longest period of importance since 1869. All trade between Europe and the American east coast to Asia, Arabia, and Australia was forced to use this route, and once again South African ports were filled.

The second Canal closure concealed another change in Cape shipping, as some countries began to ban trade with Southern Africa owing to its Apartheid policies. Trade with India, fuelled by the more than one million people of Indian extraction in Natal, almost ceased, and the growing commerce between South Africa and the newly independent nations of east Africa was reduced to a trickle. Australia and New Zealand have also instituted trade bans, although, sensibly, none of these refer to ships that have called into the Cape ports for repairs or bunkers. But whilst some trades were reduced, the eight-year closure of the Suez Canal added impetus to a trend that had already created a small increase in shipping via the Cape. This was the development of the 'super' ships. In the immediate post-war years oil tankers had been built of 25,000 to 30,000 tons, a size that could use the Canal when loaded, but in the 1950s the first oil tankers appeared that were too big to transit the Suez Canal. The Canal was deepened and widened, but as the economies of scale were realised, even larger tankers were built. The eight-year closure, at a time of worldwide expansion in transportation and a huge increase in the demand for oil products, encouraged shipowners to go a stage further. Tankers grew rapidly in size, soon exceeding the greatest passenger vessels and warships, until they reached a peak of just over 500,000 tons. Although most of the new breed of super-tankers, or VLCCs (Very Large Crude Carriers) as they are called, are at about the 250,000-ton average, they are far too bulky for any conceivable expansion of the Suez Canal in the near future, and all will see out their lives on the Cape route.

South African services had to adapt to the new traffic. In the first place the super-tankers were too big for the existing port facilities, and had to be supplied from small craft whilst stopped offshore. Later, helicopters came to be used for the re-supply operations, which included crew changes, as well as the provision of mail and fresh food. Breakdowns, which anywhere else might be dealt with by the ship's engineers, take on a sense of urgency when the ship is stopped close to land, and especially in an area renowned for its strong winds and high seas. Small wonder that two of the world's largest tugs, the *Wolraad Woltemade* and the *John Ross*, each of over 2,700 tons, capable of twenty knots and having an enormous bollard pull of 175 tons, are kept on permanent stand-by in Cape ports, ready to rush out to sea when required. But even these tugs cannot always save a ship. On 6th August 1983 the Spanish super-tanker *Castillo de Bellver* was homeward bound from the Persian Gulf with a full cargo of crude oil, and was some seventy miles to seaward of Saldanha Bay when a fire broke out. Most of the crew were saved before bad weather conditions broke the ship's back. The fire burned out, but the stern section, still full of oil, suddenly exploded and sank. Efforts by the tug *John Ross* to put a line on board the bow section, which was now standing upright, and tow it away from the coastline, were successful when the wreck was only thirty-seven miles offshore. This section was sunk 120 miles out at sea by small explosive charges, and went down with 60,000 tons of oil that is slowly being released into the sea. The ship and her cargo were lost, but the coastline had been saved from the worst of the pollution. Even so a small village close inland, Riebeek Kasteel, had suffered a rain-like fall of oil droplets.

Although the super-tankers of 500,000 tons are now becoming unfashionable, the medium-sized super-tankers and large bulk carriers continue to sail around the Cape with their vital cargoes. The numbers of ships may have decreased, but the aggregate tonnage is greater than at any time since the Suez Canal was last closed. But even today, with modern steel vessels, sophisticated electronic navigation aids, and satellite communications, the seas around the Cape still take their toll. In one recent year alone, no fewer than twenty-two large ships required assistance, either in the form of a tow or repairs, and two sank. In the same year, 1978, twenty-one vessels in total foundered off the coast. The modern ships may be much larger and safer, but their captains breathe the same sigh of relief as was uttered by the early Portuguese navigators once their ships are headed north with the mighty Cape behind them.

5

The Cape Run

Before the advent of cheap and reliable air travel, most of the world's trade and passengers were carried by sea. Although ships initially made round voyages calling at a number of different ports and countries, as trade developed companies tended to specialise on specific routes, which became known to seamen as 'runs'. The most famous of these runs were the trans-Atlantic between Europe and America, the Australian from Britain, the Indian, and the Cape run. There were many others, of course, but these were the most prestigious of the long-distance mail and passenger routes.

The Cape run has disappeared only in recent years. During its existence, however, it was the major link for South Africa, and its romantic story is an integral part of the history of the Cape.

Prior to the establishment of the modern republic, political control of the Cape was in the hands of two European maritime powers, firstly the Dutch and later the British. The Dutch rule, through their East India Company, commenced with the arrival of van Riebeeck in 1652, and came to an end with the first British invasion in 1795. Since the invasion was a part of the general war strategy during the Napoleonic Wars, and, as such, open to negotiation when the war ended, this British control was in the nature of an occupation of the territory rather than a proper takeover. The Cape was handed back to the Dutch as a part of the peace settlement at the Treaty of Amiens in 1802, but to the Batavian Republic in the Netherlands, not the Dutch East India Company, which had gone bankrupt in the intervening years. With the recommencement of the Napoleonic Wars, the British invaded again in 1806, and this time they came to stay. Their occupation was confirmed at the Congress of Vienna in 1815, and the Cape became a British colony.

The Cape was not immune from the expansion of the British Empire in the nineteenth century, but this was not a deliberate Government policy, it was a reaction to threats created by the establishment of the Boer Republics after the Great Trek in 1836. The Trekkers arrived in Natal in 1837, and in 1840 declared themselves an independent republic, thus opening up the possibility of a foreign power having a sea access to southern Africa close to the Cape colony. The British response was to annex Natal in 1842. The formation of the two inland republics of the Orange Free State and the Transvaal by the Boers created political instability in the Cape interior which Britain could not ignore. On a number of occasions it took over these republics, culminating in the First Boer War in 1879–80, which gave the republics their independence, and the major Boer War which broke out in 1899. In both these wars the population of the Cape and Natal, with a few small exceptions, remained loyal to the British. After the defeat of the Boers in 1902, the Orange Free State and the Transvaal became British Colonies, but all four colonies were united into the Union of South Africa in 1910. This Union remained a part of the British Empire, and subsequently the Commonwealth, until 1961, when it became the Republic of South Africa, and all political ties with Britain were severed.

Until 1806 very few ships sailed specifically to or from the Cape. It had been largely a place to be called at rather than a destination. When the British took control properly a direct trade began to develop, but not on a regular basis at first. Ships sailed only when sufficient cargo or passengers had been collected, similarly to the way tramps operate today. An attempt was made to run a packet service from Britain to the Cape in 1815. This service was the equivalent of the modern liner services where a ship left at a pre-advertised time for a specific port, but it failed through lack of custom after a year. The trade generated by the area at that time was small, and was easily handled by passing ships.

The more liberal attitude of the British Government in the Cape did act as a spur to certain trades, particularly the wine industry, which expanded with the advantage of imperial preference, but wool slowly became the principal export during the first half of the nineteenth century. Imports consisted largely of manufactured goods from Britain. In the early part of British colonisation, Cape Town was the only port, and cargoes for the whole colony were landed there and proceeded by ox cart if they were consigned for elsewhere. This was an expensive and slow method of transportation, and a coasting trade slowly developed, connecting Cape Town with anchorages along the coast which were closer to the final destination.

As the British Empire expanded, communications between the motherland and the far-flung territories became increasingly important. The British Empire did not depend for its security upon vast numbers of troops being stationed permanently within its territories; it relied on small garrisons and upon its ability to strengthen these when danger threatened. The speed with which the reinforcements arrived could often prove decisive. Sufficient troops could always be found to deal with a small war or insurrection, but if the extra men arrived quickly, they could often prevent the problem from growing to the point where an expensive full-scale expedition might be required. In the days before the development of the telegraph, the only means of communication was by sea, and sailing ships, subject to the vagaries of the wind, were not reliable. The voyage from London to the Cape in the small sailing ships of the time could vary between forty-five and 100 days. The Navy could be used in an emergency, but the Navy's strength had been rapidly run down after the Napoleonic Wars, and warships were not always available.

To encourage an improvement in sea communications, a series of subsidised mail services were inaugurated, administered by the Admiralty, who gave the contract to the lowest bidder with the best offer of service. For their relative dependability steamship companies were chosen to undertake these contracts whenever possible.

The people of the Cape began to agitate for their own direct steam mail service from 1847, and this pressure, and the Empire's increasing needs for good communications, eventually persuaded the British Government to put a mail service out to tender in 1850. The contract, worth £30,750 per annum, was awarded to the General Screw Steam Shipping Company, and the monthly service between Plymouth and Cape Town was inaugurated on 18th December 1850 by the *Bosphorus*, a steamer of 500 tons with eighty-horsepower engines. Two sister ships were added, the *Propontis* and the *Hellespont*, to maintain the intended thirty-five-day outward and homeward passages. In 1852 the Company won an extension of their mail contract to India, and built a series of much larger ships of 1,750 tons for their new service. The first of these ships, the *Queen of the South*, set a new record from Britain to the Cape of thirty-one and a half days on her maiden voyage in 1853, beating the previous record set by the P & O steamer *Singapore* in 1851 by five days and twenty hours. The discovery of gold in Australia in 1851 brought a large increase in shipping calling at the Cape, and a demand for improved services to that continent. The General Screw Steam Shipping Company built five more ships, this time of 2,500 tons, for a new round-the-world service, calling at the Cape, in Australia, and then round Cape Horn and back to Britain along the well-established sailing ship routes. The first of the new ships, the *Argo*, was the first steamer to circumnavigate the globe, and made the voyage in the very respectable time of 121 days in 1853. Unfortunately this large shipbuilding programme, which included three ships built for the Cape coasting trade, the *Sir Robert Peel* of 233 tons, and the *Cape of Good Hope* and *Natal* of 500 tons each, overstretched the Company's financial resources, and it went out of business at the end of 1854.

The year 1855 saw the Cape without a mail service, but in 1856 W. S. Lindsay negotiated a contract with the Government to carry mails to the Cape and India for a subsidy of £28,000 per annum. The contract called for a time on passage of thirty-eight days, but his ships were powered by sail with auxiliary engines, and never proved capable of this achievement. The first to arrive, the *England*, took fifty-four days because she had run out of coal on her way, and apart from the *Scotland* which managed to make the voyage in thirty-nine days, none of the seven ships he bought for the service managed to complete the voyage in under fifty days. A passenger, Mr MacLeod, travelling out in the *Ireland* in 1856, found that his cabin was only six feet by five feet in size, and he had to sleep on the deck. There were no lights, and the candles were too large for the cabins, the stewards were inexperienced and suffered from sea sickness. In the absence of servants the gentlemen passengers waited at the tables. The pumps were inadequate, so baths were almost impossible, and the water tanks had not been cleaned, which meant fresh water had to be rationed and filtered. If that was not enough, the poultry put aboard live for food died of neglect, and the passengers had to take it upon themselves to ensure that the dead birds were thrown overside and not served up at meals. After other similar complaints, bookings fell off dramatically, and the service was not a financial success. Lindsay abandoned it in 1857 when he was able to charter his ships more profitably to the Admiralty as troop transports during the Indian Mutiny.

The Admiralty re-tendered the contract and it was awarded to the fairly new Union Company, which had been formed in 1853 to transport coal from South Wales to Southampton. During the Crimean War, the Company's fleet of six steamships had been occupied with Government work, but with peace once more, it had become necessary to find new trades. The contract came in the nick of time for the Company. It had attempted to run a service with Brazil, but this proved uneconomic, and by 1857 its liabilities of £80,000 exceeded its assets by £12,000. However, its chairman was one of the remarkable group of men from humble origins who were beginning to dominate British shipping. A Shetland Islander, Arthur Anderson, had played an important part in the development of the P & O Company, and the Union Company was just one of his many interests. His reputation and presence as a shareholder in the company would not have discouraged the Admiralty, and the contract, valued at £33,000 per annum, was awarded on 4th September 1857. The first ship, the *Dane*, sailed from Southampton on the 15th, re-establishing the regular steamer service with the Cape.

The *Dane* was a screw steamer of 530 tons, with engines of sixty nominal horsepower. The mail contract called for the voyage to be made within forty-two days, and she arrived two days late. Even so, the Union Company had started the service so quickly that no one in Cape Town even knew that a mail ship was due. The delight of the people in the Cape once they realised that the service had been resumed is expressed by an article in the *Cape Town Monitor* of 31st October 1857:

> The arrival of the Royal Mail Steamer *Dane* on Thursday has thrown new life and vigour into the community. When our hopes were lowest the intelligence burst upon Cape Town that mail communication with England had been resumed. The old country has not yet begun to forget the interests of her dependencies. At a time when all attention might have been supposed to be absorbed in providing for the ominous struggles now proceeding in the Indian Empire [the Indian Mutiny], the British Government, instead of withdrawing Mail communication with the Cape, has only renewed it on the most satisfactory of terms.

The second ship, the *Celt*, arrived on 27th November, and the *Dane* started her return voyage three days later, via St. Helena and Plymouth, with a full cargo, and the largest mail delivery from the Cape so far: 10,867 letters and 3,671 newspapers. The total earnings by the Company on the return voyage were £980. The Union Company bought two slightly larger ships, the *Phoebe* and the *Athens*, and these, with the *Norman*, *Celt* and *Dane*, formed the first reliable steamship service between Britain and the Cape.

If the inhabitants in the western Cape were delighted to have a regular contact with London at last, the pleasure in the eastern Cape was tempered by the delays in the mail reaching them from Cape Town once it had been landed. They particularly resented the fact that whereas the Capetonians had three or more days to answer incoming mail before the next ship departed, they sometimes had to wait weeks before their letters could catch the next boat home. A coastal mail delivery was operated by John T. Rennie for a short time, but it was not until the British mail contract was renewed in 1862 that a regular service was introduced. The Union Line won the new contract, against negligible competition, which included an extension of the service to Port Elizabeth, for the sum of about £20,000 per annum.

In 1864, the mail service went as far as Mauritius for a short time, where mail from the Cape was collected with that from India, Australia and New Zealand and put aboard a P & O ship, and taken up the Red Sea to Suez, where it was transferred across land to the Mediterranean. There another P & O ship awaited to take it on to Britain. This provided a slightly quicker service for people in the eastern Cape, provided that the Cape ship arrived in time to make the connection at Mauritius, but the cost of a half-ounce letter was 1s.4d. by this route, 4d. more than from Cape Town, and the service proved less reliable.

Rivalry to the Union Line first appeared in 1864 when the newly formed Diamond Line ran its inaugural voyage from Falmouth to Port Elizabeth with the *Eastern Province* in thirty-two and a half days, as fast as the latest Union Line steamers. Initially the new line provided some competition, but it did not have the security of the mail contract nor the resources of the

Union Line. After a short time its service became unpredictable, and ceased altogether in 1867. As the Diamond Line faded from the scene, the Cape of Good Hope Steam Navigation Company appeared, but it only lasted until 1871.

The number of vessels calling at Cape ports was down by about ten per cent in 1870, the year after the opening of the Suez Canal, but that was the low point. The Suez Canal proved to be too expensive for sailing ships, since they had to be towed by a tug from one end to the other. As only sixteen per cent of the world's shipping was in steamers, sailing ships continued to use the Cape route until the demise of commercial sail at the end of the First World War. But just as a gradual decline in shipping services seemed inevitable, South Africa experienced a remarkable piece of good fortune which was to change its pattern of trade completely.

The Orange Free State and the Transvaal were pastoral economies, trading their livestock and crops with Natal, the Cape and Portuguese East Africa in return for the hardware they required. In 1867, a child playing on the Orange River discovered what it thought was a bright pebble, which turned out to be a large diamond, and was sold for £500. This was followed in 1869 by an even larger find in Griqualand, near the Orange River, the 'Star of South Africa Diamond' of 83½ carats (16.7 grammes), which was bought by the Earl of Dudley for £25,000. In an era when the rags-to-riches stories from California and Australia were fresh in everyone's minds, this led to an almost immediate influx of fortune hunters from all over the world. By 1870, more than 10,000 people had moved into the 'River Diggings' along the Orange and Vaal Rivers. In 1871 diamonds were found at Jagersfontein and Dutoitspan, far from the rivers, in what came to be called the 'Dry Diggings'. Shortly afterwards diamonds were unearthed in the red surface soil at Kimberley, near Dutoitspan, and in the fifty-foot-thick layer of yellow clay which lay beneath. Subsequently, it was discovered that the bluish rock, known as the 'Blue Ground', below the clay was also diamondiferous. In a very short space of time Kimberley had a population of 50,000 workers, roughly equivalent to the entire white population of both the Orange Free State and the Transvaal before the discoveries.

Gold was also discovered in small quantities at Tati, north of the Limpopo River, in 1868, and other finds followed, culminating, in 1886, in the discovery of the largest goldfield in the world on the Witwatersrand, where the town of Johannesburg, named after the Surveyor General of the Transvaal, Johannes Rissik, grew up overnight. The white population of the whole of southern Africa, which had been about 330,000 in 1875, rose to 1,120,000 by 1904, mostly through immigration. The resulting influx of people created a demand for good communications and provided the money to pay for them. Railways, which had been restricted to the small

Durban line and the Cape Town to Wellington line, were extended, opening up the country and providing a relatively cheap, but fast and easy connection with the ports on the coast. The economy which had been stagnant for a number of years, suddenly started a very rapid expansion. Imports doubled between 1870 and 1875, and diamonds were soon the most valuable export, rapidly overtaking wool and other agricultural products.

This new prosperity came too late for the Cape of Good Hope Line, but another shipping company appeared on the scene in 1870: the Cape and Natal Steam Navigation Company. The new Company was organised by G. H. Payne, a figure who was to appear prominently in the story of Cape shipping. Payne was a loading broker with vast experience of the Cape route, and able therefore to guarantee cargoes for his ships. The Company's initial efforts came to nothing when the *Westenhope* was wrecked in Algoa Bay on her first trip in 1871, but its second ship, the *Beethoven*, arrived safely, and its third, the *Sweden*, reached the Cape in April 1871 in twenty-seven and a half days, a good ten days faster than the Union ship which sailed at the same time. The Union Line's reputation received further blows when the *Cambrian* ran out of coal as she approached Table Bay, and had to struggle into Saldanha Bay in September, using her wooden decks as fuel to keep pressure on the boiler, and three of its ships, the *Northam*, *Norseman* and *Celt*, each had to spend three weeks anchored at Saldanha because of a smallpox epidemic the same year. However, the Union Line fought back and purchased a ship, the *Syria*, much superior to its existing tonnage, which set a new record of twenty-six days and eighteen hours for the outward trip.

The competition soon forced the Cape and Natal Steam Navigation Company into financial difficulties. It had ordered four new ships to provide an even better service, but when these were ready, did not have the money to pay the builders. In a desperate effort to keep his company afloat Payne chartered two ships from the Castle Line, but even as these ships were on their way to the Cape, he had to tell the owner of the Castle Line, Donald Currie, that he could not settle the charter fees. Rather than lose his money, Currie decided to take over the voyages for himself, and thus was brought into the South African trade one of its dominating personalities, a man who was to leave his mark on the run for the next 100 years.

Donald Currie was born in Greenock in 1825, and spent his early life working for the Cunard Line. In 1862 he established his own company, Donald Currie & Co., and took up trade with India via the Cape, with four iron-built sailing ships of 1,200 tons named after British castles. When the opening of the Suez Canal sounded the death knell for sailing ships on the India route, Currie began to build steamships, and placed his sailing ships on longer routes where they could still compete. Significantly, he was able to make a profit, and his last sailing ship, the *Cluny Castle*, was launched as late as 1883.

Currie had some experience of the Cape from his voyages to India, and he was always ready to examine a new route if he thought it would pay. He took over the charters from G. H. Payne at a time when many of the shippers to the Cape felt that competition to the Union Line would benefit freight rates, and encouraged Currie to enter the direct trade with the Cape. Currie hardly hesitated, and with the decisiveness that was typical of the self-made shipping entrepreneurs of the time, had his first ship on the route in a couple of months, with G. H. Payne acting as the loading broker. Although other steamship companies tried to compete on the route at about the same time, none of them lasted for long.

The field was thus left open for a straight fight between Currie's Castle Line and the Union Line, and Currie got off to a good start when his chartered steamer, the *Penguin*, came into Cape Town in a new record time of twenty-four days and eighteen hours on 2nd May 1872. A year later, the first of his new ships designed originally for the India run, the *Windsor Castle*, came into Cape Town in twenty-three days. Records created great excitement, and gave the owner enormous publicity and popularity at a time when ships provided the only link with what was still looked upon by many as home. Donald Currie, who was a brilliant publicist, fully appreciated that this meant full ships, and therefore profits. In 1875 the *Dunrobin Castle*, the first Currie ship built specifically for what was known as the Colonial Trade to the Cape, reduced the record by a further twelve hours. The Cape Government was delighted with the new service and its record times, and to encourage Currie to keep running until the mail contract came up for renewal in 1876, it agreed to pay him £150 for every day his ships saved on the voyage under thirty days. However, they wisely put an upper limit of £12,000 on this arrangement.

The Cape Government was keen to encourage competition, and when the contract was renewed, it was split evenly between the Union and the Castle Lines, with each company sailing on alternate weeks to give the Cape a weekly mail service. The time stipulated for the contract was twenty-six days per voyage, and the subsidy was withdrawn; instead, each company was paid 10d. for every letter carried.

The Natal Government was quick to follow the Cape in awarding a joint mail contract to the two lines, and Currie soon had a fleet of small, specially built ships operating on this trade as well. The Union Line in the meantime had managed to obtain an eight-year contract to carry mail from the Cape to Zanzibar, where it was transferred to a British India Steam Navigation Company vessel to be taken to Aden and so on to Britain by P & O. This east coast mail route had been created largely as an attempt to discourage slavery rather than to provide an alternative for the mail. It was felt that, by letting the Africans see large, fast, modern steamers belonging to another power, it would be possible to destroy their fear of the Arabs, who dominated the slave trade through Zanzibar and Mombasa. In this the policy was highly successful, and it also led to the opening up and colonisation of the east African coastal territories of Kenya, Tanganyika and the landlocked Uganda, which were still very much as the Portuguese had known them.

These were exciting times for the Cape shipping run. There was the elation of the races between two rival companies, and trade and prosperity were increasing rapidly. This was due in part to the discovery of diamonds, but also to the fact that superior shipping services provided the reliability of delivery and stability of prices that trade demands. The improved services were not achieved without a high price in ships and lives, however, and the toll amongst even the crack liners, in the days before lighthouses were a regular feature around the coast, was heavy.

The Union Line, having lost its monopoly of the mail contract, started to fight back. The *German*, of 3,028 tons, recaptured the Cape record in 1877, and four new ships were ordered for the Cape run, the *Pretoria* and *Arab*, of 3,200 tons, and the *Trojan* and *Spartan*, of 3,500 tons. In reply Currie built the *Kinfauns Castle* and the *Grantully Castle*, of 3,500 tons, and the *Drummond Castle* and *Garth Castle*, of about 3,700 tons. All these ships entered service between 1878 and 1881, and the *Pretoria* had the distinction of bringing the first reinforcements after the Battle of Isandhlwana at the start of the Zulu War. An entire regiment of nearly 1,000 men, the 91st Highlanders, was shipped aboard and taken from Southampton to Natal in twenty-four days and eight hours.

The upsets caused by the First Boer War scarcely affected the shipping scene. The continued expansion of trade was bringing in rivals to the Union and Castle Lines. Bullard and King, who had run sailing ships to Natal for twenty years, introduced a steamer service, and John T. Rennie re-entered the trade sailing from Aberdeen, both running direct services from Britain to Natal. In addition, the newly formed Clan Line started a steamer service to the Cape from Liverpool and Glasgow in 1881. The Clan Line had been established in 1878 by Charles Cayzer, yet another of the self-made British shipowners, and the association with South Africa was to continue throughout the Company's existence. All this was good news for the Cape Government, and when the mail contract came up for renewal in 1883, they were in a far stronger position to negotiate. The new terms were for a joint service between the Union and Castle Lines, but the time was cut to twenty-one and a half days, and penalties were imposed if the voyage exceeded twenty-three days. Each of the companies was to be paid £25,000 per annum, and the upper limit for total bonuses for faster-than-contract runs was limited to £15,000 each. Some idea of the increase in trade between Britain and the Cape since the mail contract system was established can be drawn from the high value of the contract, despite the competition.

In 1882, two further companies started Cape services, the South Africa Line and the International Line. The latter caused consternation amongst the mail contract companies because they had managed to obtain the Government Immigration contract at very low rates. The introduction of so much independent competition on the Cape run could only lead to one thing, a freight war. As each shipowner found that his regular shippers were being enticed away by cheaper offers from other lines, he lowered his own rates, with the result that in a very short space of time, none of the companies involved were able to make a profit. The International Line was quickly in difficulties, and had to seek assistance from Donald Currie. It was Donald Currie who suggested that they should get together and come to some sort of an arrangement that assured that all the parties involved could make a profit, and in September 1883 the first South African Conference was formed to regulate the competition and the rates of freight. Not surprisingly, the agreement favoured the established lines. The problem with trade from the shippers' point of view was that although there were large cargoes for the outward voyage, South Africa produced little for export in return, except for diamonds and gold which did not take much space in a ship. In order to make a decent profit, the ships needed cargoes both ways. To avoid conflict over these it was agreed that Clan Line would only load three ships homeward from South African ports in each year, and the company sent its ships on to Mauritius and India for return cargoes.

The Conference was formed just as the South African trade entered its worst depression of the century. The boom following the discovery of gold and diamonds and the demands of the army came to an end in 1883, and merchants found that they were heavily overstocked. South African trade with Britain fell from a value of £21 million in 1882 to £13 million in 1886. The opening of the Witwatersrand goldfields that year fuelled a recovery, but until the depression passed, many ships were laid up or transferred to other routes, and it was not until 1889 that the companies had all their ships fully employed on the Cape run again.

The Conference of shipping companies was put to its first test in 1885, when the Natal Merchants Line was formed, and attempted to breach the agreed terms. The response was to offer loyal shippers a deferred rebate, whereby a percentage of their shipping costs was returned to them after a certain period of time. This was the first occasion this device was used in South Africa, although it had become common elsewhere. The new company found that it could not obtain sufficient cargoes once the shippers realised that if they transferred their business away from existing companies, they would lose their rebate, and it went out of business in 1886. The system of rebates was to become a very thorny problem in South African trade, and developed into what has been called the South African shipping question. It was not finally resolved until 1904.

In 1889 G. H. Payne reappeared on the scene, having broken with Donald Currie in 1885. He persuaded a friend, Edward Lloyd, who was manager of a firm of ship charterers, Bucknall Brothers, to enter the Cape trade. Realising that to tackle the Conference lines cold would have small chance of success, Lloyd put in a very attractive tender for the 100,000 tons of cargo about to be shipped out to Delagoa Bay for the construction of the railway line to Pretoria, which would guarantee that he would not operate at a loss. This railway was being built by President Kruger in an attempt to free the Transvaal from dependence upon the Cape ports, and liberate his country from British influence. Lloyd won the contract, placed an order for nine new ships and announced his plans to enter the South African trade. The Bucknalls were a wealthy and powerful family, and no one was in any doubt that they would fight the Conference lines if necessary, and they were unlikely to be driven from the scene easily like the Natal Merchants Line.

The Conference responded with a rate cut and an increase in the shippers' rebate, but these measures, although attractive from a financial point of view, could only lead to disruption of shipping services in the long run. It was in all parties' interests to avoid the impending conflict, and a compromise was reached eventually whereby the two smallest members of the Conference were persuaded, on favourable terms, to cease operating and their place was taken by the Bucknalls' British and Colonial Line in 1892.

The 1890s were a decade of growth. The railway from the Transvaal to the Cape was completed in 1892, the Delagoa Bay line opened in 1894, and the Transvaal to Durban line in 1895. On the sea the size and speed of ships were also increasing. In October 1890, the new *Dunottar Castle* of 5,625 tons set a new record of sixteen days and fourteen hours, which she reduced by nearly a day the following year. In 1891 the Union Line replied with the *Scot* of 6,844 tons, which reduced the time to fifteen days nine hours and fifty-two minutes, and in 1893 lowered it to fourteen days eighteen hours and fifty-seven minutes, bringing in the mail on a Sunday instead of the following Tuesday. This time was to remain unbeaten for nearly fifty years. Larger vessels followed until by 1900 the newest additions to the Union fleet were 12,000 tons, and they had brought into service no fewer than ten 'G'-class ships of 6,250 tons for their intermediate operations. By 1900 the tonnages of the two rivals were: Union Line 114,000, Castle Line 107,000.

Competition proceeded to grow steadily but the Conference lines did

A late nineteenth-century view of Cape Town Docks.

A view of Cape Town Docks with ships alongside the quays and others at anchor in the bay.

The infamous baskets used on the east coast to discharge passengers aboard tenders or barges before ships were able to go alongside in the ports.

their utmost to keep the trade to themselves. In 1895 the subsidised German East Africa Line, which had been formed to connect the German colony of Tanganyika with the homeland, found it could not find sufficient cargoes, and extended its services to Portuguese East Africa and later to Durban. Inevitably this led to another freight war, which was resolved only by an agreement when the Conference put very low freight rates on fertilisers and machinery, the main cargoes of the German company. The Conference lines also started runs to the United States, partly to provide competition with the American companies that were moving onto the route, and because trade between the United States and the Cape had started to grow. In just over forty years shipping had changed from being a rather casual business, when a cargo was dispatched and no one could guarantee when it would arrive, to a situation where a new service, with advertised sailing and arrival times, could be attempted by anyone who owned the necessary steamers.

From the launch of the original ship in 1802, steam-propelled vessels had made steady progress. The merchant shipowners had been the first to adopt iron and then later steel for construction. The early engines were unreliable and not very efficient, and ships, particularly on the longer routes, were still equipped with masts and sails. Part of their problem was that their engines required vast amounts of coal, and this was not readily available at convenient depots around the world. In 1865 the compound steam engine was introduced at sea. Instead of one cylinder, this engine had two, and the steam, having passed through the high-pressure cylinder, continued to provide extra power in the low-pressure cylinder. Coal consumption was reduced by almost fifty per cent. This saving was amply proved by the first ship fitted with these engines, the *Nestor*, owned by Alfred Holt, which steamed the 8,500 miles from Britain to Mauritius without having to take on any coal bunkers. The reduction of coal required to be carried left more space available for cargo. This dramatic improvement in the economy of the steam engine was one of the factors that spelt the end of sail in the long term. It was followed in 1881 by the development of the triple-expansion engine which was even more efficient. Steamers ceased to be rigged for square rig from about the mid-1880s onwards, although they could and did set fore and aft sails for some time. The change in the make-up of the world's shipping tonnage from wood to iron and sail to steam was slow, but by 1870 eighty-three per cent of all construction in British shipyards was in iron, and three-quarters was steam-powered. Steel was being introduced in place of iron at the same time, and since it was stronger and half the weight, it led to another increase in ships' carrying capacity.

By 1890 most of the ships on the Cape route had been re-engined with the triple-expansion engines, and all new tonnage was equipped with them as a matter of course. Sailing ships no longer featured on the premium runs and Donald Currie sold the last of his sailing ships in 1886. By 1900 sailing vessels were outnumbered by steamers on the world's oceans, although sailing ships were chartered in large numbers by the Admiralty for war deliveries to South Africa, this was partly due to the lower cost when they were delayed.

The steady expansion and orderliness of the Cape trade was blown apart by the advent of the Boer War in 1899. At the outset the British Government chartered a vast number of ships, both for troops and supplies, and these quickly clogged the Cape ports. At one time there were more than 200 ships at anchor in Table Bay awaiting their turn to go alongside and discharge their cargoes, and other ports were in a similar situation. Only the mail ships were given priority for berthing, and this enabled them to turn round with the minimum of delay. All others had to queue and the losses to some companies were considerable. Bucknalls', who reckoned that a medium-sized cargo ship cost them £80 to £100 a day to run, estimated that their losses due to port delays amounted to £250,000 and even transhipped cargo in Saldanha Bay to speed up the process. Sir Charles Cayzer of the Clan Line calculated his losses to be £70,000 a year. In 1900 alone his forty-four ships that sailed to the Cape were held up a total of 968 days. The *Clan Robertson* lay at anchor off Port Elizabeth for three months, and when she sailed, her speed had been reduced from eleven to six knots. Subsequently fifty tons of barnacles and weed were scraped off her hull when she was dry-docked in Calcutta. In order to reduce these delays, Cayzer founded the Caledonia Landing Shipping and Salvage Company, with three tugs and eight lighters, to service the anchored ships and offload their cargoes.

There were compensations of course; Government charters were usually lucrative but no shipowner was ever going to admit that he made money from them. Bucknalls' put in a claim for compensation of £200,000 for delays incurred during the war, but the Government was not very sympathetic! The total sum paid by the Government for ship charters during the war amounted to £12,700,000, of which the members of the Conference shared £1,750,000, between them. The combined Union and Castle Lines received ninety per cent of the Conference payout. The huge difference between the total payments to the Conference lines, who had plenty of ships between them and were best placed to take on the work, and the overall figure for chartered ships indicates the enormous volume of shipping diverted for the war effort.

In 1900 the mail contract was due for renewal again, but this time it was opened for a single tender. Neither the Union nor the Castle Line offered, nor did any other of the Conference lines, and the Government was forced to split it between the two big companies. This time the contract did not contain a clause forbidding an amalgamation between the companies. Sir Donald Currie and Sir Michael Evans, the respective Chairmen, had probably already started talks, Sir Donald in any case had shares in the Union Company, and in 1901 the shareholders agreed to a merger. The new company hoisted its house flag, a combination of the two lines' flags, for the first time on 17th March 1901. The great contest that had done so much to promote better Cape services was over, and from now on the combined Union–Castle Line became the unchallenged passenger carrier on the South African run.

At the close of the Boer War, it was expected confidently that there would be another boom in the South African economy as the gold mines returned to work, but, as after the previous war, a serious depression occurred. The shipping companies, who had been looking forward to expansion as the economy became buoyant, were faced with a shortage of cargoes, just at the time that other companies decided to join the Cape route. The new Union–Castle Line, which had had all its ships employed whilst the war raged, was particularly affected. The combined fleet had more ships than were necessary to run a full mail service. Some were disposed of, but others which they intended to keep were laid up in Southampton Water because of the shortage of cargoes. In the expectations of a greater trade the Conference had been expanded by the addition of the Ellerman and Harrison Lines in 1902. John Ellerman was a financier who had bought the City Line and the Hall Line in 1901. Shortly thereafter he also acquired Bucknalls', who were a member of the Conference. The Harrison Line was already well established on the Indian trade, as were the City and Hall Lines, and part of the agreement to join the Conference was that they both paid the Clan Line five shillings a ton on an agreed rate of twenty shillings a ton as compensation. In 1904 this was abolished in return for a lump sum of £20,000 paid on their Cape cargoes to the Clan Line. Admission was refused to the Houston Line, however, when it applied to join later the same year. The Conference no doubt thought that there were sufficient ships on the run, and that they were, in any case, strong enough to squeeze out a newcomer, but they picked on the wrong man.

R. P. Houston, a Liverpool shipowner who had started life as an engineer, had established himself on the Argentina trade in the 1880s, and this was proving very profitable. During the Boer War his ships had been employed regularly with Admiralty contracts, and he had gained some experience of the South African trade, and made some good contacts. Houston's reaction to the Conference shut-out was to enter the trade and offer lower rates. Just as cargoes were drying up, another freight war was developing.

The battle between the one independent operator and the might of the

Conference lasted nearly two years, but its effects lasted much longer, and led ultimately to a diminution of the Conference's hold on the Cape trade. The Conference lines used every weapon at their disposal, including larger rebates, and the threat of shutting out cargoes from any shipper who used Houston's line. This had the effect of alienating the shippers, but they were tied economically. Eventually, Houston started a passenger service, just at the same time as the White Star Line began calling into the Cape to collect passengers on its routes to Australia. The Union–Castle Line, which had been less affected by the freight war than the other members of the Conference, now saw a real danger to their services, and took the lead in patching up a peace. Under the terms of the settlement Houston became a member of the Conference, but he paid a price by surrendering a number of his sailings and his passenger service. No one was a real winner, as everyone lost money whilst the conflict was on, and the shippers were left with a feeling of deep dissatisfaction at the way they had been bullied by the Conference.

The new Conference agreement limited each of the companies to a certain number of sailings each year:

Union–Castle	160
Clan Line	90
Bucknall	48
Ellerman–Harrison	38
Bullard, King	38
John T. Rennie	38
Houston	28

This total of 440 sailings each year by the Conference lines, plus additional sailings by tramps, and ships on other routes to the Cape not included in the Conference, indicates the extent to which trade with South Africa from Britain and some Continental ports had grown after the post-Boer War depression. However, Houston did not last long in the trade, and retired completely in 1911 owing to poor cargoes. His short appearance on the scene had disrupted the Cape trade, and left it with a bitter controversy that was not resolved finally, and then at the Conference's expense, until after the Union of the four colonies, when the new Union Government became strong enough to tackle the Conference head on.

Whilst this wrangle was continuing, Sir Donald Currie died on 13th April 1909, aged 82, and the shipowners lost their most powerful and experienced advocate. There was no one person with the stature to replace him, and his death marks the end of an epoch in the South African trading history. His absence also led to another change in the management of the Union–Castle Line, which was taken over on 18th April 1912 by the Royal

Mail Steam Packet Company, under its Chairman Sir Owen Philipps, later Lord Kylsant.

Local businessmen had been involved in the sphere of coastal shipping from soon after the British occupation of the colony, but in 1909 the first South-African-registered foreign-going ship was bought by De Beers. The 1,981-ton *South Africa* was built to bring nitrates from Chile for the manufacture of dynamite by the Cape Explosive Works at Somerset West, owned by De Beers. She continued in this trade until after the First World War, when an improved method of obtaining nitrogen was discovered and the *South Africa* sold.

At the start of the Great War in 1914, Britain, as usual, had only a small standing army, and the troops stationed in the Colonies and Dominions were required urgently to fight on the Western Front in France. There were still about 4,000 British troops left on garrison duty in the Union, but it was agreed quickly that the Union would take responsibility for its own defence in future. The last British soldiers to serve in South Africa were accordingly shipped out from Cape Town aboard six Union–Castle steamers on 27th August 1914. Shortly afterwards the Union Government mobilised its troops to invade South-West Africa, and a force was dispatched by ship from Cape Town on 15th September to take Port Nolloth. At the same time another Union–Castle converted cruiser, HMS *Armadale Castle*, shelled the radio station and occupied Swakopmund. This campaign came to a temporary halt in November due to a rebellion in the Transvaal. The rebels seized vast quantities of guns and ammunition, and General Botha put out a call for assistance. No troops could be spared from the European theatre, and Australian troops bound for the Middle East were stood by to be sent to South Africa, but Portugal came to the rescue, and the *Kildonan Castle* was diverted to Lisbon to take aboard a cargo of rifles and ammunition which was rushed to the Cape. With the rebellion crushed, and the danger of interference from German warships removed by Admiral Sturdee's victory off the Falkland Islands, the campaign was resumed, and the Germans surrendered to the Union of South Africa's forces on 9th July 1915.

Services to the Cape were disrupted severely by the war, but it was possible to maintain a mail service until 1917, when the British Admiralty took over all passenger ships. From then on mail came out to the Cape in whatever ships might be available. Apart from those taken up for conversion to armed merchant cruisers, no fewer than thirteen of the seventeen Union–Castle intermediate passenger ships were converted for use as hospital ships. The losses were heavy, particularly after the commencement of the German unrestricted U-boat campaign in 1917. One of the most tragic losses to this campaign was the *Llandovery Castle*, a hospital ship torpedoed on 27th June 1918. The ship sank within ten minutes, and the U-boat, *U-86*, surfaced and shelled the lifeboats. Only one boat and twenty-eight of the crew survived this attack which was in total breach of international law. In all, the Union–Castle Line lost eight ships, the Clan Line twenty-eight, and Ellerman's over fifty.

Although there had been a British Government programme to build ships during the war, it took time for the Cape trade to adjust to the peacetime conditions again. Three years after the signing of the Armistice in 1918, Ellerman's had managed to replace only forty of their lost ships by purchase and rebuilding, and the Union–Castle's intermediate routes were not re-established at their pre-war levels until 1922. With the South African economy buoyant after gearing up during the war, other lines quickly moved into the trade. The Germans made a rapid recovery and had established sailings using chartered tonnage by 1920, and this was soon replaced by new ships. The Dutch also reappeared on the scene at the same time after a gap of over 100 years. A new company was formed, the Nederlandsche Zuid-Afrika Stoomvaart Maatschappij, which started its services with three second-hand 5,000-ton cargo ships. Two years later it added two new 6,000-ton ships to its fleet, capable of taking passengers and cargo, the *Springfontein* and the *Klipfontein*. In 1924 it combined its services with the Holland–Oost Afrika Lijn, and eight years later the two companies amalgamated to form the Holland–Afrika Lijn.

As an effect of the war, and the difficulties of obtaining ships to suit Union needs, was founded a small Government-owned shipping company, under the management of South African Railways and Harbours, which became known as Sarships. Three 5,000-ton cargo ships were bought, the *Huntress*, *Apolda* and *Seattle*.

South African exports were growing steadily, and an increasingly important part of them was made up of fruit, which required specialised freezer storage. Fortunately for the country, when the worldwide depression arrived in the late 1920s, demand for fruit continued although most other produce was severely affected by the slump.

In 1933, in an effort to expand the market and lessen its dependence on Britain, the South African Government entered into an agreement with two Italian shipping companies whereby the Government gave them a subsidy of £150,000 a year for five years, to be matched by £380,000 a year by the Italian Government. These companies were amalgamated by Mussolini into the Lloyd Triestino Line. In return the companies agreed to run freight and passenger services to the Mediterranean. Not unnaturally the entrenched companies, mainly British, many of which already ran Mediterranean services, felt that they were being given a poor reward for their loyal service to South African trade over the years, and through bad as well as good times. However, this action came at a busy time for the

Union–Castle Line, which, following the collapse of Lord Kylsant's shipping empire, was in the process of regaining its independence, and was about to embark on a new shipbuilding programme designed to reduce the mail run to fourteen days. The first of the mail ships, the diesel-powered *Stirling Castle* of 25,000 tons, broke the *Scot*'s record of 1893, by making the run in thirteen days and nine hours in August 1935. Her two sister ships, the *Athlone Castle* and the slightly larger *Capetown Castle*, were equally fast.

The period between the great depression and the Second World War saw enormous investment in ships for the South African service as trade expanded. In addition to the new Union–Castle Liners, the Deutsche–Ost Afrika Line built two passenger ships of 17,000 tons, the *Pretoria* and *Windhuk*, the Holland–Afrika Line built two 10,000-ton ships, the *Bloemfontein* and *Jagersfontein*, and Lloyd Triestino added two passenger liners of 22,000 tons, the *Duilio* and *Giulio Cesare*. The largest regular caller at the Cape became the Shaw Savill and Albion Liner *Dominion Monarch*, of 27,155 tons, when she made her first visit in 1939. During the period between the wars the first cruise liners began to appear in South African ports. The first of these was the *Orca* in 1926, but ten years later the biggest ship to visit the Union since the *Great Eastern*, the *Empress of Britain* of 43,500 tons, came to Cape Town. The increase in the sizes of ships and the numbers in the trade led to the expansion of South African ports to handle the traffic.

The most obvious sign of the outbreak of the Second World War was that the ships changed suddenly from their peacetime liveries to battleship grey, to make them less conspicuous. But not so apparent was the change from the individual peacetime operation of companies' fleets to war emergency centralised management by the Admiralty of all British merchant shipping. Whilst hostilities continued, South Africa was served by shipping that was primarily devoted to the prosecution of an all-out war, and its industry expanded to help in the effort. The Cape became a vital strategic route again, as the alternative Mediterranean/Red Sea route via the Suez Canal was threatened by the Italians. Simon's Town, the British naval base at the Cape, went onto a war footing immediately, as, apart from the alterations necessary to merchant ships as they were converted to a war role, it was expected that the dockyard would have to undertake vital repair work to ease the workload on the busy yards in Britain. One of its first tasks was the conversion of the *Carnarvon Castle* which was taken over by the Admiralty in Cape Town, and sent round to Simon's Town to be equipped as an armed merchant cruiser with a main armament of eight 6-inch guns, the first of many services to be rendered by the dockyard during the next six years.

One by one the ships that were such a familiar sight on the Cape run were removed for war service as captains received their requisition telegrams. Passengers and cargo were hastily discharged so that the ships could take up their new duties. Union–Castle Line's entire reserve fleet of ships, which had lain at anchor off Netley, in the Solent, was quickly back at sea, and the venerable *Gloucester Castle*, which had been built in 1911, was soon the only ship continuously employed on the Cape run until she was sunk in July 1942. Because of their size, speed and range, the Cape passenger ships were high on the list for conversion to armed merchant cruisers and for use as troop transports. A ship like the *Stirling Castle*, which carried nearly 800 passengers in her usual role, could be changed easily into a troopship capable of carrying more than 5,000 soldiers. The *Pretoria Castle* was initially converted into an armed merchant cruiser, but in 1943 was taken into a shipyard and emerged a short time later as an aircraft carrier. After the war she reverted back to her peacetime role and was re-christened *Warwick Castle*.

One of the regular round-Africa service ships of the Union–Castle Line, the *Llandaff Castle*, was torpedoed off the coast of Zululand, about 100 miles south-east of Lourenço Marques, whilst carrying troops to Durban on 30th November 1942. All the passengers and crew, except two who jumped overboard, took to the liferafts and lifeboats and were eventually rescued. One lifeboat sailed itself to the coast where the crew were given assistance by a Zulu farmer until transport arrived to take them to Durban.

The Union–Castle Line lost a total of thirteen ships during the war, and were lucky not to lose the *Langibby Castle* in January 1942, when a torpedo hit her stern, blowing the gun into the air, killing twenty-six of the crew, and damaging the rudder. The ship struggled on in gale force conditions, steering herself with her engines, and three days later managed to anchor at Horta in the Azores. An escort of destroyers arrived, and the ship set sail for Gibraltar, where the troops were landed. As repairs were not possible in Gibraltar, the ship had to steam back to England, still without a rudder. She was subsequently repaired and took part in the D-Day landings.

Even before the war in Europe was ended, a new mail contract was signed between the South African Government and the Union–Castle Line. It took effect on 1st January 1947 and was for a period of ten years. The fourteen-day voyage was stipulated as before, and it was agreed that the Company would register some of its ships in South Africa. The *Good Hope Castle* transferred to the South African Flag on 14th July 1946. The full mail service started again as soon as ships were refitted after their war work, initially in fast cargo ships, as the liners were still engaged in the repatriation of troops. The first of the passenger liners to sail with mail again on the direct route was the *Capetown Castle* in January 1947, and four months later the round-Africa service was re-started by the *Llandovery Castle*. With the loss of nearly half Britain's merchant fleet, companies undertook an enormous rebuilding programme, their problem being not so much of paying for the new ships, but of finding space in the shipyards that were booked to capacity. Nevertheless the Union–Castle Line ordered two new 28,705-ton passenger ships at three million pounds apiece, capable of carrying 278 first and 478 cabin class passengers, and four new intermediate ships, the *Bloemfontein*, *Rhodesia*, *Kenya* and *Braemar Castles*, of about 18,000 tons to replace wartime losses. The *Pretoria Castle* and the *Edinburgh Castle* came into service in 1948, the intermediates between 1950 and 1952. Ellerman and Bucknalls built the four beautiful cargo/passenger ships of 13,400 tons, the *City of Port Elizabeth*, *City of Durban*, *City of York* and *City of Exeter*, which came into service between 1952 and 1954. However, owing to the huge demands for war replacement tonnage from shipyards, it was not until the mid-1950s that most companies had rebuilt their fleets to their pre-war levels.

Immigration from a war-weary Britain still suffering from the rationing of most essentials, was encouraged by both the British and South African Governments. Rhodesia was expanding rapidly, and there was a large demand for skilled workers in the Union. Some of the passenger ships' refits were delayed so that they could carry these new citizens at a special low rate and the Union–Castle Line alone kept three ships employed for nearly three years in this trade, bringing out nearly 30,000 people in total.

Whilst the Union–Castle Line was best known for its large passenger-carrying mailships, it also had a fleet of cargo ships which competed with other members of the Conference on the South African trade. One of its principal rivals since 1881 had been the Clan Line, but when Sir Vernon Thompson, the autocratic Chairman of the Union–Castle, died in 1955, the moment seemed opportune for a merger. In 1956, after a legal wrangle, the British and Commonwealth Shipping Company was established, specifically to purchase the shares of both companies. This was just the beginning of other major changes that were to affect shipping in the post-war years, as competition increased from countries that had recently received their independence, and were determined to secure and protect their own shipping interests.

As at the end of the previous war, the main lesson for the people of South Africa was that they were very largely dependent upon British and foreign shipping for their trade. The volume of tonnage under the Union Flag was small, only 35,485 tons, and the Government was keen to develop its fleet. Such shipping would be under its own control, and not subject to the demands of other countries' war efforts, or the vagaries of their sanctions. A number of companies were formed with Government assistance in the immediate post-war years, the most important being Safmarine (The South African Marine Corporation), which started a service to the United States in 1947 with three ex-United States war emergency programme Victory ships of 7,500 tons each. In 1950 Safmarine was admitted to the

South African Shipping Conference, and launched its services to Europe. In 1955 the first new ship was delivered to the Company, the *South African Merchant* of 9,900 tons, and three chartered vessels of roughly similar size were bought outright. The year 1961 saw the purchase by the British and Commonwealth Company, which was now the parent of Union–Castle, Clan Line, Bullard–King's Natal Line, and the Springbok Line, of some American-held shares in Safmarine, and the six ships owned by the Springbok Line were added to the Safmarine fleet.

During the 1960s a major expansion of Safmarine occurred after which the Company became the major player on the South African routes. A large new building programme was started by the Company, six fast refrigerated cargo ships (Reefers) of 10,200 tons, and eight dry-cargo ships of 12,500 tons being added to the fleet by 1969. In 1966 two Union–Castle Liners were transferred to Safmarine, the *Transvaal Castle* and the *Pretoria Castle*, which were re-christened the *Vaal* and *Oranje* respectively, and the mail contract was shared subsequently between the two companies. A joint company with A. P. Moller, Safbulk, was established in 1964 to operate four ships for the carriage of bulk cargoes, and an agreement arranged with the Royal Dutch Interocean Line to operate four ships on an Australian and Pacific service. As the decade came to a close, Safmarine entered the tanker trade, although some of these ships were registered abroad to avoid the sanctions policies of some Arab states where the oil was loaded, which refused to allow South African ships into their ports.

In 1974 it was announced that the cargo operations of the British and Commonwealth Shipping Company, and other members of the Conference, were to be containerised from 1977. Until this time cargo had been loaded piecemeal into a ship's hold, and removed item by item at the destination. With the introduction of containers, cargo arrived pre-packed in steel boxes which were quickly placed on board ship. The large investment in new ships especially designed to take containers, together with the sudden redundancy of the other types in use, many of which had not reached the end of their expected life, faced shipowners with costs that few could individually afford. A series of amalgamations of services and clubbing together to set up new companies were the only solution. The British and Commonwealth Group took a financial interest in Overseas Containers Ltd, and the cargo side on the South Africa run was absorbed into the new company.

As container ships came onto the scene, passenger shipping also became uneconomic. The passenger ships on the Cape service had been built to combine a certain amount of cargo with passengers. Since this cargo was now to be transported more economically in containers, they lost this useful form of revenue. At the same time, air travel had become cheaper and much quicker, and although the passenger ships were still popular as a relaxing method of travelling between the Cape and Europe, they had lost the bulk of their business. A further blow to their profitability came in 1973 when the price of oil rocketed. The combined Union–Castle/Safmarine service was wound down in the mid-1970s, the *Windsor Castle* completing her last voyage on 19th September 1977, and the SA *Oranje* on 10th October. The last mail-ship voyage was completed by the fast cargo liner *Southampton Castle* on 24th October the same year.

Although mail continues to be carried with cargo by sea, it travels today on the first convenient ship, instead of a selected mail ship. Containers have revolutionised sea transportation to the extent that the cost, size, speed and organisation behind a modern container ship is so high that very few commercial organisations in the world could afford to take the buccaneering attitude towards entering the Cape trade against the established companies that was such a feature of the nineteenth century. The vestiges of a passenger service are still continued by the liner *Astor*, registered in Mauritius, and owned by Safmarine, but there is no longer the regular mail and passenger service which contributed so much to the development of South Africa, and was such a dominant part of the Cape shipping scene for 120 years.

Part II

6

The Cape Coast – Orange River to Table Bay

There are many ways to view the Cape coast. Some areas are geographically significant, others have been the scene of great activity both in the past and at present. To avoid the confusion of leaping from one area to another, the following five chapters cover the coast geographically from west to east, describing it through the eyes of the Portuguese and as a modern mariner might find it, and pausing where events of historical significance occurred. The geographical descriptions are brief, but if large areas may be described as featureless, with their rich maritime history they can never be described as boring.

The Cape coast owes its unenviable reputation amongst seafarers to the severity of the weather and its lack of shelter. Since records were started at the time of the Portuguese more than 1,400 ships have been lost on and around the coast, and the cost in lives is probably fifty times higher. The death toll is comparatively greater than for other areas of the world because although coastal shipping was slow to advance, most wrecks occurred initially to large, well-manned ships *en route* around the Cape to other destinations. Later, as the coast was developed and local shipping services began to connect outposts with Cape Town, the losses amongst the coasters were inevitably high, given the lack of navigational aids and the absence of port facilities. Nevertheless shipowners and seamen continued to persevere with their dangerous trade, and it is largely due to their determination that the opening up of southern Africa was effected.

All around the Cape coast small ships pulled into any place where there was a good landing for their boats, and where they could place cargo and passengers ashore. Ships' masters were accustomed to anchoring off a coast or in a river. They would choose an area, preferably free of swell, where the holding ground for their anchors was good, mud and sand being favoured. For sailing ships in particular, it was also important that the ship be anchored so that she could sail clear regardless of the wind direction. It was a constant nightmare for captains that whilst at anchor the wind might rise or change direction. If the anchor dragged, or the cable parted, the ship might be swept down onto a shore before she could hoist sail unless she

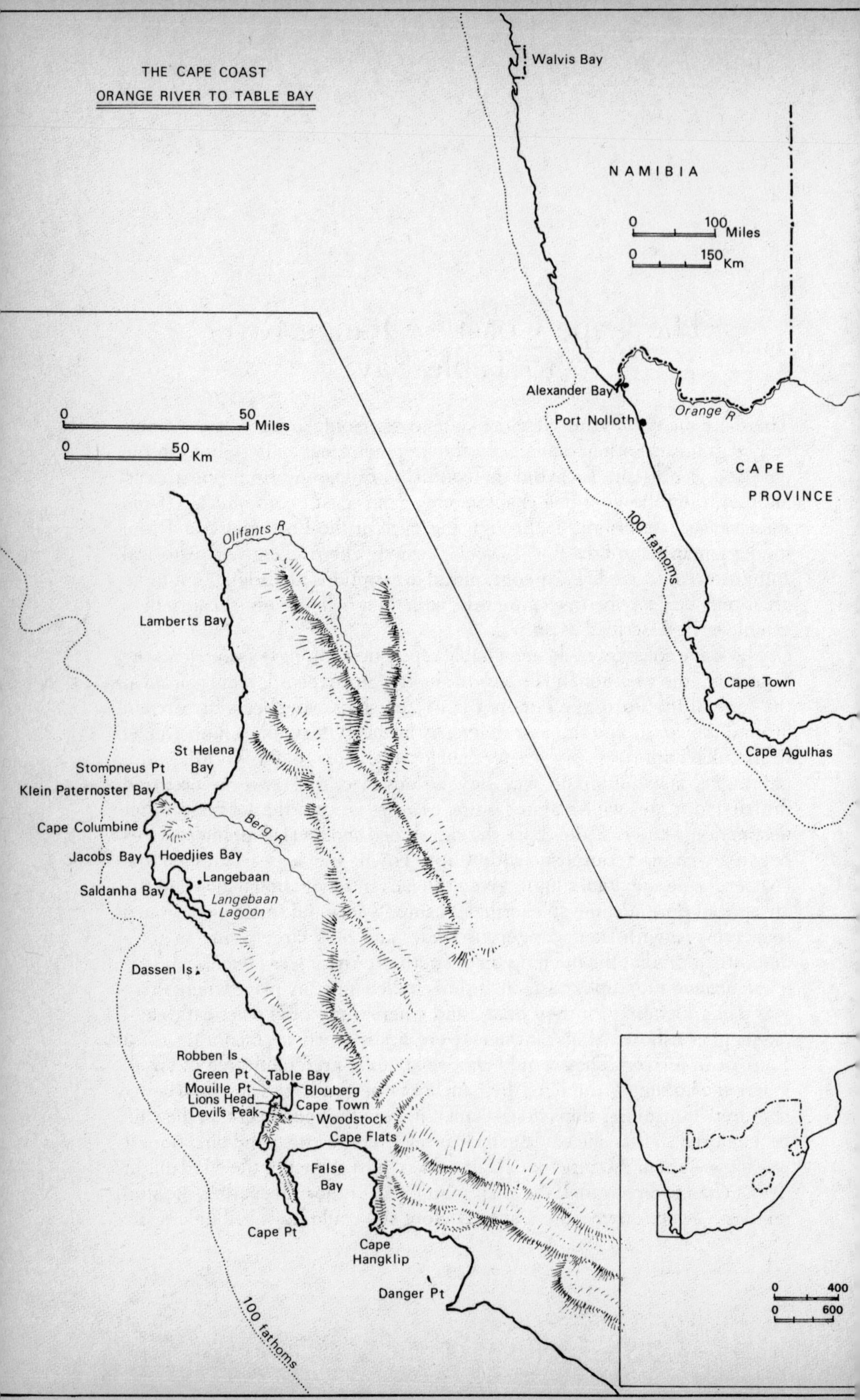
THE CAPE COAST
ORANGE RIVER TO TABLE BAY
Walvis Bay
NAMIBIA
0 100 Miles
0 150 Km
Alexander Bay
Port Nolloth
Orange R
CAPE
PROVINCE
100 fathoms
Cape Town
Cape Agulhas
0 50 Miles
0 50 Km
Olifants R
Lamberts Bay
St Helena
Bay
Stompneus Pt
Klein Paternoster Bay
Cape Columbine
Berg R
Jacobs Bay
Hoedjies Bay
Langebaan
Saldanha Bay
Langebaan
Lagoon
Dassen Is
Robben Is
Green Pt
Table Bay
Mouille Pt
Blouberg
Lions Head
Cape Town
Devil's Peak
Woodstock
Cape Flats
False
Bay
Cape Pt
Cape
Hangklip
Danger Pt
100 fathoms
0 400
0 600

had been anchored leaving enough sea room to manoeuvre herself clear. Ships did anchor off some very exposed beaches, but provided the wind was not blowing onto the shore, they were perfectly safe.

Some of these anchorages evolved into harbours and became great ports; others, as ships grew in size, and man advanced his engineering ability to create protection for shipping, fell from use, or became small shelters for fishing or pleasure craft. The 1,250-mile stretch of the coast of South Africa from the Orange River in the north-west to Ponta do Ouro on the border with Mozambique has only one natural harbour at Saldanha Bay, and most of its modern ports had to be created, either by building breakwaters as in Cape Town and Port Elizabeth, or by dredging through sand bars as at Durban, East London, and Richards Bay. With the obvious exceptions of Cape Town and Simon's Town, nearly all the ports were developed after the British finally took over the colony in 1806, partly owing to their more open attitude towards trade, but also owing to the developments in engineering and particularly the railways.

Starting in the north-west, the Orange is southern Africa's largest river, but it is very shallow and has a large bar across its entrance. The depth within the entrance varies with the run-off of water from the interior, and it has never supported anything but small craft. No port developed in the area but just south of the entrance, at Alexander Bay, an undersea pipeline was built out to a buoy in 1963 so that tankers could offload oil directly for use in the diamond mines, situated just inland. For many years the shallow waters off the north-west coast have also been dredged for diamonds, which are found in the deposits between the ridges of rock which extend seawards. The ships are anchored and lower a large suction pipe to the seabed. The deposits are pumped on board, and pass through a series of screens from which the diamonds are extracted. Some idea of the quantity and value of the diamonds recovered by this method can be gauged by the fact that the costs of adapting and operating ships for this purpose is extremely high, and yet three or more are currently employed in the process.

South of the river, and almost all the way to Table Bay, the coast is backed by a range of hills whose tops indicate their volcanic origin, which sweep down to a low sand and rocky foreshore. It is an inhospitable coast, with one or two exceptions, and open to a westerly sea and swell. Fog is frequent owing to the cold Benguela Current that sweeps up from the Southern Ocean, and is only reversed occasionally by strong and consistent northerly winds.

Port Nolloth, which is now the northernmost port in South Africa, apart from Walvis Bay, which, although South African territory, is a small enclave in Namibia, lies almost 300 miles north of Cape Town. Originally it was known as Robbe Baai (Seal Bay), but the name was changed to its present title in honour of Commander Nolloth, who carried out a survey of the coast in 1854 from HMS *Frolic*. The earlier name was given by the sealers who found this part of the coast a rich hunting ground in the days when seal blubber was a major source of oil. The port developed as an anchorage for copper shipments out from Okiep to which it was connected by a railway in 1876. A number of small ships were employed in this trade, the earliest steamer being a German named the *Namaqua* in 1868–69. Some confusion must have been felt a few years later when two more steamers, each with the name *Namaqua*, were operated between Cape Town and Port Nolloth. Both entered the service in 1873, but the Union Line's ship was wrecked at Port Nolloth in 1876, whilst the other, owned by Berry of Cape Town, lasted until 1886, when she met the same fate. In 1885 a channel was blasted through the rock bar across the entrance into the inner anchorage and quay, and provided some security.

The German Woermann Line operated a coastal service from Swakopmund to Cape Town between 1896 and 1914, calling at all the intermediate ports including Port Nolloth. The first ship on the run was the 300-ton *Leutwein*, but this was replaced in 1900 by the larger *Gertrude Woermann*. In 1903 the *Gertrude Woermann* was wrecked close to Port Nolloth, and replaced by the *Eduard Bohlen*. This latter ship lasted until 1910, when she went aground near Conception Bay. She remained almost intact for many years, an eerie sight amongst the sand dunes that slowly engulfed her. The German service ceased at the outbreak of the war in 1914, and was never re-established. In recent years the Namaqualand diamond workings have provided an added industry, but the port has a limited depth of water, and is still only used by small coasters and fishing vessels.

To the south of Port Nolloth there are two small harbours, but no real protection for large ships. The Olifants River, 150 miles down the coast, was surveyed by Captain Morrell, RN, in 1828, and he reported that if the bar, which has only two feet of water over it, could be dredged, an area for two miles within the river mouth would provide the finest harbour in South Africa, but the demand for a port in the vicinity has never arisen. Twenty miles to the south, the small settlement of Lamberts Bay has the distinction of having been the scene of a naval engagement during the Boer War, when members of General Hertzog's Commando rode to the coast in an effort to make contact with a shipload of supplies dispatched by sympathisers in Europe. When they rode up to the coast they saw a ship; it was the small cruiser HMS *Sybille*, which promptly opened fire. The Boers galloped away and returned to the Orange Free State. However, they must have smiled grimly a few days later when they heard that their antagonist had run ashore in the bay in a heavy sea and become a total wreck with the loss of one member of her crew.

Some twenty-four miles north of St. Helena Bay, the Dutch East Indiaman *Goude Buys* anchored in October 1693 on her way out to the

Cape. This was because so many of her crew were ill that there were insufficient hands left on board to manage the ship. Seven of the crew landed to seek assistance, but they all died of starvation except one, Daniel Stillman, who managed to walk to Saldanha Bay. Another vessel, the *Dageraad*, was sent north to help the stricken ship, but found that she had drifted ashore in the intervening period. Only one man was found alive on board, and he died soon afterwards. The first priority of the rescuers was to save the Company's seventeen treasure chests and as much of the cargo as they could, and then they set sail for Table Bay. During the second night of the voyage, after a thick fog had descended, the ship's crew alerted the captain that they could hear breakers ahead. The captain ordered the anchor to be let go, but the cables cut on the rocks, and the ship drifted onto the rocks of Robben Island, at the entrance to Table Bay. The only survivor of this tragedy was Stillman, who was hauled clear of the surf by some convicts. The Company lost all its treasure, which still lies somewhere off the west coast of the island.

St. Helena Bay was first described by Pacheco Pereira in his *roteiro* written sometime between 1506 and 1508:

> A bay called Angra de Santa Elena. It is fairly large and dangerous because of its many reefs of rock. The whole of this coast is foul with rocks. On the south the bay runs into a point, where there are shallows and here one must be careful. Its latitude is 32 degrees 30 minutes south of the equator. [In fact 32° 42′ south.]

St. Helena Bay does provide a good and safe anchorage in the summer when the prevailing wind is southerly but is exposed to the northerly winds of winter. Nothing more than a small fishing community was formed here because of the proximity of the safe anchorage at Saldanha.

Between Stompneus Point, the western headland of St. Helena Bay, and North Head at the entrance to Saldanha Bay about twenty miles to the south, lies Klein Paternoster Bay, which houses a small village and is one of the few bays offering any shelter on this coast. Just off the coast lies the Soldiers Reef, named after the troopship *St. Lawrence* went aground there in 1876. The ship was carrying a battalion of the 'Buffs' when she struck, but, very fortunately, no lives were lost. Thirty-four years later, the largest vessel in the Portuguese merchant fleet grounded on the same reef. The *Lisboa*, a liner of 7,500 tons built that year, was on her way from Lobito to Cape Town with 300 passengers and crew when she struck at 11 o'clock on the night of 23rd October 1910. Fortunately the night was calm, and everyone was put overside in the lifeboats, the only losses coming when the falls on one of the boats broke and seven people were drowned. Next day the boats were rowed ashore and the survivors were transported to

Cape Town. The loss of the *Lisboa* is of interest because it is the first time that wireless was used in the rescue. The *Lisboa* was fitted with wireless, as was the German ship *Adolph Woermann* which was in Cape Town at the time, and was able to relay messages from the stricken ship to the agents ashore.

If these ships had obeyed the first pilotage instructions written by Pereira, they would have avoided trouble. 'He who sails beyond Angra de Santa Elena should stand three leagues out to sea because of the presence of some reefs of rock here. All this coast has a sandy beach. Twelve leagues beyond Angra de Santa Elena is a point called Ponta da Praya [Green Point in Table Bay].'

Just south of Paternoster Bay lies Cape Columbine, and then the coast takes a more or less southerly bearing fifteen miles to Saldanha Bay. It was off Cape Columbine that the new 6,000-ton trooper *Ismore* went aground in a violent south-easterly gale on 3rd December 1899 whilst carrying soldiers and horses to Cape Town. All the soldiers and crew managed to get ashore, but none of the horses were saved from the wreck which broke up in a few days. A few miles further south is Jacobs Bay, where in 1850 the bodies of three of the crew of the small iron schooner *British Settler* were washed ashore. No trace of the ship or the remainder of her crew has ever been found.

Saldanha Bay, lying fifty miles to the north of Cape Town, was the site of the second European settlement at the Cape. Enclosing an area of roughly eighteen square miles, the northern part of which takes very large ships, it is the finest natural harbour in southern Africa. It was first reported under its present name by Joris van Spilbergen in 1601, who thought that this was Saldanha's Bay, the name then given to Table Bay. Van Spilbergen must have been on his first voyage to the East, because it is hard to understand how he could otherwise have mistaken the very distinctive Table Bay. However, the name stuck as far as the Dutch were concerned, because from then on they called Table Bay by the more descriptive name we use today. Saldanha Bay would have developed as the major stopover port for ships passing the Cape had it had a source of fresh water. Its shelter is far superior to that of Table Bay, but Table Bay has the fresh water which was one of the principal requirements of passing ships, and so Saldanha has been largely ignored except as a haven for ships requiring repairs, and a certain amount of seal hunting, fishing and farming until quite recent times.

Van Spilbergen did not explore the bay; this was left a further eleven years, when the British ship *Pearl*, captained by Samuel Castleton, anchored there on 17th April 1612. Castleton was after water, but discovered that there was little available, and what he thought might be a fresh water stream proved to be a salty lagoon. He did manage to trade with the local tribe of Hottentots, however, obtaining meat in exchange for a piece of iron hoop and a hatchet blade.

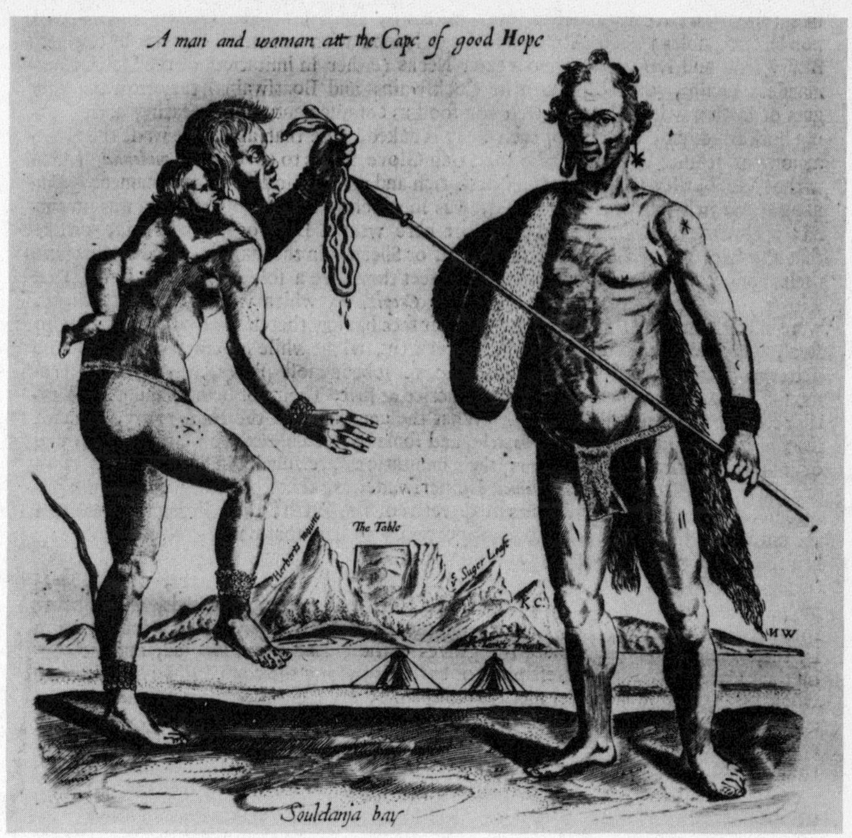

A Table Mountain Hottentot couple from a travelogue by Sir Thomas Herbert (1634).

The bay was rich in seals and fish, and the area of waters around the Cape supported a large whale population. French sealers and whalers certainly knew and used the area from quite an early time, and kept the information very much to themselves, no doubt wishing to keep such a rich hunting ground a secret for their own benefit. Evidence of their activity was discovered by others who used the bay from 1620 onwards, and in 1623, two Icelandic vessels, under a Captain Olafsson, who called in to make repairs and careen, found barrels of oil left by a French ship on Schapen Island. The earliest French written account of Saldanha Bay comes from Etienne de Flacourt, Governor General of Madagascar, who arrived in the *Saint Laurent* in October 1648. His arrival was almost a disaster as the *Saint Laurent* went aground off Meeuw Island, and was lucky to refloat without too much damage.

De Flacourt described Saldanha Bay as

seven or eight leagues long and two or three wide. There are several good anchorages, where the tide does not reach and a ship is like on a pond, shielded from the wind. It looks like a lake, and the exit is invisible until about a league away. The passage to the sea lies to the north-west and is about three leagues in width. To the north a quarter north-east there is a point Pointe à Feu [Hoedjies Point], where there is a little Island named L'Isle à Margaux [Marcus Island] on account of the enormous number of birds of that name which make this place their home. To the south quarter south-west lies the Isle de Sansy [Malagas Island] to which we sent men to kill seals for the boiler. A league further into the bay to the north-east lies Isle de Thomas Pan [Jutten Island?] where seals can be obtained and behind this island there is an inlet where the anchorage is excellent [Jutten Bay]. It is almost a harbour, being sheltered from the winds and hemmed in by a high hill, the bottom, like the shore, being all loose sand. It is a good three leagues from where we lay.

There are five islands in all, to wit, the three aforementioned, the Isle à la Biche [Schapen Island] and the Isle aux Cormorans [Meeuw Island] near which we were anchored. These islands are very small, being about the size of the Isle Louvier [on the Seine]. The Biche and Sansy islands are about twice as big as the Isle de Notre Dame. The Isle aux Cormorans is thus named because of the large number of cormorants that live there.

Elephants and other large animals have made it their home, coming there at low tide from the Anse à Flamens [Riet Bay]. Each Island has its particular species of birds, which live on the fish abounding in the bay, for all sorts of sea creatures live there – whales, porpoises, dogfish, mullets and a thousand other kinds.

All the land on these islands and all the soil on the mainland in the vicinity is excellent, and were it to be cultivated, would grow anything. The greater part is black earth, and it is covered with the verdure of different flowering plants and bushes. There are no big trees.

Reading de Flacourt's description, one receives the impression that Saldanha Bay was a small paradise just waiting to be colonised, and no doubt that is what he had in mind, because the French were aware of the necessity of a base somewhere towards the extremity of southern Africa for their ships travelling to the East. However, the Dutch settled there first, and although the French had the military power to take the bay if they wanted, it would appear that the lack of fresh water persuaded them to use Madagascar as a temporary alternative.

Shortly after his arrival at Table Bay in 1652, van Riebeeck sent a small ship to Saldanha to explore as far north as St. Helena Bay just north of Saldanha, including the islands on the coast. The purpose of this expedition was twofold, to obtain greater knowledge of the area, and to see if there were any opportunities for trade or hunting that might bring benefit to the Company. Captain Sijmon Pieterssen Turver of the *Goede Hoop*, was not too impressed with the land about Saldanha, although he commented favourably on the sheltered anchorage. On one of the islands, however, he found a large stack of seal skins, together with some tools, all of which pointed to activity by the French. He removed the seal skins, some 2,700 in number, and returned to Table Bay.

Seals were hunted for their blubber which was rendered into oil and their skins were a marketable commodity. In Europe they were used for gloves, hats and boots, and van Riebeeck, who had been instructed to make the colony self-sufficient as quickly as possible, sent the *Goede Hoop* back to obtain a cargo of seal skins. The expedition was not a success because the Dutch lacked experience, and it was decided to let this enterprise wait until after the rainy season. However, in 1653, two Hottentots arrived at the settlement in Table Bay with the news that a large ship was at anchor in Saldanha, and van Riebeeck sent a boat to investigate. There they found another Frenchman, which had been sealing for the past six months, during which time her crew had collected 39,000 skins. The Dutch managed to persuade four of the French crew to desert, bringing with them the knowledge of this industry.

There were now two good reasons for van Riebeeck to keep men occupied at Saldanha. The first was to discourage the French from installing a more permanent base, the second was to obtain seal oil and skins. In 1655, he had a boat specially built for the purpose. In the same year Etienne de Flacourt, returning from his duties in the East, called into Saldanha again and, finding no Dutch there, left a message on one of the islands for another French ship. The message was found by the Dutch, and by now thoroughly alarmed by the attentions of their powerful European neighbour, the Dutch East India Company put up two posts to claim the bay as their territory. In 1658, when the first Freeburghers were being created in the Cape settlement, some were encouraged to go to Saldanha and establish themselves as sealers and traders. The Company had decided that although sealing had become a less profitable operation for them, partly owing to the seals looking for safer areas to breed, it might be worthwhile for individuals.

The first settlers at Saldanha, who had to agree to stay for a minimum of twenty years, were allowed to trade provisions directly with the ships that called into Table Bay; however, certain items like rhinoceros horn and elephant tusks had to be sold to the Company at the Company's prices. They were quick to take advantage of this unusual freedom, and within sixteen days returned to Table Bay with their boat loaded with a large quantity of eggs, dried fish and birds, upon which they made a good profit.

In less than a year the Freeburghers had bought a larger boat of thirty feet in length from van Riebeeck for 300 guilders. This sum was equivalent to half a year's salary for the Governor himself, and must have been a small fortune to the traders, which gives an indication of just how well they were faring. The boat was sold to them on the understanding that they would guarantee supplies of seal meat for the Cape Town settlement, where it was used for feeding the slaves. In the same year the traders provided a further service to the Company when the Indiaman *West Vriesland* crawled into Saldanha Bay with over 150 of her crew down with scurvy. Fresh meat and eggs were supplied from their own stocks, and eventually when vegetables came from Table Bay eighty of the sick recovered. Such was the success of the Freeburghers at Saldanha, that van Riebeeck became convinced that ships were calling at Saldanha Bay rather than at Table Bay so that they could purchase provisions there rather than at Cape Town as stipulated by Company rule, and he sent a small detachment of soldiers to keep them under surveillance.

In 1666 the French arrived in force, still seeking an alternative to Madagascar, but with the full backing of their Government, which wished to see the French East India Company, formed in 1664, achieve some of the success of its British and Dutch counterparts. The Governor at the Cape, van Qualberg, treated the visitors with every possible kindness, an action that subsequently cost him his job, as the Dutch East India Company was far from pleased at this encouragement of a potential enemy. An element of high farce developed when one of the French ships slipped from Table Bay, and was followed by a Dutch ship to Saldanha. The two sides watched each other closely for nearly three weeks, the Dutch putting soldiers ashore and claiming that these were only a part of the detachment they regularly kept in the area, and the French exploring, and erecting their own post to establish a claim to the bay. This action stung the Dutch into action. Additional troops arrived and destroyed the French marker, claiming, to avoid any diplomatic difficulties, that when they got there lions had already torn it down.

Undeterred by a less than enthusiastic report from the 1666 fleet, Colbert, the French Minister of Finance, instructed the outgoing fleet to make a proper survey of Saldanha Bay. The first frigate, the *St. Jean Bajou*, arrived on 22nd August 1670, and was soon followed by the rest of the fleet under Admiral de la Haye. Corporal Calmbach, in charge of the small Dutch detachment, immediately sent a message to Table Bay relaying the news. Whilst he waited for reinforcements, he started to remove the sheep which had been established in the area, as they were being stolen by the French. To his surprise he was joined by about forty Hottentots who had come armed with bows and spears to help him to repel the invaders. Although grateful for the show of support, Calmbach dispersed these auxiliaries, knowing that they were no match for trained troops. A

Sergeant Cruse arrived from Table Bay to take over in time to surrender the small Dutch detachment to an overwhelming force of French soldiers which had been landed. Things were not looking very good for the Dutch, their posts claiming the area had been destroyed deliberately just as they had demolished the French posts, and the French showed every intention of marching on Table Bay and capturing the base. At this point Sergeant Cruse managed to escape, and made his way overland to Table Bay, where Governor Hackius put his settlement in readiness for a fight. Fortunately he was not tested, as the French sailed on for Madagascar, contenting themselves with erecting new posts. Had they returned, they could easily have taken the Cape from the Dutch, but the subsequent decline of Colbert shifted French interests elsewhere. The Company, however, seriously alarmed, entered into a contract with the local Hottentot chief, described as Prince Manckhagou, on 19th April 1672 whereby they bought all the coastland from Cape Point to St. Helena for 4,000 reals of eight, which they hoped would clearly establish their claim.

The sale of land was opposed by the Chief Gonnema, head of the Cochoqua, one of the Hottentot tribes, who claimed Saldanha as a part of his territory. He reacted by killing a hunting party of eight Dutchmen, and then attacked the small settlement at Saldanha. Only three fishermen escaped the massacre, and sailed to Table Bay to report the disaster. Sergeant Cruse was already hunting for Gonnema, who evaded capture, but was forced to sue for peace in 1677. With this peace, Saldanha was resettled by Freeburghers, and under Governor Simon van der Stel, considerable encouragement was given to expand the post.

One of the new Freeburghers at Saldanha was William van Dieden, who between January and May 1677, with two Company ships, the *Boode* and the *Haagman*, accomplished the first survey from the Cape right up the west coast as far as Ponta do Sombreiro, just south of Lobito, in Angola, a round distance of 2,500 miles.

With the active support of van der Stel, Saldanha developed gradually as a safe base for ship repairs, and for fishing, whaling and herding, although there was a setback when it was discovered that lions were capable of swimming as far as Schapen Island and attacking the sheep. Other dangers came from visiting ships that might be unfriendly. In 1693, the British barque *Amy* was arrested on suspicion of being a pirate. She was taken into the Company's service, and the crew sent to Holland to stand trial. Subsequently, the crew was released on lack of evidence, and successfully sued the Company for 30,000 guilders. This was not the end of the story, however, as two years later another pirate sailed into Saldanha, and ransacked the post and the ships at anchor. The mate of the second ship was recognised by some of the settlers as the Captain Drew who had commanded the *Amy*. The pirate ship was lost off the coast of

Madagascar in 1701, whilst the *Amy* remained in the Company's service until 1722.

In 1702, a large Dutch East Indiaman, the *Meresteijn*, was making for the Cape with most of the crew sick with scurvy. As night fell the ship headed in towards Saldanha Bay, aiming for the channel between Jutten Island and the land to the south before a strong south-westerly wind. Close to the entrance the captain let go his anchors, instead of hardening onto an easterly course, and the ship swung round and went ashore on Jutten Island. Only ninety-eight of the crew survived. They managed to scramble ashore on the island, and at daybreak there was no sign of their ship; she had been battered to pieces on the rocks. Two of the crew succeeded in reaching the mainland on a makeshift raft, and alerted the guard post. Help was summoned, and a rescue ship was sent from Cape Town, to collect the survivors, but only after the cargo and sixteen money chests had been recovered. All attempts to find the stern section of the ship failed, however, and the disconsolate crew was taken back to Cape Town to explain the loss.

The *Meresteijn* might have remained just another Cape casualty, except that in 1728, she became the object of attention for one of the world's first deep sea salvage divers. In 1722 the Dutch East India Company had lost most of its homeward-bound fleet, many lives and a fortune in specie during a storm in Table Bay. John Lethbridge, an English salvage diver, who had previously found 265,000 guilders for the Company from another wreck, was commissioned in 1727 to go out to Table Bay and endeavour to recover some of the lost treasure. He had limited success in Table Bay, and in January the next year, sailed north to Saldanha to inspect the *Meresteijn*. He spent six weeks waiting for weather calm enough to launch his operations, which were carried out from a raft, but with the weather remaining uncooperative he retired and returned to Cape Town. Quite what equipment Lethbridge used is not known. The diving bell had been improved in the previous century, and Dr Halley had developed an ingenious method of replenishing the air in a wooden, lead-sheathed bell by means of barrels, which, filled with air, were hauled down to the bell and the air forced out by the water pressure. Men had worked comfortably under water in Dr Halley's bell for over an hour and a half. Other salvage attempts were made but it was not until 1972 that the Bay began to surrender the treasure from the *Meresteijn*; 1,300 silver coins, a bronze cannon bearing the Company's insignia, and chinaware were discovered by divers using modern scuba equipment. So finally part of the Company's treasure did raise a good price 250 years later, but for its salvors in the auction rooms in Cape Town.

Crop growing began after 1713 when a smallpox epidemic annihilated the local Hottentots and left the land free. This cleared the way for further white settlement, but growth was slow. The great storms of 1722 and 1728, which created such havoc with shipping in Table Bay, caused Saldanha to be re-examined as an alternative anchorage for shipping, but once again, the lack of a proper water supply proved to be a major obstacle. Saldanha remained an occasional port of refuge for large ships, and a relatively small outpost for fishermen and a few farmers.

The wars between Holland, France and Britain brought back Saldanha to prominence for a short time. The Dutch fleet which was sheltering there in 1781 was captured at Saldanha by Commodore Johnstone, with the exception of the *Middleburg* which, in accordance with Company instructions, was set alight and blew up when the fire reached her powder magazine. Commodore Johnstone was in command of an invasion force, but indications that the French were already entrenched and the Cape reinforced made an attack too risky, and he sailed away with his prizes, the loss of which was one of the causes of the Dutch East India Company's eventual bankruptcy. In 1796, also in Saldanha Bay, Admiral Elphinstone captured the entire Dutch Fleet which had been sent to retrieve the colony from the British, thus putting an end to military threats to British control of the Cape.

During their first occupation of the Cape between 1795 and 1803 the British inspected Saldanha Bay with a view to using it as a naval base. The entrance, suitably protected by heavy batteries, would be almost impossible to force, and the bay was well known for the excellence of the shelter it offered. The problem of the water supply was investigated, and surveys were made to see whether it would be possible to pipe water from either the spring at Witte Klip a short distance north, or the Berg River, some thirty miles away. Neither scheme was pursued, probably because of the high costs of creating a canal for the fresh water, and the Royal Navy appeared quite satisfied with the facilities it found at Simon's Town.

Life continued in its quiet way until the realisation that the vast deposits of bird dung, known as guano, found on islands regularly used by seabirds for nesting, were rich in phosphates and nitrates and thus a valuable fertiliser. Deposits up to seventy-five feet thick were found at Ichaboe Island, just to the north of Lüderitz on the Namibian coast, and sparked off a guano rush. As Ichaboe Island was worked out, attention turned to alternative sources, the islands at Saldanha Bay being an obvious choice. The Government issued licences to ships to take guano from Malagas Island in 1845. Ships poured into Saldanha Bay, and, as was the custom of the time, the crews were employed in excavating the guano which was up to thirty feet deep in places, and loading it aboard the ships. A scene of indescribable confusion developed, as hundreds of seamen from every country in the world dug into the well-matured guano and loaded it from scaffold jetties. The bar keepers of Cape Town were quick to take advantage of all these potential customers, and makeshift canvas taverns sprang up, adding intoxication to the risks in the cosmopolitan community. Fights were frequent, and when one trader attempted to introduce Indian labourers, the sailors threw them all into the sea. Once the sailors had achieved success in keeping the digging to themselves, they got beyond control. Marines were sent from Cape Town to restore order, but as soon as they departed, anarchy erupted again. Peace was achieved finally by the timely intervention of the Reverend James Bertram, who had himself rowed across to the island and, alone, talked these tough and undisciplined men back to their work through force of personality.

The guano rush lasted only a few months, during which time Malagas Island was cleaned down to the bare rock, and then, as quickly as they had come, the ships disappeared, and the bay reverted to its backwater existence. Further plans for development were projected, usually by companies started specifically for the purpose, but none of them matured, and the only break in the routine was the occasional arrival of ships of interest and shipwrecks. In the former category one of the most interesting visitors must be the Confederate warship *Alabama*, which called into the bay between 29th July and 5th August 1863 to replenish her coal bunkers, whilst hunting for Northern shipping during the American Civil War. Built on the Mersey in 1862, she had evaded arrest by the British Government which had declared itself as neutral, and sailed to the Azores to collect her armament. For two years she plagued the sea routes, and sank 57 Federal ships before being sunk by the USS *Kearsarge* off Cherbourg on 19th June 1864. The British Government eventually paid the United States three and a half million pounds as compensation for the damage caused by the *Alabama*, since it was decreed by arbitration that Britain had been lax in trying to stop the ship from sailing when newly built. The incident is still remembered in South Africa because of the very popular folk song 'Daar Kom die *Alabama*' (There comes the *Alabama*).

The greatest danger for ships comes as they approach land or a port, and Saldanha is no exception. Seventeen ships are known to have foundered on the rocks around the approaches to the bay, each casualty bringing with it the need to save and shelter the survivors, and to recover the cargo before the ship broke up. Not all the contents salvaged found their way to the Receiver of Wrecks. Many locals became the owners of silverware after the Portuguese liner *Lisboa* went ashore on Soldiers Reef in 1910, and the disappearance of cargo from the *City of Hankow* in 1942 led to a number of prosecutions.

Another incident that must have brought a great deal of excitement to the area was the arrival of a Boer Commando, under General Maritz, on 10th October 1901. The bay was being used by a number of companies, not least Ellerman's and Bucknalls', for the transhipping of cargoes, as the congestion in Cape Town was causing expensive delays to their ships. At the news of the approach of the Commando, most of the inhabitants fled by taking to fishing boats, and a gunboat, HMS *Partridge*, was sent to Saldanha. A small Boer patrol opened fire on the *Partridge*, but a couple of shells in return persuaded them to move elsewhere although they helped themselves to any horses that they could find as they departed.

Fishing continued on a regular if fairly minor basis, mainly because until the introduction of a rail connection with Cape Town in 1913 it was not possible to get the fish fresh to the market. Canning, which started at Baviaans Bay in 1903, and moved to Hoedjies Bay in 1905, put the industry on a firmer footing, particularly when a world market developed for crawfish. As the numbers of crawfish declined, the Second World War suddenly supplied an enormous market for just about any fish that could be caught and canned. Few people who lived in Britain during that war will have forgotten canned snoek! Fish canning thrived, and has continued since the war, but the most important development for the industry in the bay has been the establishment of the Sea Harvest Corporation in 1964, a combine of the existing canning industry, the Spanish fishing company Pescanova, and Imperial Cold Storage. A large processing plant was built and frozen fish from Saldanha was available in the markets all over the country. Also the bay has become the home port for some thirty Spanish fishing vessels.

Whaling around the Cape had been a spasmodic affair until the growth of the American whaling industry during the eighteenth century from Newfoundland, Nantucket and New Bedford. American and British whalers were taking rich harvest in Cape waters by the end of the century, as part of their general expansion into the Antarctic Ocean. The first locally based industry was established by a Scot, John Murray, during the first British occupation, and although he lost this whilst the Batavian Republic ruled, he re-established himself once the British returned for good in 1806. In 1807 it was reported that there were between six and ten whalers operating in Cape waters, the best season being February, and Saldanha was one of the ports used, mainly between April and May each year. In 1909, a shore station was set up at Donkergat in the bay by a Norwegian, Johann Bryde, who brought with him three whale-catchers from Sandefjord, and in 1911, Carl Ellefsen built another shore station in Salamander Bay, using three ex-Icelandic catchers. The First World War pushed the value of whale oil up from £18 to £90 per ton, which gave the industry an added boost, but in the post-war depression, the price fell to £9, and both stations were closed down in 1930. The industry returned for a short time after the Second World War, and catches in 1967, the last year of operation, rose to 874 whales, but the introduction of the highly efficient whaling fleets, complete with purpose-built factory ships and tankers that could follow the whales around the Antarctic, meant that a shore-based operation could no longer compete economically.

The demands of maritime war transportation during the Second World War gave Saldanha a major boost. The facilities at Cape Town were soon overwhelmed by the number of ships trying to find berths, and an alternative port had to be found in a hurry. The advantages of Saldanha, safe and sheltered, and close to Cape Town itself, were recognised, and an enormous effort was put into its defence, and the development of facilities for shipping. Boom defences were laid between Hoedjies Point and Eland Point via Marcus Island, and a coast defence battery was installed. A temporary jetty was constructed by casting a concrete slab over the remains of the German passenger ship *Präsident*, which had been captured in Tanganyika in the First World War whilst supporting the cruiser *Königsberg* and later brought to Saldanha Bay to be broken up. Her bow and stern protruded from each end of the jetty. The building of a new jetty was started, but not completed until 1945. Perhaps most importantly, the problem of a large and regular water supply was tackled at last. A pipeline was laid from the Berg River, which, via pumping stations along the route, was capable of supplying a million gallons a day into reservoirs. No longer was the settlement dependent upon small springs and rainwater collected on the roofs of the houses, augmented by supplies shipped from Cape Town.

At the war's end, the military moved away, and only their large bases were left, which provided buildings and jetties for the fishermen and whalers. The bay might have reverted to its rather quiet existence had it not been for the decision in 1973 to build a large ore terminal, to export iron ore from the Sishen deposits in the north-west Cape. Sishen was connected directly with Saldanha by a new railway line, 534 miles long. A large jetty, with a depth of seventy-five feet alongside, capable of taking vessels of up to 250,000 tons, was constructed in the bay, and a breakwater to protect the bay was built between Hoedjies Point and Marcus Island. Plans for a proposed steel plant, capable of producing three million tons a year, have been tabled, which would greatly add to the population of the area, now called Greater Saldanha. The industrial development has been kept largely to the north of the bay, most of the southern part of Langebaan lagoon being designated as a nature reserve, and the town of Langebaan has developed as a holiday resort.

From Saldanha to Table Bay is a distance of about fifty miles along an inhospitable coastline which provides no natural harbours, although there are a few good anchorages when the wind conditions allow. A danger to shipping along this coast is an eddy current that runs southwards between four and five miles off the coast during the winter months of June, July and August, whilst further out to sea the main current usually sets northwards at between half a knot and two knots. These currents, which are not always consistent, have, when combined with the fog, led to a number of ship losses in the area.

The main features on this section of coast are Dassen Island and Robben Island. Dassen Island lies about five miles offshore, almost halfway between Saldanha and Table Bay. It was given the name 'Lisla d'Elizabeth' by Joris van Spilbergen, on his voyage east in 1601, although the Portuguese probably knew it under a different name.

Van Spilbergen describes the island as follows:

> This island lies about two miles off-shore on 35¾ degrees approximately [33° 26′ in fact], and about 19 to 20 miles to the north of the Cape bon Esperance. [Van Spilbergen is using the Hollandse Mijl here, which is 1/20th of a degree or three nautical miles, and so his position is about right. The Hollandse Mijl is only 360 yards less than a league, and used prior to the introduction of the Nederlandse Mijl which equals a kilometre.] It is about a mile around, very low [its highest point is sixty-three feet] and very rocky around the shore, but inland is sandy, adorned with good pasture and very sweet smelling flowers, though without any shrubs or firewood, and with no fresh water to be found, but with a quantity of sea wolves, better called sea-bears since they more resemble bears than wolves, having the colour and heads of bears except that their snouts are sharper, and very like them in all their movements except that they are quite lame in their hindquarters and drag their hind feet or paws after them, these being in shape like hands. But nevertheless they move so quickly that they are almost as fast as a man. The beast is also very savage in appearance, and bites so fiercely that it can bite a ship's pike in two as we ourselves experienced. Also it will not give way to a man or two or three and will even attack them boldly enough. We clubbed many of them to death. Besides these we also found a quantity of other little beasts in shape like a stone badger [*Steen-Dasch*, or *Dassie*, here we can see the origins of the name subsequently given to the island], reddish in colour, of which we also clubbed many since we could run fast enough to overtake them. They are very tasty, like lamb or mutton, since they feed only on the herbs and grass. Furthermore there is also a great abundance of birds, such as a sort called penguins, of which there was an innumerable quantity, these being very crisp of flesh and tasty. The Cormorants are black birds the size of a duck, these also we found in innumerable quantities, and had enough ado to keep them away from us since they were not accustomed to men. As far as we could judge of it this island would indeed be very convenient for ships to refresh there if there were fresh water. Oil could also be obtained in quantity from the many sea-bears that dwell there so that a ship of 600

> tons or more could be loaded in a short time. We found no fresh water but considered that it could be had by digging wells.

A few years afterwards in 1605, the English fleet under Sir Edward Michelbourne stopped at the island, and the Admiral and John Davis were stranded ashore for two days when their fleet was driven off by a storm. The English gave the island the name 'Cony' Island after the large number of these birds they found there. Ten years later, when Davis wrote his pilotage instructions, the island is still being referred to as 'Connie' Island. Incidentally, Davis gives the position as 33° 27′ south latitude, which is within a mile. The early mariners were quick to appreciate the sheltered anchorage on the eastern side as protection against westerly winds, but also noted the dangerous rocks that existed around the rest of the island.

Van Riebeeck was not slow to take advantage of the source of oil from the sea-bears on the island, and sent men there, as well as to Saldanha, to collect oil and skins. It was not a popular task, and he ordered his overseer not to spare the lash in order to achieve results, but by the end of his tenure as Governor, oil was being supplied regularly on a more satisfactory basis by Freeburghers for the tanneries in Batavia.

Considering its location on the approach to Table Bay, there have been surprisingly few wrecks on Dassen Island itself. The first recorded one was of the small cutter *Shylok*, which struck a reef off the island in March 1839, fortunately without loss of life. Eleven years later the full rigged ship *Childe Harold* was wrecked on the south-eastern point, but only the captain was drowned as he tried to swim with a line to the shore. The most serious wreck was of the Currie liner *Windsor Castle* on 19th October 1876, which hit a reef some two miles west of the island at 2 a.m. whilst making her approach to Cape Town from England. Fortunately again, the weather was calm, and since the ship was in no danger, it was decided to keep everyone on board until daybreak. In the meantime two passengers were rowed ashore to carry the news to Cape Town. At daybreak the rest of the passengers were rowed to the island where three Portuguese, who were collecting penguin eggs and guano for shipment to Cape Town, gave them a breakfast of bread and fried eggs. At noon on the 20th, when everyone was helping to build a camp to provide shelter, the *Florence* arrived from Cape Town to rescue nearly everyone, the remainder being collected the next day. The weather conditions remained calm for long enough to allow all the baggage and most of the cargo to be removed from the wreck, which broke up a week later.

Nearby on the mainland, the Dutch East India Company's ship *Reygersdal* ran ashore on 25th October 1747. This loss was due to a very severe outbreak of scurvy on the voyage out from Holland, during which 125 of

One of the great mysteries of the sea: the Blue Anchor liner *Waratah,* lost without trace in July 1909 somewhere off the south-east Cape coast with 211 souls aboard.

The Union Castle liner *Cluny Castle,* built in 1903 as an 'Extra' steamer for the cargo and passenger trade between Britain and the Cape.

The author, just visible on the port bridge wing, taking the *Congella* out of Durban Harbour in 1966. The *Congella* was typical of the small ships used on the south-east African coast.

the crew of 206 died, and the rest were too weak to handle the ship. Only twenty men were recovered alive from the wreck.

Losperd's Bay was the scene of the final British invasion of the Cape in 1806. The Napoleonic Wars had resumed in June 1803, and Britain declared war on the Batavian Republic in the same month. However, Britain was in no position to mount an attack against the Cape for some time. Her fleet had been disbanded in 1802, and although an immediate mobilisation was ordered, the demands for ships and men to contain France by blockade meant that there was no spare shipping available for operations elsewhere. The Cape's importance was recognised, but first the European seas had to be made safe for British shipping, and Napoleon's threatened invasion thwarted.

Slowly Britain's maritime might was assembled, and started to regain mastery of the seas. Final control was not achieved until the Battle of Trafalgar on 21st October 1805, when a British fleet under Vice-Admiral Lord Nelson destroyed a larger combined fleet from France and Spain. Even before this battle took place and established British supremacy at sea, a fleet of fifty-nine ships had been dispatched to recapture the Cape under Admiral Sir Home Popham, with General Sir David Baird on board in command of 5,000 seasoned troops. Admiral Popham was unaware of Trafalgar when he came into sight of Table Bay on 5th January 1806. He did know that a large Franco-Spanish fleet had been at sea when he sailed, and possibly could have sailed to the Cape itself. He was thus under considerable pressure to take the Cape as quickly as possible and provide a protected anchorage for his fleet and its vulnerable troop transports. He had intended to land in Table Bay, but a storm prevented this, so he dispatched some ships to Saldanha to disembark. On the 6th the weather had moderated, and after beaching a small brig to provide a breakwater, the troops were sent ashore at Losperd's Bay (Melkbosstrand), against light resistance.

The Governor of the Cape, Janssens, formed up his troops, perhaps 5,000 strong, and advanced to the vicinity of Blouberg. The battle was a foregone conclusion. Unlike the British soldiers, the Dutch Cape army was inexperienced. It had only two professional units, the German Waldeck Regiment, and the European-recruited Jagers; the rest of its numbers consisted of burgher militia, some French marines, and a recently formed regiment of Hottentots. As the British advanced and closed with their enemy, the Dutch line gave, and a general retreat ensued. The Battle for the Cape was over, the British sustaining some 204 casualties to the Dutch 347. Quite why Janssens came out to fight instead of staying behind his strengthened fortifications is a mystery. Undoubtedly he would have lasted longer had he sat behind his lines, but perhaps he knew that he could not expect reinforcements, and that the only chance of retaining control of the

Cape was to hope to defeat the British in a battle. If that was his plan, his gamble failed. He withdrew with about 1,200 men to Hottentots Holland, leaving Cape Town to be defended by Colonel von Prophalow. Faced by overwhelming force, the colonel asked for a truce, and capitulated on 10th January. The surrender was signed at Papendorp (Woodstock). Three weeks later, Janssens finally laid down his arms. The Cape was once more in British hands, and to legalise the situation Britain paid the Prince of Orange six million pounds for the whole colony in 1814. The British occupation was confirmed at the Treaty of Vienna in 1815.

Robben Island, which lies north-west of Table Bay, is first referred to in the accounts of Dias's voyages; one account states that it was used as a base to avoid the Hottentots on the mainland, but this does not tie in with other reports. Antonio de Saldanha certainly called in at the island in 1503, where he reports killing many penguins, sea-wolves and tortoises, but after the slaughter of sixty-five of their most renowned soldiers close to Table Mountain in 1510 there are no records of any further Portuguese visits. Sir James Lancaster, on the first English voyage to the East in 1591, took his pinnace to the island to obtain food when he found difficulty in obtaining any by barter with the Hottentots. In all, three visits were made, each resulting in a full boatload of seals and penguins, and before he departed he put two rams and four ewes on the island in the hope that they would supply meat for any other sailors passing that way. Van Spilbergen does not mention these sheep in 1601 when he visited the island, which he described as being very similar to Dassen Island, only larger. He gave it the name Isla de Cornelia, after his mother, but Robben Island, from *Robbe*, a seal, quickly became the better-established Dutch name.

The first wreck occurred in 1611, and was probably a small sealer, the *Yeanger of Horne*. John Saris, who was in the English fleet that year, reported trading some rope for sheep with nine 'Flemings' shipwrecked on the island who were building a pinnace from the remains of their ship so that they could complete their adventure by taking a cargo of oil back to England. Unfortunately there is no further record of these men, but when Thomas Best's small fleet of two ships visited the island the following year there was no trace of them, nor were there any sheep, so it looks as if these indomitable seamen had completed their boat and set sail. There is no evidence of their arrival in Europe, although this would be difficult to trace as the name of the boat is unknown.

Robben Island (under its current English name of Penguin Island) became the base for the first attempt to establish a settlement at the Cape when John Crosse and nine other convicts were put ashore in Table Bay from the 1615 English fleet. They soon found that the Hottentots made life so unpleasant that they were forced to beg for a boat and flee to Robben Island, the island being safe as the Hottentots had no means of travelling across three miles of water. In 1616, another English ship anchored in Table Bay was advised that eight men and a boy were living on the island. They sent their pinnace to investigate, and it returned with three men, leaving another three behind. Crosse had drowned the previous week whilst trying to reach the mainland again on a raft which was upturned by a whale. Nothing further is known of the three left behind except that they may have been picked up by a Portuguese ship. The three taken aboard the *Gift* in 1616 and returned to England jumped ship the moment it reached the Downs, and were caught stealing very shortly afterwards. All three were executed.

Later a small party of Hottentots under their leader Hadah, who had been taken on a voyage to the East in the *London* in 1631, was left on the island to act as a post office for passing ships. Over the next ten years this group alternately lived on the island and the mainland, depending largely upon their relations with the Hottentot tribes ashore. In 1634, Peter Mundy, the factor aboard the English ship *Mary*, described a visit to Hadah on Robben Island.

> Here the said Hadda liveth with all his kindred and allies, in number about sixty persons men women and children. They come all about us verrie merilye rejoyceing at our comeing, better apparelled than those on the maine, though after the same manner, Hadda excepted, who that day came in English habit from head to foote. They live on seals and penguins of which there are abundance on the other side of the island.

Van Riebeeck first landed on the island in 1657, but he had already made use of it both as a source of oil from the seals and meat from the penguins. In an effort to produce an alternative source of food he tried stocking it with rabbits but these fell prey to snakes. Since the island is placed right in the middle of the approach to Table Bay from the north and west, and presents a serious hazard to ships at night or in poor visibility, van Riebeeck placed a lookout there from the early days of the settlement, whose task was to signal to the town when a ship was in sight, and light a fire as a warning at night.

Van Riebeeck's instructions to ships approaching Table Bay are typically detailed.

> When ships see these fires they may sail between the Lion Mountain shore and the island, close to the Cape shore, in order to avoid the whale rock, until at night the fire, or by day the Vuijrbergh, the highest point on the island [where the fire was lit] is to the NNW of them, when even the largest ship may sail safely SSE into the bay until he has sounded 8, 7, 6, 5 or four fathoms in a sandy bottom, according to the size of the ship.

> They have to remember however, that when the gate and the centre of the fort is general SW by S of them they will be at the proper anchorage.

Only on its north-eastern side is the island free of dangers, and vessels approaching from any other direction ran the risk of striking the off-lying rocks and being wrecked, a threat to Company property that no good Company servant could ignore. Whether it was these precautions, or the prudence and instructions given to the masters of the Company ships, but the first loss during the Company's period of rule did not occur until fifty years after they had started their settlement, when the *Dageraad* returning with some of the salved cargo from the wrecked *Goude Buys* ran onto the rocks on the west side of the island and sixteen men were drowned.

In all some ten ships have been wrecked on Robben Island since 1611, and the island still takes its toll, the most recent casualty being a large tanker that dragged her anchor and finished up firmly aground. Like those before, she will eventually be completely destroyed by the sea and the rocks, but in the meantime, to the casual view, she looks like any other of the many ships lying safely at anchor in Table Bay.

Robben Island has never proved successful for settlers as it is unsuitable for agriculture. Instead it has led a varied existence, as a lookout post and prison by van Riebeeck, later as a leper colony, more recently as a prison, and it now comes under the jurisdiction of the South African Defence Forces. But although it has little to offer commercially, it has always been an important consideration to the Governors of Cape Town and the Cape because of its strategic position at the entrance to Table Bay.

7

The Cape Coast – Table Bay

Table Bay is dominated by Table Mountain, one of the most famous and distinctive landmarks for sailors anywhere in the world. The level flat top, 3,500 feet high and almost two miles in length, culminating in steep, almost vertical sides, creates an outstanding feature clearly visible many miles out to sea. It is framed by two large peaks, Devil's Peak to the east, and Lions Head to the west, either of which would be impressive on their own, but lying so close to the Table, they are almost lost in comparison. Frequently the 'Table cloth', the white orographic cloud that appears over the top of the mountain, is the first sign to the mariner that he is about to make his landfall. The mountain, which faces north-north-west, is the northern end of a range that extends from Cape Point twenty-eight miles to the south, to the low sandy isthmus that separates Table Bay from False Bay in the north known as the Cape Flats. Nestling at its foot lies the city of Cape Town, which overlooks the large bay between the Salt River in the east and Green Point in the west, its extreme seaward limit demarked by Robben Island, just over five miles west of north of Green Point.

To understand the history and development of Table Bay it is necessary to consider its geography through the eyes of a seaman. Table Bay is wide open to winds from the north to the west, a direction that is rare except during the winter, but the prevailing south-easterly wind of the summer months is broken by the mountain, and although it can reach a strong force, it rarely creates serious difficulties for ships at anchor. For nearly 250 years after van Riebeeck's arrival in 1652, the bay was deeper to the south-east and provided greater shelter than it does today when land reclamation and the docks have encroached a mile out from the original shoreline. To visualise the extent of the bay as it used to be it is necessary to visit the castle, now well within the city, but which used to be on the seashore.

The need for fresh water, food, and an opportunity for crews to recover from the diseases brought about by shipboard life were the original reasons behind the examination of Table Bay as the replenishment station on the route to the East. The Portuguese ceased to use it after the massacre of 1510, but the British and Dutch were quick to see its possibilities.

The senior merchant in the East India Company's 1611 fleet, Thomas Aldworth, reported to his Directors:

> But to make this commerce the safer, it seems desirable to me to advise Your Worship of one thing which appears to be very important, which is to establish a settlement at the Cape of Good Hope; which could easily be done by carrying out each year in the ships coming here, a hundred men to leave here in passing. When we went ashore at Saldania [still the English name for Table Bay] which is near the Cape, I went two leagues inland with four or five others, and I assure Your Worship that I have never seen a better land in my life. Although it was mid winter the grass came up to our knees: it is full of woods and lovely rivers of fresh water, with much deer, fish and birds, and the abundance of cows and ewes is astonishing. The climate is very healthy, insomuch that, arriving there with many of our people sick, they all regained their health and strength within twenty days. Also it is a place made so strong by nature that a very few men can defend themselves there against many. And we found the natives of the country to be very courteous and tractable folk, and they did not give us the least annoyance during the time that we were there. As regards its position, it is almost halfway on the route from Europe to the Indies, and will be no less convenient for our journeys than is Mozambique for the Portuguese.

Aldworth's obvious enthusiasm for a settlement at Table Bay glosses over some of its disadvantages, not least the problems with the Hottentots and the fact that they stole anything they could lay their hands upon. Perhaps because of the numbers in the fleet, and the ability of the English to guard themselves on this occasion, the Hottentots did not cause trouble during Aldworth's stay, but most other contemporary reports, particularly by the Dutch, indicate that dealing with the natives would be a major hazard for any settlement.

Three years later the East India Company Court minuted that they would consider the dispatch of a ship annually to Table Bay, loaded with provisions and stores for the Company's ships, and that the ship should spend its time whilst waiting in fishing for seals and whales. Nothing came of this. Instead, King James was persuaded to release a number of condemned prisoners from Newgate Prison, and these were carried out to the Cape in the 1615 fleet. Nine or ten men were landed under their elected leader, John Crosse, with instructions to explore the country. It is significant that despite Aldworth's glowing description of the Cape, the East India Company was unable to attract voluntary explorers, and the condemned men were not all that happy about their plight, despite being forced to sign a declaration that they landed of their own free will. These

English gaolbirds thus became the first 'voluntary' settlers of the Cape, but their stay, as recounted in chapter 6, was shortlived.

This lack of success did not prevent the Company from trying again in 1617, but the three prisoners who were to be landed, once they heard of the fate of the earlier settlers, went to the captain and asked him to hang them rather than leave them behind. In spite of their pleas, he put them ashore, but another vessel in the fleet, delayed by a couple of days, took pity on the wretches and allowed them aboard.

The short Anglo-Dutch war of 1618–19 led to numerous engagements in the East but none at the Cape, where the two nations seem to have managed to avoid each other. On resumption of peace, the East India Company and the Dutch Company agreed to seek a suitable harbour for joint exploitation, but although Table Bay was chosen, nothing came of this admirable idea. However, on 3rd July 1620, two English fleets, one led by Captain Shilling, the other by Captain Fitzherbert, and with many Dutch in attendance, solemnly claimed title to the land. Their purpose appears to have been to prevent anyone else taking control, as there were rumours that other unspecified people intended to create a settlement and make charges for watering. Although the English did not try to colonise the land they had claimed, they were unchallenged for thirty-two years, except by the French who in 1632 laid claim to Robben Island.

From the beginning of the Dutch and English voyages round the Cape, it had become the habit of ships outward-bound for the East to leave messages and letters ashore at Table Bay for homegoing ships to collect and take back with them. This interesting custom, which had started with messages scratched or carved on conspicuous stones, known as post stones, may have been copied from the Portuguese, because the earliest stone found in the Cape is dated 1503, and was left by Captain João da Nova at São Bras. This, and many other post stones are now preserved in the South African Cultural History Museum, Cape Town. The stones give information about the name of a ship and her captain, and the dates of her stay in Table Bay, and provide a very useful confirmation of the many contemporary accounts of voyages to and from the East which are still stored in Holland and England. One, which appears to be split in two, records the visit of the Dutch outward fleet in July 1620. Part of this stone was found in 1976 during the construction of the Golden Acre shopping complex in Cape Town, and lies in Pretoria; the other piece was discovered in 1984 at the site of the old Good Hope Theatre. When put together these two appear to be part of a larger stone which was probably broken for construction work during the early years of the settlement.

Another complete stone, in much better condition, records the visit of the British ship the *Royall Mary* in 1634. The *Royall Mary* was a comparatively large ship of 800 tons, built in 1626, and obviously of some

A Table Bay post stone for the *London*, 1622. The inscription reads: 'The London arrived the 10 of (M)arch here from Surat bound for England and depar(ted) the 20 ditto 1622 Richard Blyth Captain. Hereunder look for letters.'

importance since she was christened by Queen Henrietta Maria, wife of Charles I of Britain. In 1634 she was commanded by Captain Slade, had a crew of 200, and was carrying saltpetre and indigo to England. She made a total of seven voyages east between 1626 and 1647, and spent some time sailing between the eastern trading ports. On the back of this stone is another inscription, somewhat difficult to decipher, but it appears to refer to the *Expedition*, another British ship. Frequently, letters wrapped in oilcloth were buried beneath the stones to prevent them being found by natives. The Dutch and the English also had their own trusted native who would keep letters and hand them over to the captains of homegoing ships. A ship on arriving in the bay would fire a cannon, and this would bring the 'postman' down to the beach, either in Table Bay or Robben Island. A ship's boat would be sent to fetch him and he would exchange mail and report any other useful information in exchange for a small reward.

The habitability of the Cape was emphasised in 1644, when 250 men from the Dutch ship *Mauritius Eiland*, which was wrecked in the bay, were left behind by the rest of their fleet owing to a shortage of space. Although they were given some provisions by the English *Endeavour*, the marooned men fed largely off the land and lived in a small fort, guarding their cargo until rescued by the *Tijger* sent expressly for that purpose.

In 1647, three ships, the *Haerlem*, *Oliphant* and *Schiedam*, departed from Batavia on 17th January. The fleet was separated by a storm after leaving the Sunda Strait, and the *Haerlem* made her own way to Table Bay, arriving on 25th March. She came into the bay close-hauled, but failed to respond when the helm was put over to wear ship when she reached a sounding of eight fathoms. A desperate attempt was made to tack by cutting away the sprit, but the ship failed to come into the wind, and, falling off, the foresails filled again and drove her ashore. A heavy surf was running and pounded the ship on the beach. Four guns were fired as a signal of distress, but no response was forthcoming from another ship they had seen in the bay, which turned out to be the *Oliphant*. However, the next morning the *Oliphant* sent over two boats and efforts were made to put out an anchor astern to ascertain whether the ship could be warped off. The strain was too great, and the *Haerlem* drove inexorably further ashore. By the 27th it was obvious that the ship could not be saved, and so attempts started to salvage the valuable cargo. Two homeward-bound English ships, which arrived that day, gave a hand with this operation, and when they sailed on the 30th, took about forty of the crew to land at St. Helena to await collection by homeward-bound Dutch ships. The same day the *Schiedam* arrived. A council was held, and it was agreed to build a fort ashore in which to place the cargo where it could be guarded by the crew, until another ship arrived to recover it. The necessity of a fort becomes apparent when one learns that a small party of Dutchmen, walking along the beach with cargo, were attacked by Hottentots. The other two ships sailed on 12th April, and the *Haerlem*'s crew continued to salvage what cargo they could and improve their defences.

The crew settled down and waited to be relieved. They managed to obtain some fresh meat from the Hottentots, and did some hunting and fishing. A rhinoceros was shot and eaten, its meat being described as firm and tasty. Penguins and their eggs were brought back from Robben Island, and they seine-netted for fish in the vicinity of Salt River. In the middle of August, an outward-bound fleet of three ships arrived, but declined the request to unload one of their number so that she could return home with the salvaged cargo. However, they did leave some provisions, and were asked to make a report on the state of the fort and the cargo for the Company directors. Presumably the crew of the *Haerlem* hoped that this report would stand them in good stead at the subsequent enquiry.

Their fort is described as being built on a high and steep-sided sand dune, with breastworks eight or nine feet high, and a gun in each corner. An outer rampart with three guns had been erected on the north-west side.

From various indications, the site would appear to have been at Skulpbaai. Inside, in an area of 450 square feet, lived sixty-two men with thirty muskets, commanded by under-merchant Leendert Janssen. A sixty-foot well had been dug within the fort, through sand, coral-limestone, shelly sand, clay, and finally water-bearing sand. Most importantly from the Company's point of view, the salvaged goods were under strong tents within the fort, apart from the pepper, which was in an equally robust tent near the shore. No reason was given for the pepper being outside, but perhaps it was due to the noxious gasses given off when pepper becomes wet. The list of cargo being stored gives us a clear idea of the type of goods being carried to Europe from the East at that time:

Pepper,	175 tons
Cinnamon,	7 tons
Candy Sugar,	14 tons
Gold cloth,	114 packs
Porcelain,	140 barrels
Indigo,	7 chests

The men lived ashore for nearly a year until collected by the 1648 homeward fleet. A *remonstrantie* or exposition written by Janssen gives a long discourse on the advantages of establishing a colony at the Cape. This, and the fact that he had managed to keep his crew fit and healthy for such a prolonged period with little outside assistance, and provide a surplus to provision visiting ships, finally persuaded the Company that a base in Table Bay would be to their advantage.

The obvious leader for such a settlement would have been either Janssen or Nicholaas Proot, the other merchant who had stayed with Janssen, but both declined. However, another under-merchant, Jan van Riebeeck, was kicking his heels in Holland, having been sent back from Batavia in disgrace for trading on his own account. His crime was probably not an unusual one for merchants at the time, especially as his monthly salary as an under-merchant was only twenty-five guilders, and his mistake was possibly to have been too obvious. Van Riebeeck had returned with the fleet that had collected the *Haerlem*'s crew, and so had some knowledge of the Cape. The Company offered him the position as leader of the expedition with the rank of Merchant at fifty guilders a month, and he was quick to accept, although he did extract a promise that once the colony was established he would be returned to Batavia.

The first settlers were recruited and boarded a small flotilla of five ships, the *Drommedaris*, *Reyger*, *Walvis*, *Oliphant* and *Hope*. They sailed from Holland on 14th December 1651, under their 32-year-old leader, and arrived in Table Bay on 5th April 1652.

Regrettably, no architect's drawings survive of the *Drommedaris*, a ship that has an established place in the hearts and history of South Africa, but she was described as a '*Jaght*', the term used for any light, fast vessel, and was therefore typical of the smaller Dutch East Indiamen of that time. She was probably about 100 feet long, and twenty-six broad. In order to navigate the shallow waters around the Netherlands, she would, like all Dutch ships, have had a light draught, probably no more than six foot six inches, whereas a similar-sized English ship would have drawn nearer thirteen feet. Her rig would have been familiar to Vasco da Gama, in that she would have had three masts, the forward two being square-rigged, and the mizzen still having a lateen sail. The only difference was that by this time most of the ships carried an upper topsail on the fore and main masts, and so had three square sails on each mast. The high stern of a century before had been lowered by a deck, as it had been discovered that the extra top hamper did not help the ship's sailing performance, but she would have retained a great cabin at the poop, and a smaller cabin above for the master. Like all ships of that vintage she would have had a large tumblehome, so that she was considerably narrower at the deck than she was at the waterline. For protection she would have been equipped with up to twenty iron guns, fired through gun ports cut in the hull, and small brass swivel guns on her bulwarks.

The initial concerns of the Dutch East India Company after they had dispatched van Riebeeck to the Cape were to guarantee the supply of water, and create a source of corn and meat. The Cape station was not expected to become a port for major refits, nor was it anticipated that large quantities of cargo would be landed, so that there was no requirement to build wharves and docks. Ships that had any cargo to discharge or water and stores to collect could easily do so with their boats. However, the beach was not the easiest place to manhandle large casks of water, and van Riebeeck made the construction of a small jetty one of his earliest priorities once he had built his fort and a small supporting battery called Duijnhoop near the Salt River. The jetty was created by building large wooden boxes which were sunk in position by filling them with boulders. Along the top of these boxes, beams and a wooden deck were laid to make a simple but effective landing stage. The work was a tremendous strain on van Riebeeck's small work force, and he was permitted to take carpenters and crew from visiting ships to help progress on the project, which was completed in January 1658. Van Riebeeck's jetty, which lay at the foot of Plein Street in modern Cape Town, must have been well constructed, because with occasional repairs, it served for more than fifty years. Another jetty was built in 1666, at the foot of Buitenkant Street, and these two landing stages provided the only attempt at any harbour works for nearly a century.

Although the Dutch at the Cape were kept extremely busy, they must have felt a sense of isolation struggling to create a small township in a strange continent, a loneliness broken only by the arrival of the outward and homeward fleets. To the energetic commander of the station these visits would have been something of a mixed blessing, as they usually brought with them a Commissioner from Batavia, to whom van Riebeeck was responsible, who would inspect the works, make recommendations, and write a report which would eventually find its way to the Company directors in Holland. Some of these recommendations, like van Goens's famous canal across the Cape Flats to cut off the Cape Peninsula from the rest of Africa and create a defensive moat for the settlement, were impracticable, but nevertheless had to be taken seriously by a Commandant several ranks junior in the Company hierarchy.

Once the basic work of erecting fortifications, shelter and the jetty were completed, the Company planned to decrease the garrison from a maximum of 125 to less than fifty, but continual demands on this small force for work, defence against the Hottentots, and the effort to make the settlement self-supporting in food prevented this reduction. It was as well that it did, because every able man was required in May 1660 when the French warship *La Marichale* was driven ashore near the entrance to the Salt River by a strong north-westerly. The ship was carrying the new Governor for the French settlement in Madagascar, together with more than 150 armed men, a force that outnumbered the Dutch garrison. Van Riebeeck was faced with an extremely dangerous problem from the point of view of the safety of his little settlement, and he decided to take a firm line from the outset. As the survivors of the French ship came ashore, they were met with the demand that they should hand over all weapons, and in return they would receive assistance and shelter. The French had no choice but to accept these conditions, and were then divided into small parties and set to work around the colony. Perhaps fortunately for van Riebeeck, about thirty-five of the Frenchmen proved to be Huguenots, who were sympathetic to the Protestant Dutchmen, and stayed behind when the others were removed by passing vessels.

Van Riebeeck's successor in 1662, Zacharias Wagenaer, is chiefly to be remembered because he started the work on a new stone fortification, the Cape Town Castle that still stands today, to replace the earlier turf structure. The work was completed in 1676, and a part of the armament came from guns salvaged from *La Marichale*. The site of the castle was criticised by some, including a visiting Commissioner, on the grounds that it was open to bombardment should an enemy manage to manoeuvre guns up the Devil's Peak or Lions Head. One of the castle gunners injudiciously remarked on this, and was challenged by Governor Isbarand Goske, who had originally laid out the site. The story goes that a gun was manhandled up the Devil's Peak and the gunner allowed to fire it at the castle. The shot fell well short, but of course the gunner may have realised that there was no future in proving the Governor a fool! But even if the castle might have been vulnerable to a land bombardment, it adequately served its main purpose of providing military protection over the anchorage.

The first serious loss of shipping, after *La Marichale*, occurred in May 1692, almost the middle of the southern winter. Eleven ships were at anchor in the bay, the Dutch homebound fleet of eight, two British Indiamen, and an old frigate converted into a convalescent ship, when a north-westerly wind sprang up. It soon reached gale force, sending large seas rolling into the anchorage. The strain on any anchor cable in these conditions is immense. As a ship pitches, one moment running forward and letting the cable go slack, and then being thrown backwards, its full weight comes on the cable and anchor. Modern anchors and chain cables frequently give in these conditions, but the rope cables in use until the middle of the nineteenth century had far less strength, and were more liable to chafe through on obstacles on the bottom. The first vessel to break her cable at about 2 a.m. was the *Hoogergeest*. She let go her sheet anchor, but this could not hold and she drifted rapidly towards the shore. At dawn, she and the *Goede Hoop*, whose cable had also parted during the night, were ashore near the mouth of the Salt River. The British Indiaman *Orange* followed soon afterwards, stranding close to the others. Whilst the remaining ships in the anchorage did their utmost to hold on as the gale blew throughout the day, the people on shore could only watch helplessly as the three ships were slowly battered to pieces and their crews mostly drowned as they tried to swim ashore. At this point, Jochem Willemsz, the quartermaster of the *Spierdijk*, who had been ashore when the storm rose, approached Governor Simon van der Stel, and asked for permission to swim out with a line through the surf to the *Hoogergeest*. Consent was given, and tying a light line around his waist, Willemsz waded out into the sea. One can imagine how difficult a swim in those conditions must have been, but despite disappearing from the view of the spectators ashore, Willemsz reached the *Hoogergeest*, and a stronger line was attached to his line, and the crew hauled ashore on makeshift rafts. Most were saved, and it would be nice to report that Willemsz was rewarded for his bravery, but although he was recommended for promotion, there is no record that he ever received it.

The convalescent ship, the *De Swarte Leeuw*, survived the 1692 storm, but was blown ashore four years later in another north-westerly. She was filled with boulders to provide a breakwater off the jetty for the ship's boats, but the first storm in May 1697 smashed her to pieces. The same storm was responsible for wrecking two more Dutch East Indiamen, the *Waddringsveen* and the *Oosterland*, which both went ashore near the Salt River mouth.

The prevalence of wrecks in this area caused the new Governor, Willem Adrian van der Stel, on succeeding his father in 1699, to examine the river and the lagoon inside the entrance, the Rietvlei, to see whether a harbour could be created which would provide better shelter for shipping, but the task was beyond the financial or human resources of the time.

The loss of five ships within five years in what was considered a safe anchorage, should have alerted the East India Company officials to the dangers of Table Bay from a north-westerly gale in the winter months, but although False Bay was considered as an alternative, nothing was done to implement its use, and the ships continued to anchor in Table Bay all the year round. For the next twenty-five years the gales missed the fleets, but in June 1722 the odds ran out. On the 16th of that month the bay was full of shipping at anchor including six Dutch and three British East Indiamen, plus the little *Amy*, the small vessel recovered from pirates and used for coastal work at the Cape, when the north-west wind began to rise. All day the ships strained at their anchors, whilst the small craft and fishing boats were thrown onto the beach near the jetties. Soon after sunset the first distress gun was heard, and the population of the town was summoned to watch the beaches. Very soon the first ship grounded, and by morning no fewer than eleven were lying wrecked along the shore. Fate played a fickle game with the ships, the lighter ones were pushed far enough up the beach for their crews to wade ashore, but others struck rocks and rolled over and were soon battered to pieces by the surf. Seven hundred men died during that evil night, and an immense value in cargo and money was lost. Some of the missing equipment was recovered by the English diver Lethbridge, but the valuable money chests were never found, and this fortune in specie is probably still buried under what is now the reclaimed land around the docks.

Six years later, in 1728, another winter north-west gale caught the Dutch homebound fleet. It might have been thought that after the previous experiences the ships would have anchored further out from the shore so that they would have the room to set sail and claw out of danger when a north-westerly threatened. However, anchoring at a greater distance from the jetties added considerably to the time required to make the journey between the ship and the shore, and also exposed the ships to the south-westerlies. Three ships went ashore, and although one of them, the *Haarlem*, was refloated, she did not escape the next north-westerly gale that sprang up soon after she had returned from Saldanha Bay for repairs.

The wrecking of so many richly laden vessels on such an accessible beach would have provided a source of rich pickings for beachcombers, but at the Cape the Company jealously guarded its property, and took possession of foreign goods if they were not claimed. So strict were the rules against individuals helping themselves from the wreckage, that one of the first actions undertaken by the soldiers who were always ordered to the beach as soon as it was known that a ship had gone ashore, was to erect gallows, on which looters were summarily hanged. This discouraged the population from assisting in saving cargo but, more damaging, it also prevented ready help being given to the drowning sailors. People, however, were less valuable to the Company than the precious cargoes, which were always the Governor's priority. As a small compensation for the loss of the ships, the Cape settlement, which was extremely short of wood, was able to salvage considerable quantities as timbers from the ships were washed ashore on the beach.

Although the 1722 and 1728 losses were a serious blow to a company even as rich as the Dutch East India Company, little action was taken. A number of options were considered, including banning ships from visiting the Cape at all. This was not adopted as the loss of crews from scurvy and typhus without the break at the Cape would have been equally threatening to the safety of the ships. However, captains were released from the obligation to call at the Cape if they felt that their ship was making a fast passage, and it was decreed that stops during the winter months of May, June and July, if they could not be avoided, were to be kept as short as possible. In the meantime False Bay and Saldanha Bay were investigated again as substitute anchorages, and a study was put in hand to see whether a protective mole could be built out across the harbour from its western end at Green Point. When none of these three options was deemed practical, ships were directed to be provided with better and longer anchor cables.

The measures taken after 1728 could hardly be described as very positive, but for nine years all was quiet and, lulled by the lack of disasters, the Dutch captains began to stretch the rules and prolong their stays in the bay during the winter months. Sooner or later another tragedy was bound to happen and it occurred on 21st May 1737. Lying at anchor in the bay at the time was the entire homebound fleet, and when a north-wester began to blow it was already too late for the ships to sail clear. Eight of the ten ships were lost, either drifting ashore, or, when the captains realised that they could not save their ships, by being sailed towards a safe part of the beach, which offered a better chance of survival for the crew and cargo. It is said that one vessel, the *Paddenburg*, was lifted by a huge wave clear over another wreck and deposited on the beach so heavily that the stern was shattered, but most of her crew survived.

The Directors of the Dutch East India Company were stung into activity at last by the almost total loss of one of their two returning fleets, and firm instructions were issued that all ships passing the Cape between 15th May and 15th August must anchor at Simon's Bay, whilst improved protection for the Table Bay anchorage was effected. Earlier plans for a mole from Green Point were re-examined, and a further survey discovered that a reef which had formed part of the plans produced by Michiel Lantsheer did exist, and would provide a foundation for a protective mole as well as reduce the quantity of materials required. Almost six years after the disaster, Governor Swellengrebel was told to start work on a 2,300-foot breakwater behind which ships would be sheltered from the devastating north-westerly waves. The work was entrusted to the Port Captain, Jacobus Moller, using slaves borrowed from the burghers, and carts and oxen from the farmers, who carried stone quarried from Lions Rump and deposited it along the reef to construct a mole 100 feet wide at its base and forty feet across its top.

Progress was extremely slow, partly because of a shortage of labour, and also because the burghers chose their old or sick slaves to fill their quotas. In an effort to speed the work a request for a ship to sail to the east coast to fetch more slaves was made to the Directors, but was turned down. Building stopped in 1747 when the mole had reached a length of 330 feet because a storm in May swept away the outer end and a swarm of locusts ate the crops, threatening a famine throughout the Cape. The outgoing Commissioner in 1748, Daniel Nolthenius, was asked to examine the breakwater, but although he found that Moller had been exaggerating the difficulties he was experiencing, he also realised that the mole would have to be made much larger if it was to survive the winter storms, and a massive expenditure would be required for its completion. The Company gave up the contest with the sea, and the waves and the citizens of Cape Town soon removed all trace of the mole. All that remains of these first major engineering works attempted in the bay is the name, Mouille Point, a corruption of the old Dutch word *Moelje*, meaning a mole.

Simon's Bay was developed as the winter anchorage, but ships occasionally disobeyed the Company's instructions and anchored in Table Bay during the winter. It was the disaster that befell one of these vessels, the *De Jong Thomas*, that gave the Cape one of its great seafaring legends, 'The man who rode the water'. The homecoming fleet had anchored in the bay against all advice in June 1773 when the almost inevitable north-wester began to blow. When it became apparent to her captain that the *De Jong Thomas*'s last anchor was about to part its cable, he had it cut, set some sail, and ran his vessel into the shore. It struck close to the Salt River mouth. Soldiers were dispatched to the beach to guard Company property, but no endeavour was made to help the poor wretches on board the wreck on account of the heavy surf. Amongst these soldiers was a corporal, whose father Wolraad Woltemade rode up during the day with his son's meal. Seeing the plight of the sailors aboard the ship, he rode his horse straight out into the sea, and managed to swim to the ship. He called for two sailors to jump into the water, and grab the horse's tail so that they could be brought ashore. With the first two men safely on the beach, Woltemade

The Union Castle passenger liner *Pretoria Castle* after conversion into a light aircraft carrier during World War II. In 1946 she was reconverted, and resumed service as the *Warwick Castle.*

The Union Castle liner *Windsor Castle,* built in 1960 and sold when the mail/passenger service was discontinued in 1977.

The *John Ross* (right), one of the largest tugs in the world, which towed the bow section of the *Castillo de Bellver* (below) away from the west coast of the Cape when the Spanish super-tanker had broken in two after a fire on board in 1983.

headed back to the ship and rescued two more. On his eighth trip, when his horse was tiring, the men on board must have feared that this would be his last attempt and six of them jumped into the water. The load was too much for the exhausted horse, and it went under, dragging all seven men with him.

Although the losses by Dutch ships decreased dramatically after the great storm of 1737, and only six ships were lost until the British takeover thanks to the more rigid enforcement of the rules regarding Table Bay, the wrecks did not cease. Other nationalities were either unaware of the dangers, or did not apply the same rules concerning winter anchoring, and their ships continued to suffer. The British were affected less than the French, who lost four, because although there were more British ships passing the Cape, many of these chose to make their homeward stop at St. Helena Island.

One famous British visitor during the eighteenth century was Commodore Anson, and his ship the *Centurion*, on her way home having almost circumnavigated the world and captured the Spanish Manilla galleon. He called in at Table Bay in 1744 and described it in his log.

> The Cape of Good Hope is situated in a temperate climate, where the excesses of heat and cold are rarely known, and the Dutch inhabitants, who are numerous, and who here retain their native industry, have stocked it with prodigious plenty of all sorts of fruit and provision, most of which, either from the equality of the seasons, or the peculiarity of the soil, are more delicious in their kind than can be met elsewhere: so that by these, and by the excellent water that here abounds, this settlement is the best provided of any in the known world for the refreshment of seamen after long voyages.

Anson's crew had been reduced by sickness, and he managed to sign on forty men from the settlement for his voyage home, although the nationality of these men is unknown it is quite possible that some were British, left behind from their ships to recover from illness.

Frequently British ships had to avoid the Cape altogether because of wars with the Netherlands. It was such a war in 1781, when Holland joined France against Britain, that led to what was almost a French occupation of the Cape and a major effort to improve the fortifications.

The British had dispatched a large invasion fleet under Commodore Johnstone, which had an indecisive battle with the French fleet under Admiral Suffren on the way. Johnstone paused at Porto Praya to effect repairs, but the French fleet, unhampered by so many transports, sailed on and reached the Cape first on 11th July 1781 and immediately set about strengthening the defences of Table Bay. The greatest innovation was a fortified line from Fort Knokke, which lay halfway between the castle and Salt River, and halfway up Devil's Peak, which became known as the French or Munnik Lines. Additionally, new batteries were erected between Fort Knokke and Salt River, and another one built at Mouille Point. A second line of entrenchments was started to support the French lines, which could be outflanked by an enemy if he managed to climb halfway up the Devil's Peak, but these had not been completed when the French withdrew in 1784. After the French had left, the Dutch built another large battery, named the Amsterdam, which was finished in 1787. Table Bay had never been so well protected, and although there were doubts as to how effective these defences might be against a landward attack, they made the anchorage a very hazardous proposition for an enemy fleet.

Between 1784 and 1793 the Dutch East India Company was to lose four more ships in the bay, all during the winter months, which would indicate that the strictures against anchoring there were still sometimes ignored. In 1784, the *Hoop* ran onto Mouille Point, and in 1788 the *Avenhoorn* was swept ashore by a north-westerly. On 20th May 1793, five days after the official time to be clear of the bay, two ships out of a fleet of eleven were driven onto the beach. The *Zeeland* lost her anchors and sailed herself onto the beach where most of the crew got ashore safely. The story of the *Sterrenschans* which went onto rocks south of the castle has a touch of romance as the captain had just married a Cape Town girl who was on board at the time. The girl's family, seeing the ship hopelessly aground and being battered by the waves, offered a reward for anyone who could save their daughter. None of the local boatmen would take the risk, but the captain of an American whaler which was in the bay summoned his boat's crew and pushed their boat out through the surf. They managed to reach the stricken ship, and arranged that the bridegroom would lower his wife over the stern on the end of a rope, and the whaler's boat would then row alongside, cut the line, and take her ashore. For some fifteen minutes the poor girl hung on the end of the line, one minute beneath the waves, the next suspended many feet above the sea, whilst the Americans slowly manoeuvred their boat into position. Miraculously the operation was a complete success, and the girl was brought safely to the beach to be reunited with her relatives. The story ends on a happy note, as the wind died later that day, and her husband and most of his crew were rescued.

As a result of these calamities the Company extended the closed period for Table Bay to between 10th April and 1st October each year. But the Company's decision had been made too late in the day to have any bearing upon their own shipping. Events in Europe, and in particular the effects of the long series of wars between France and Britain, which, whatever excuse was used, were fundamentally about mercantile superiority, placed a newly republican Holland on the side of revolutionary France, and the

British were not prepared to lose the opportunity of acquiring the useful facilities at the Cape a second time. When the British arrived in 1795 they did not risk their ships against the formidable batteries in Table Bay, but chose instead to land at the poorly protected Simon's Bay, and the campaign was over in a few weeks.

It was not long before the British Navy were to experience some of the dangers of Table Bay. Two frigates, the *Sceptre* and the *Jupiter*, and the Danish 3rd rate *Oldenberg*, were anchored with a number of others on 5th November 1799, when an unseasonable north-westerly storm arose. The *Sceptre* lost three anchors despite reducing her windage by striking her topmasts and lowering the fore and mainyards to the deck. Her remaining anchor was only just holding so she sent away her launch to the *Jupiter* to borrow another one. Unfortunately the launch broached and sank with all hands. In an attempt to give more hold to the remaining anchor, the ship's two bow cannons were attached to the anchor cable, but as darkness was falling, the cable parted. Helplessly the frigate drifted ashore and grounded on rocks about 330 feet from the beach. She was quickly followed by the *Oldenberg* and a British whaler, the *Sierra Leone*. For the 400 men on board the *Sceptre* there was little chance of swimming to the shore, so they hung on, hoping that their ship would stay in one piece until the wind subsided or changed direction. Sadly the ship was in need of repair, and soon she began to break up. Some men tried to float ashore on broken pieces of their vessel, but very few survived. When a roll-call was taken the next day it was discovered that only about 130 of the crew were alive. The losses from the other ships driven ashore in the storm were remarkably small, mainly because their ships ended up on a softer beach, and their hulls were stronger and so remained intact until the wind abated.

An unusual survivor of the *Sceptre* was one of her seamen, Joshua Penny. Penny was an American citizen pressed into the Royal Navy who feigned sickness until he was sent to the hospital in Cape Town a few days before the ship was lost. As he was being carried ashore he managed to escape, and ran away up Table Mountain. For fourteen months he evaded capture and lived on the mountain, eating anything he could find. Eventually he risked coming back down into the town and his first question concerned the whereabouts of his old ship, because he did not wish to run into any of his shipmates and be recognised. Desertion in those days was punished by 1,000 lashes with the cat-o'-nine-tails administered around the fleet, and very few endured even half the punishment. His relief at discovering that his ship had been wrecked can be imagined, because the record of his desertion had most probably been forgotten. However, he wasted little time in signing on aboard a Danish ship and putting as many miles as he could between himself and the Cape.

The Treaty of Amiens and the Dutch repossession of the Cape in 1803 did not materially affect Table Bay. Some modifications were made to the defences, but nothing was done to improve the facilities for shipping, which still consisted of little more than van Riebeeck's frequently refurbished jetty. The old rules for ships to winter at Simon's Bay were reintroduced, and no losses occurred. When the British returned again in 1806 trade began to increase, and it expanded dramatically once the Napoleonic Wars finished in 1815. By this time van Riebeeck's jetty had become unsafe, and cargo was having to be carried across the beach from boats once more. A tonnage duty was introduced, and levied against ships that anchored in the bay, but the monies received were too small to pay for the upkeep of the jetty, let alone the cost of building a new one. The problem received a considerable amount of attention from succeeding administrations and a number of investigations were made, but no action was taken.

The problems of Table Bay as a winter anchorage were highlighted again in 1822 when, despite all the warnings, it was in full use. On 10th July the wind rose and two ships were driven ashore. Eleven days later in a similar storm seven ships lost their anchors and ended on the beach. This salutary reminder led to a number of plans being drawn up for the creation of a breakwater, and one plan, proposed by Captain Knox, included two moles around a sheltered harbour. His cost of £32,000 was based upon the use of convicts for the work, which Lord Charles Somerset, the Governor at the time, enthusiastically supported. It was even suggested that in order to help pay for the works, the Royal Navy might be persuaded to move their base round from Simon's Bay. The Royal Navy was not at all keen, and none of the projects came to anything because of the unwillingness of the Colonial Office to spend the money. Local politics also interfered with a firm decision being made, as the local merchants were more interested in the building of a new jetty which would help them get their goods across the beach in greater safety.

Whilst discussions proceeded, ships continued to be lost during the north-westers, the worst occasion being in 1831 when six ships came ashore, although five were later refloated. The damage caused was in excess of £40,000, and led at last to some action being taken. A stone quay was started in 1832, but work was stopped the following year when it had reached a length of 790 feet because of the high estimated cost of completion. However, Cape Town was now too important a port for the need for facilities to be ignored, and six years later the North Jetty was started at the foot of Bree Street, and this time both it, and another smaller jetty, were finished.

Although the jetties pleased the merchants, and aided the transhipment of cargo because they allowed boats to unload without having to go through the surf, they did not solve the seamen's problem which was

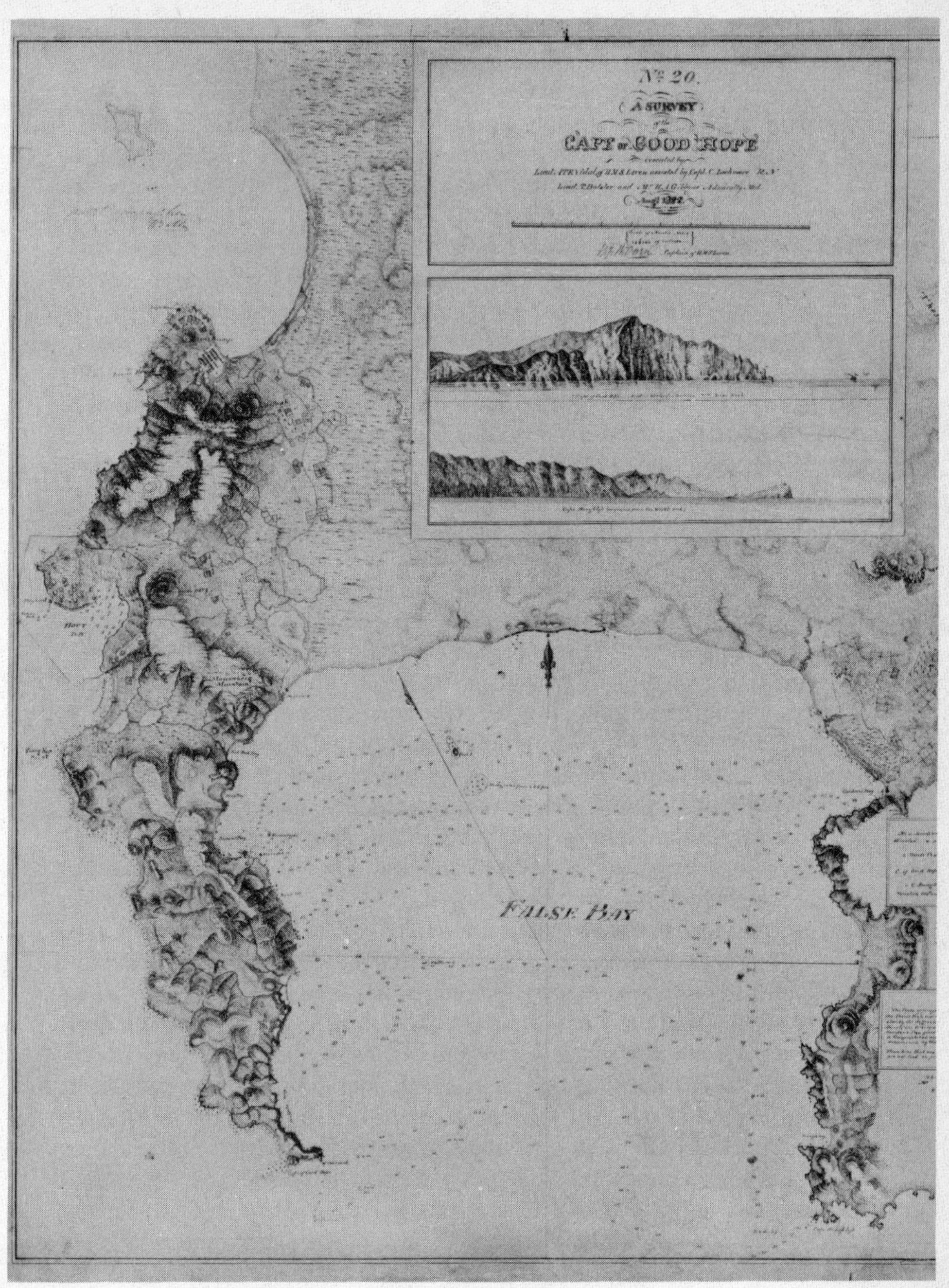

The Cape of Good Hope and False Bay, an 1822 survey by Lieut. A. T. E. Vidal of HMS *Leven*.

principally the open nature of the bay to the north-west. There was some criticism of the way in which ships were anchored, the Port Captain stating that many of the losses were due to ships putting out too short a length of cable, or using inferior materials for their ground tackle. It is interesting to note that he also blamed some of the problems on iron anchor chains, which appeared to part more easily than hemp cables, no doubt because of the brittle nature of the iron of the time.

But it was not the quality of the anchor cable that helped the crew of one of Table Bay's more famous wrecks, it was the discipline of those on board and the chance which allowed the ship to remain upright after she went ashore near the mouth of the Salt River. The *Abercrombie Robinson* was a troop transport of 1,415 tons on her way to Algoa Bay with a replacement regiment. When she arrived in Table Bay on 25th February 1842, she anchored close to a convict ship, the *Waterloo*, well to the south of the normal anchorage. The Port Captain went on board and advised the ship's captain to move to a safer berth, but the captain decided to stay put for the night and move at daybreak. On the 26th a freshening wind delayed the move, and by the 27th the winds were gusting heavily and the barometer was falling. At four o'clock on the morning of the 28th distress guns were heard from the shore and shortly afterwards the ship went aground. The rescue was organised by Captain Bance, the Port Captain, who immediately sent two surfboats to the site by waggon which began the arduous task of taking off the more than 600 crew and passengers, only a few at a time, on account of the dangerous surf. By mid-afternoon the entire complement of the ship had been safely brought ashore, thanks to the quick action of the Port Captain, and the remarkable discipline of those on board who patiently waited their turn whilst the waves buffeted their vessel.

The convicts and their guards aboard the older *Waterloo* were not so fortunate as their ship beached broadside to the waves and began to break up at once. One surfboat was manhandled along the beach from the *Abercrombie Robinson* and put to work, but already many of the souls on board had thrown themselves into the sea in an effort to swim to the shore, and had either been drowned or maimed by the large chunks of floating wreckage that were being thrown around in the surf. Only ninety-eight out of the 288 people on board managed to reach safety. All the other vessels at anchor, numbering nearly twenty, had managed to stay out of the surf because, although some dragged, they had sufficient room for the gale to subside before they reached the beach. The only good to come out of this appalling loss of life was that Captain Bance was able to raise £104 the next day by public subscription to build a proper lifeboat for the port.

Another risk that faced ships' masters when calling at Table Bay, and one which caused several casualties, was involved in finding the entrance safely at night. The fire placed on Robben Island by van Riebeeck helped, but the usefulness of such a guide depended upon the sailors knowing where it was placed in relation to the port, and there being no other fires lit within a number of miles which could cause confusion. Unless a captain was fully confident of his position, and conditions were particularly favourable, most ships would heave-to out at sea at night, and await daylight before trying to enter. The ship losses due to this cause had been small whilst the Dutch were at the Cape, mainly because night arrivals were discouraged, and the *De Visch* grounding on Mouille Point in 1740 is one of the few on record. After 1815 the volume of traffic increased enormously, under flags of many nations, and although the Colonial Government could advise against entering in darkness, it could not apply penalties for those ignoring this advice. From 1819 when the *Feniscowles* was wrecked on Green Point, the number of losses suddenly became a spate, and the Government was forced to consider building a lighthouse to guide shipping around the western edge of the bay. The loss of two more vessels in 1821 convinced the Governor that a lighthouse had to be constructed at Green Point, and a contract was awarded to the Inspector of Government Buildings, Herman Schutte. The original estimates by the Governor of £200 were wildly over-optimistic, as Schutte's quote was for £1,000, but the building went ahead and commenced on 12th April 1824.

Lighthouses as an aid to navigators date back to very early times, and there is mention of a simple beacon as early as 660 BC at Troad in the Mediterranean. The Pharos at Alexandria, perhaps the most famous of all, and one of the seven wonders of the world, was built between 283 and 247 BC and lasted until it was destroyed by an earthquake in the thirteenth century AD. The early lights were simple braziers containing inflammable material often coated in pitch, but there was considerable development during the eighteenth century when reflectors were fitted to increase the intensity of the light. This had the combined effect of making the lights visible over a greater distance, and also making them less easily confused with other lights ashore.

It became clear fairly quickly that Green Point was not the ideal situation for the light as it was too far to the south of Mouille Point. Ships coming into the anchorage assumed that they were clear of the rocks if they ran in slightly to the north of the light itself, with the result that five ships went ashore close to Mouille Point within the next thirteen years. A recommendation was made that another light be erected at Mouille Point in 1837, but this was ruled out for financial reasons because of the Colonial Government's debts. So the wrecks continued, one in 1839, five in 1840, until public indignation forced the Government to act, but not before a further two vessels had been lost. The Mouille Point Lighthouse was opened in July 1843, nearly a mile from Green Point, and on the northernmost point of the western side of the bay where it gave mariners a clear lead into the anchorage. Wrecks caused by vessels not knowing their exact positions did not cease, but they became much less frequent after the new light was opened.

The increase in trade and traffic through Table Bay continued steadily throughout the nineteenth century, but the provision of proper wharf facilities and a longer breakwater continued to be postponed by changes in the Government in Britain, and the lack of availability of sufficient funds in the Cape. A Commission was formed in 1844 to examine the feasibility of building both. It reported that a harbour with a 1,800-foot-long breakwater extending from the Chavonne Battery, enclosing alongside berths for twenty-six ships with further space for sixty vessels to shelter in bad weather could be built for £700,000. This was far too great a sum for the colony, but the British Colonial Secretary, William Gladstone, offered a Government loan of £300,000 for the project, provided the colony paid the interest on the sum. Unfortunately by the time the Governor's representative reached England the Government had changed and Gladstone had been replaced by Lord Grey, who felt that the colony should fund the harbour. With the arrival of Sir Harry Smith as Governor in 1847, plans for a breakwater were again taken down from the shelf and dusted off. This time it was proposed that in order to keep the costs to a reasonable level, convicts should be used for labour, and a request was sent to London. Unfortunately a misunderstanding arose as to the eventual fate of the convicts. The colony wanted them to be housed on prison hulks in the bay until the work was finished and then either sent home or on to Australia, whilst the British Government expected them to be released into the country as free men at the end of their sentences. Since many of these convicts were Irishmen sentenced for rioting and considered to be no better than traitors, the people of the colony were unwilling to accept them as future citizens. When the first convict ship, the *Neptune*, arrived at Simon's Bay in September 1849, the inhabitants refused to allow any food or stores to be supplied to the ship. For five months the ship languished at anchor until Lord Grey gave way and it was ordered on to Australia.

Losses of ships from storms and the waste of time whilst ships awaited suitable weather to load or discharge their cargoes continued to affect shipping. As the reliability of steamers and the regularity of their services improved, particularly after the introduction of a proper mail service by the Union Line in 1857, the delays and risks of leaving ships out in the bay to work their cargo, particularly during the winter months, became a source of grievance to the people of Cape Town, and of frustration to the shipowners. A ship might make a fast passage out to the Cape, which was expensive in coal, and then find she was forced to lie idly for days until weather conditions permitted the safe transfer of her passengers and cargo.

The arrival of the mail ship was a major event in the calendar. A lookout was kept from the station on Lions Head, and anxious eyes in the town watched for the signal that the mail steamer was in sight. When the ship came into the bay it fired a salute with its two cannons, which was answered from the castle, and then the Port Captain would go out in his launch to meet the new arrival and give her port clearance. This was an important procedure in the days before the wireless, when the only way of knowing whether the ship was free of disease picked up during her voyage was by the display of flag signals from her masts. If there were infectious diseases on board, the ship would be left at anchor, and isolated from all other shipping and the shore until the safe period had elapsed after the last outbreak. Assuming that the ship was healthy, the mails were the first items to go ashore, together with a special 'English Supplement' which had been printed just before sailing from England to bring the latest information to the news-hungry Capetonians. Delays in the delivery of the mails were not popular, and there was a strong local feeling that it was time that something was done to make Cape Town into a safe port.

Throughout the 1850s new plans were produced and discussed, but the high cost continued to be the prime reason why nothing happened. In 1855 James Rendel produced a plan for a north breakwater of 4,300 feet and a southern one of 4,600 feet for a cost of £485,000, but the Admiralty, who were asked for an opinion, replied by producing a plan by Captain James Vetch that would have enclosed double the area at a cost of a million pounds. Such a project could only be considered if the Colonial Government saddled itself with an enormous long-term debt which it hesitated to do, but in the meantime losses continued to mount and eventually the Government decided that it had to act. John Coode, who was building Portland Harbour to Rendel's design in England, was appointed Engineer-in-Chief, and produced a scheme to build a basin close by the Chavonne Battery which would provide 4,300 feet of quay space, complete with a dry dock and breakwater for a cost of £400,000. The first truck of rubble for the breakwater was tipped into the sea on 17th September 1860 by Prince Alfred, the second son of Queen Victoria. To contain costs, local convicts were used for labour, but even so the work cost more than budgeted and took ten years to complete.

Even as the basin was being constructed the north-wester continued to exact its toll, and 1865 saw the largest total of shipping lost to this scourge of Table Bay. The storm rose on 16th May, and during the night a number of sailing ships piled onto the beach. The next day, as spectators looked on powerlessly from the shore, others broke free of their moorings and were driven remorselessly onto the rocks. As evening approached, the Union mailship *Athens*, which had been due to sail to Mauritius the next day, was seen to lose her anchor and started to put out to sea, her captain having taken the precaution of raising steam the moment the storm started. The ship struggled against the steep mountainous waves as she slowly made her way out of the Bay, but once round Mouille Point even larger seas swept right over her and water poured down the engine room skylight and extinguished the fires in the boilers. Without power the *Athens* was doomed, and she was slowly swept onto the rocks between Mouille and Green Points. The people onshore could hear the cries of the twenty-nine people on board, but it was impossible to provide help and by daybreak on the 18th the only remains of the ship were her engine and boilers, the sea had totally destroyed the rest of the ship and her crew. A part of the engine is still visible on the rocks to this day, and is a sad memento of the fifteen ships that were lost in the worst shipping disaster ever to strike Table Bay.

The storm was so severe that the waves shifted 60,000 tons of stone on the breakwater, but although it was only partially completed, it had given complete protection to the existing jetties, and when the next storm swept the bay in 1867 work was sufficiently advanced so that no damage was caused. Eventually the Alfred Basin, containing 4½ hectares of water and protected by a 1,790-foot-long breakwater, was opened on 4th July 1870, the Union Liner *Saxon* being the first vessel to moor alongside the new quays. Cape Town could at last offer proper alongside berthing for ships, enabling cargoes to be loaded and discharged directly onto land instead of having to be double handled and transhipped by lighters, resulting in a saving in costs and less harm to goods. To pay for the works, an additional charge was levied on all goods handled in the port.

The new Alfred Basin and its breakwater at last gave shelter from the north-westerlies, but it had been built primarily to provide a harbour for shipping with cargo for the Cape and not for shipping that was calling at the Cape. Many of these only visited to collect coal bunkers, water and stores, and they still had to await out in the anchorage whilst lighters brought their requirements to them. The 1860s were a period of expansion in the size of ships which had hitherto been limited by the physical inability of shipwrights to build a ship of more than about 3,000 tons from wood. Iron was becoming the universally accepted material for ships, and with this material came new shipbuilding techniques which allowed much larger vessels to be constructed. Already in 1843 the iron-built *Great Britain* had measured 3,448 tons and was a foretaste of things to come. Her visit to Cape Town in 1852 on her way to Australia was a great event.

It was ten years after the *Great Britain* was launched before a ship of similar size, the *Himalaya*, was built. Within a year the largest ship the world had ever seen, and the greatest to be built until 1899, the *Great Eastern* of 18,914 tons designed by Isambard K. Brunel, was under construction in London. She was intended to transport 3,000 passengers between England and India at a time, but her owners went into liquidation and so she was put on the Atlantic run for which she proved unsuitable. Subsequently she was converted into a cable-layer and in this guise laid the first trans-Atlantic cable. In 1869 she called into Cape Town on her way to lay a cable between Bombay and Aden and spent a week at anchor in Table Bay, providing a great cause of excitement. People came from all over the colony to inspect the remarkable ship which was opened to visitors. When she sailed on 30th December 1869, every vantage point was taken by the immense crowds of sightseers. It is interesting to note that the *Great Eastern* reached Bombay on 27th January 1870, and had laid the cable and returned for a short stop at Cape Town by 30th April 1870. She had an unlucky career, and was eventually broken up in 1887, but she did prove that extremely large ships could be built using iron, and gave encouragement to other builders and owners to increase the size of their ships.

The Alfred Basin served its purpose well, and although it was too small to harbour vessels like the *Great Eastern*, it was of sufficient size to take the 3,000-ton ships that became common on the mail run in the 1870s. Another severe storm in July 1878, during which five ships anchored outside the breakwater were driven ashore, led to a scheme to extend the breakwater to provide more sheltered room for ships to anchor, but by 1880 shipping and trade had increased to such an extent that a further expansion of the entire port facility had to be planned. Sir John Coode was asked to produce plans for an extension in 1880, but the slump in trade after the First Boer War caused a postponement until 1886 when the first rubble was tipped to build what came to be called the South Arm. The dock extension, christened the Victoria Basin, was built out from the entrance to the Alfred Basin. Although the basic quays had been completed by 1895, the new basin was not finally opened until 1905 when it added a further twenty-seven hectares of enclosed water and provided an additional wharf length of 5,000 feet. The work would have taken even longer than nineteen years to finish had not the discovery of the Transvaal goldfields created such a demand for goods from abroad that berth space in all South African ports was put at a premium, and progress was accelerated in 1890.

The facilities of the port were found again to be totally inadequate with the outbreak of the Second Boer War in 1899, when the British Empire rallied men, horses, guns and supplies from the four corners of the Earth. Liners from the crack Atlantic run, such as the White Star Line's *Majestic* and *Brittanic*, were requisitioned as troop carriers and the bay was soon so crowded that some of the less important vessels found themselves waiting at anchor for up to six months before there was berth space or lighters available to discharge their cargoes.

There is an interesting account of sailing into Cape Town harbour at this time, given by Commander Woollard, who was an apprentice aboard the three-masted barque *Penrhyn Castle*.

We had taken 65 days to reach Capetown, having sighted land only once, and the distance we had covered was 8,516 miles. Had we made the journey by steamer, in a direct line, the distance would have been shortened by some 3,000 miles. An astounding feature about this passage was that we had never had an occasion to tack, all the winds having, except in the south-east trades, been in our favour. Table Bay was full of sailing ships awaiting their turn to unload, and I imagine there must have been well over fifty.

The congestion in the harbour was also acute, and although we had an important cargo destined for use in the prosecution of the Boer War, we had to wait several weeks before we could go alongside.

Anchored near us were the *Philomene*, *Sardomene*, *Buckingham*, *Glenpark*, *Eivion*, *Englehorn*, *Windlatter*, *Erin's Isle*, *Raglan Castle* and many other fine sailing vessels, which, during their enforced wait in the bay, had taken the opportunity of painting their sides, so that they looked very smart.

Whilst waiting our turn to go alongside, we did a good deal of sailing in the ship's boats and visited many of the other vessels, and when we landed in Capetown it was either to visit the Missions to Seamen Institute for a concert or a service, or to take part in a picnic organised by the Missions to the top of Table Mountain, which in those days had to be undertaken on foot, being a long days outing.

Troopships were frequently arriving and the soldiers in khaki (then a newly coined uniform) were to be constantly met with when we went ashore, and there was much activity about, especially in the docks and railway station, particularly in the latter, where troops were constantly entraining for the seat of military activities against the Boers.

At last we went alongside and unloaded, ballast being taken in gradually as the last of the cargo was being discharged, in order to keep the ship upright. The ballast consisted of 900 tons of rock and earth which had been excavated from the new dock then in course of construction.

Very shortly afterwards, the unloading having been completed, we were towed out into the bay to await orders from home as to our next destination, and these came several weeks later, which were that we should make for Caleta Buena in ballast and there take in a full cargo of nitrate of soda, commonly known as saltpetre, a mineral found on the slopes of the Andes and brought down to the coast by rail.

Many of the less urgent stores for the war were carried in sailing ships and 1900 was the last year when sailing ships outnumbered steamers in Table Bay. Only the mail ships were allowed any priority over the needs of the army, and this led to arguments later between the members of the shipping Conference who felt that the newly amalgamated Union–Castle Line had been thus given an unfair advantage in the South African trade. Almost inevitably the north-westerlies claimed a victim with so many ships anchored in the roadstead, and the Houston Liner *Hermes* was driven ashore on Blouberg beach in a gale on 12th May 1901. She had just arrived from Argentina with forage, but, seeing the large number of ships in the anchorage, had banked the fires in her boilers so that when the wind arrived she was unable to raise steam quickly enough to save herself. The only other loss in the area was the Union–Castle Liner *Tantallon Castle*, five days before the *Hermes*, which ran onto the rocks on the north-west side of Robben Island in fog. All the passengers were disembarked safely, and, since the ship had been going at slow speed at the time, it was hoped to tow her off. However, despite the efforts of tugs and the *Braemar Castle*, *Raglan Castle* and *Avondale Castle*, which all came out from Cape Town to assist, the ship would not move, and the gales which drove the *Hermes* ashore smashed her to pieces.

The mail ships had continued to grow as the nineteenth century came to a close, reaching 12,000 tons by 1900. There was only a very small increase up to the beginning of the First World War, the largest mail ship at the time being the *Balmoral Castle* of 13,361 tons, built in 1910. However, the post-war shipbuilding programme incorporated ships of 20,000 tons, and Cape Town harbour had only one quay capable of taking ships that big, so a further expansion was put in hand, with work starting in 1926 on a new basin to the south-east of the south arm of the Victoria Basin. The new scheme, completed in 1932, enclosed a further seventy-nine hectares of water, and provided three new berths on the south arm, but when in 1934 the 43,500-ton *Empress of Britain* docked, it was found that even Cape Town's three most powerful tugs could not pull her off the quay in a strong south-easter. The berths for such large ships needed to be placed in line with the wind, and this required a different layout. Accordingly, a new plan was announced in 1937, which involved the removal of the southern breakwater for a dock containing 118 hectares of water, with quay space of 6,000 feet and a minimum depth alongside of forty feet. As part of this scheme an area of foreshore between the castle and the new docks, totalling 195 hectares, was reclaimed, most being used for an extension to the city, but a part supplying a wide quay and railway marshalling yards. A small boat basin was built at the eastern end of the dock, which is now occupied by the Royal Cape Yacht Club and the Defence Forces, and a huge new dry dock, the Sturrock Dry Dock, capable of taking very large ships, was commenced. The new Duncan Dock, named after the Governor-General Sir Patrick Duncan, and the Sturrock Dry Dock were officially opened in 1945, but much of the dock was available for use in the hectic war years when Cape Town became a major convoy collection-point for shipping whilst the Mediterranean was closed.

During the war years Cape Town was crowded with shipping once more, and played a vital part in forming and supplying convoys. The world's two largest ships, the *Queen Mary* and the *Queen Elizabeth*, both called, but they had to anchor outside the port as even the Duncan Dock did not have sufficient depth of water to take them at low tide.

The shipping boom during the post-war years, and the expectation that the expansion would continue, led to a committee being formed in 1957 to examine proposals for expanding the docks even further. Whilst the committee was sitting, the port was enlarged by the building of specialised tanker berths, capable of taking loaded tankers of up to 65,000 tons, but the committee foresaw the need for yet further expansion. The new dock, called the Ben Schoeman Dock, is as large as the Duncan Dock, and was originally designed to provide twenty-two more dry cargo berths. The advent of containerisation and Roll-On/Roll-Off ships meant that these plans were changed whilst construction was taking place to provide berths for the new types of vessels coming into service.

Whilst the Ben Schoeman Dock has given the port facilities as modern as anywhere in the world, containerisation has reduced the number of ships required to carry the same amount of cargo, and it is now very rare to see all the berths in the docks occupied as was common in the 1950s and 1960s. The bustle that used to be a feature of the docks where ships were crowded close to warehouses and much of the cargo handling was done by hand has been replaced by acres of parking for large metal containers, and the sole activity seems to come from the enormous gantries that move around the park shifting the containers to and from the ships. Only in the Albert and Victoria Basins is the atmosphere anything like the old days, and this is due to the large number of fishing vessels that make Cape Town their home.

Despite sanctions, and the changes in world shipping, Table Bay still lies at the junction of a number of the great shipping routes. Tankers passing round the Cape call in for stores, and on any single day the flags of many maritime nations can be seen hanging from the sterns of ships berthed in the port. Although the British flag is now quite a rarity, the flags of Japan, Panama, Russia, Poland, India and of course of the growing South African Merchant Marine are quite common, and Cape Town still justifies its title as the 'Tavern of the Seas'.

8

The Cape Coast – Green Point to Cape Hangklip

South of Table Bay the coast is steep-to, and initially backed by the range of mountains known as the Twelve Apostles, varying between 730 and 915 metres (2,400 and 3,000 feet) in height. The mountains, although less dramatic, continue beyond Hout Bay, the only indentation in the twenty-eight miles between Green Point and Cape Point. After the mountains the land descends before rising once more to the two peaks at Cape Point. The only river of note is the Krom which flows into a small lagoon near Olifantsbos Point, but it is not navigable. The coast is rocky and dangerous, and frequently shrouded in fog, and ships are advised to keep well offshore in at least twenty fathoms of water. This area has taken more than twenty ships over the years, and is still claiming victims today.

One of the earliest wrecks recorded is of the *Huys te Craijestein*, a Dutch East India ship that went ashore in thick fog on 27th May 1698. The ship was bound for Batavia from Holland when she sighted land south of Lions Head, and, because of the fog, the captain anchored in eighty fathoms of water. During the night the anchor cable chafed, a fact not noticed by those in charge on deck, although a seaman can usually tell quite quickly from the vibration on the cable whether it is holding or not, and the ship began to drift. The captain called away the largest of the ship's boats in order to tow his ship away from the breakers which could now be heard quite clearly, but it was mobbed by frightened seamen, who rowed away leaving the ship with no means of propulsion. Shortly afterwards, as the rest of the crew were trying to clear away another anchor, the ship went aground at Oudekraal. In the calm conditions, the ship did not break up, and the crew managed to land taking sixteen of the nineteen money chests on board with them. Not a life had been lost, because the crewmen who had deserted made their way to a French ship at anchor off Robben Island, and were landed safely at Cape Town the next day, where we can be sure they received a pretty rough reception from the Governor, Simon van der Stel. An intensive search was conducted for the missing money chests, and the investigation discovered the remains of one of them, together with some of the pieces-of-eight which it had contained. But of the other two chests, not

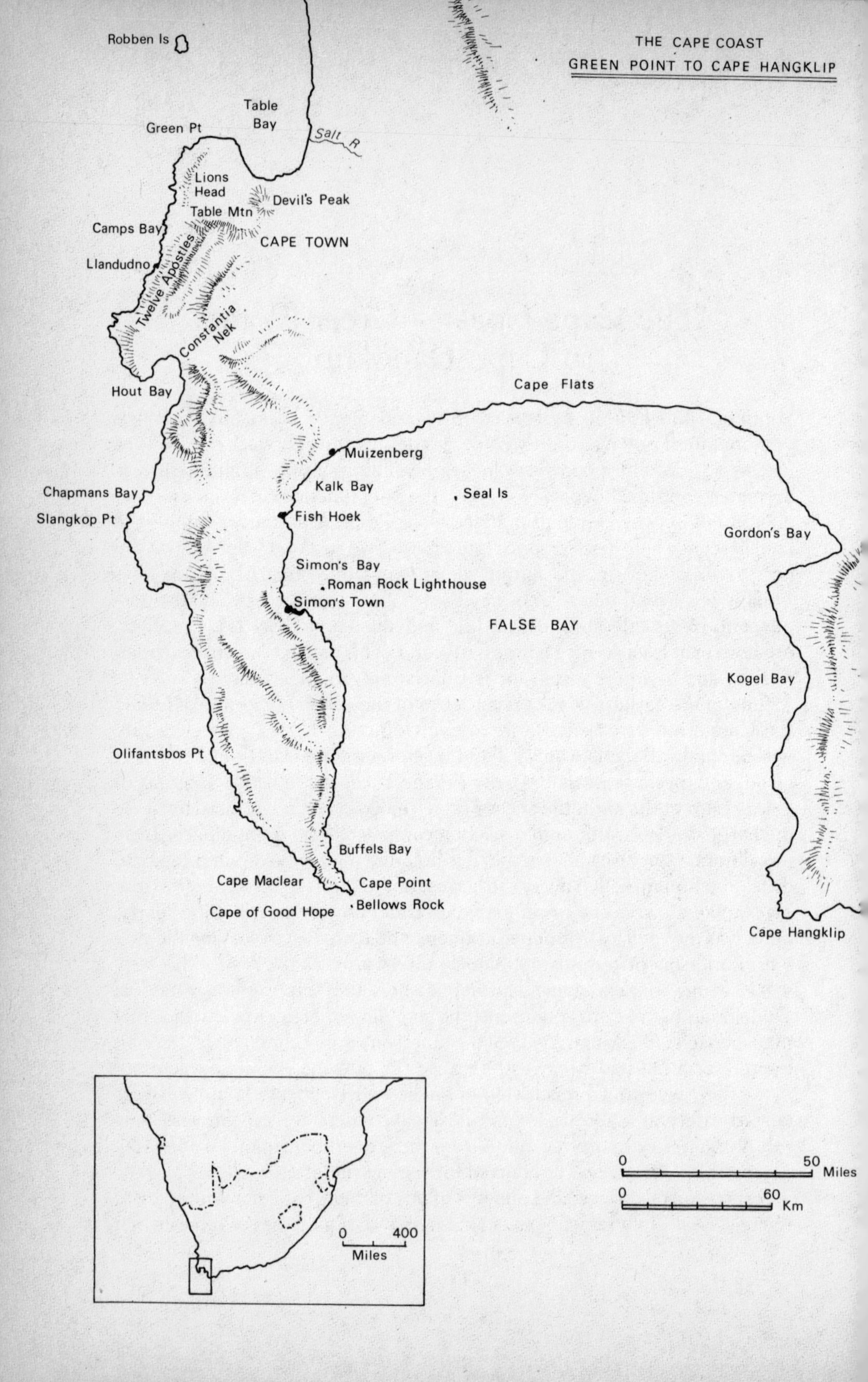
THE CAPE COAST
GREEN POINT TO CAPE HANGKLIP
Robben Is
Table Bay
Salt R
Green Pt
Lions Head
Devil's Peak
Table Mtn
Camps Bay
CAPE TOWN
Llandudno
Twelve Apostles
Constantia Nek
Hout Bay
Cape Flats
Muizenberg
Kalk Bay
Seal Is
Chapmans Bay
Slangkop Pt
Fish Hoek
Gordon's Bay
Simon's Bay
Roman Rock Lighthouse
Simon's Town
FALSE BAY
Kogel Bay
Olifantsbos Pt
Buffels Bay
Cape Maclear
Cape Point
Cape of Good Hope
Bellows Rock
Cape Hangklip
0
400
Miles
0
50
Miles
0
60
Km

a sign has ever been found. If the crew stole them, then they were very careful as to how they hid and spent their treasure. Assuming, as was suspected at the time, the chests slipped over the stern as the ship settled, then the hoard is still lying on the bottom near Camps Bay, where other items such as bottles and cannons have been located.

About five miles south of Camps Bay lies the small village of Llandudno where, in the early hours of the morning of 29th July 1977, the tanker *Romelia* came ashore on Sunset Rocks. The *Romelia* of 32,913 tons, and another tanker, the *Antipolis* of 42,050 tons, were under tow from Greece to a scrapyard in the Far East, when the weather deteriorated. The Japanese tug tried to anchor in the lee of Robben Island, but the towing cables snagged and broke and both tankers were set adrift. The *Antipolis* went aground at Oudekraal, and the *Romelia* followed further to the south soon afterwards. For a while there was concern that some of the oil left in the ships would cause pollution, but this was pumped aboard small tankers before it could leak into the sea. Ten years later, the double bottom section of the *Antipolis* was still visible, whilst the whole stern section of the *Romelia* acted as a tourist attraction to the south of Llandudno beach.

Hout Bay provides the only port along the western side of the Cape Peninsula, and although it is open to the south-west, modern breakwaters have been built to create a well-sheltered fishing port in the north-west side of the bay. The area was named by the Dutch for the timber they found growing there, but the bay was never developed into a port by them, owing to the lack of a good road access. Its entrance is exposed to the south-westerlies, and the south-easterlies, which blow with great force down the mountains into the bay itself, and provide very strong but variably directional williwaws, which make anchoring extremely dangerous. About three miles south of Hout Bay lies Chapmans Bay, another unfavourable anchorage, where the new steamer *Kakapo* went aground in a gale on 25th May 1900, and the remnants of her boilers are still visible.

The southern end of Chapmans Bay is marked by Slangkop Point, which is distinguished by a tall lighthouse where the *Clan Monroe* went ashore on 2nd July 1905 whilst trying to make the Cape. Some of the crew tried to reach the shore with a ship's boat, but it was overturned by the large seas. Miraculously all survived, and although attempts to save the rest of the crew using a breeches-buoy succeeded in bringing only two more ashore, the rest reached safety the following day when the seas subsided. Nine miles further south lies Olifantsbos, the scene of the wreck of the French frigate *Napoléon* driven ashore by the British frigate *Narcissus* on Christmas day 1804. The surviving members of the French crew were pressed into defending the Cape against the British invasion the following year. Two miles further south the Union Line's *Kafir* was wrecked on 13th February 1878. Some of those on board managed to get ashore at once, but then the seas rose and the rest were stranded on board whilst the ship broke in two. Ultimately all but four crewmen were rescued, including a native bearer who had accompanied H. M. Stanley on his travels through Africa.

In this area, too, the French brig *La Rozette* came to grief in 1786, in circumstances that at once aroused the suspicions of the local French agent. The wreck of a ship was first reported to Christoffel Brand, the Dutch Company's Resident in Simon's Town, who rode over to investigate, but finding no one on board, left a guard and informed the Governor in Cape Town. Eventually the French agent, a M. Percheron, was told and rode down the coast to check for himself. He managed to get on board where he found some documents that gave him the name of the ship, and the fact that she had sailed from Bordeaux in May 1786 bound for Mauritius with a crew of twelve. More importantly he also came across the records of a *Procès verbal* which indicated that action had been taken against one of the crew. The agent returned to Cape Town and, after making enquiries, discovered that three men, two French and one American, had just signed on board a Dutch East Indiaman which was waiting to sail. A warrant for their arrest was issued, and amongst their belongings were found gold watches and coins, the former the unlikely property of a seaman. Furthermore, one of the men had the name Stefano Tailjasco, the same as the man mentioned in the *Procès verbal.* An interrogation followed, which in those days of the Dutch East India Company's control at the Cape meant questioning under torture, and Tailjasco soon broke. It appeared that Tailjasco and his brother had led a mutiny during which all the officers were killed. Then they tried to sink the ship to destroy the evidence, but, unfortunately, the ship floated long enough to go ashore instead. At the subsequent trial all six survivors were found guilty, four were sentenced to be broken at the wheel and then hanged, the fifth just hanged, and the American to be whipped and deported. The authorities at that time took a very dim view of mutiny.

A more recent wreck at Olifantsbos whose remains can still be seen, was of the *Thomas T. Tucker*, a liberty ship that went ashore on the rocks of Olifantsbos on 27th November 1942. The ship, which had been completed two months before, was on her way to Suez via the Cape with war supplies, when she reported being aground in thick fog, on Robben Island. How the master managed to be some twenty-three miles from his estimated position has never been explained, but the enquiry discovered that his compass had an error of 37°. The cargo and crew were saved, but bad weather drove the ship higher onto the rocks before a tug could try to haul her off.

All along the western peninsular coast there are large beds of kelp, a thick, brown, ropy seaweed, that can often exceed fifty feet in length. The weed, whose strands are often thicker than a man's arm, is quite strong enough to snag the propeller of a small boat. Kelp fastens itself to rocks on the sea bottom, but often long strands break off and are found floating miles out to sea. The early visitors to the Cape coast used the sightings of kelp as an indication that they were approaching land.

The southern point of the Cape Peninsula terminates in two peaks, Cape Maclear to the west and Cape Point to the east. These two capes are divided by a small sandy beach, of which the *Admiralty Sailing Instructions* states: 'There is a small sandy bay, called Buffel's Bay, between Cape point and Cape Maclear in which vessels in a sinking condition may be beached in greater safety than on any other part of the adjacent coast westward of Cape point.' Pacheco Pereira tells us of the Cape:

> It is with good reason that this promontory was called Cabo de Boa Esperança, for Bartolomeu Dias, who discovered it at the command of King João in the year 1488, when he saw that the coast here turned northwards and north-eastwards towards Ethiopia under Egypt and on to the Gulf of Arabia, giving great hope of the discovery of India, called it the 'Cape of Good Hope'. Its latitude is 34 and a half degrees south [nine miles further south than the actual position]. The land is very high indeed and shaped as in our picture [unfortunately this picture, and a large part of Pereira's *roteiro* are missing]. During the winter, from the month of April till the end of the month of September, it is very cold and stormy . . . Some say that this Cape is the promontory called Plaso of which Ptolemy spoke, but I do not think so. I rather think that it must be the Montes Lunae in which Ptolemy says the Nile rises, for in the very position that Ptolemy gave to these mountains, in 34½ degrees south of the equator, there the promontory of Boa Esperança is found. At this promontory Africa comes to an end in the Ocean, and is divided from Asia.

Although the Cape lies in latitude 34° 21′ south, Cape Point is not the southernmost point of Africa. That distinction belongs to Cape Agulhas, which is also the dividing point between the Indian and Atlantic Oceans. Nevertheless it has always been looked upon as the major navigational feature of the entire coast since Bartolomeu Dias first christened it Cabo Tormentoso and subsequently changed its name to Cabo de Boa Esperança. It was described as the 'fairest Cape' in Drake's account, and is 'a beautiful promontory' according to Pereira. For sailors, it is the rounding of the Cape of Good Hope, not Cape Agulhas that really counts. It used to be said that a seaman could put one foot on the table when he had rounded Cape Horn, and both when he had rounded the Cape of Good Hope as well. The southernmost part of the Cape is a short spine of rock that points southwards across the vast ocean wastes of the Southern Ocean, and no land lies between it and Antarctica. The original lighthouse on the point was constructed in 1860, but it was placed too high, and its light was frequently hidden by the fog that obscured the upper parts of the point even when the sea was clear below. A new lighthouse was built lower down, but only after a serious loss had emphasised the dangers from having the light in the higher position.

About two miles to the south of Cape Point lies Bellows Rock, a sharp pinnacle that rises some five feet above the sea at low water. The sea always breaks over this rock so that it shows clearly in daylight in good visibility. At night, however, the only navigation mark to guide the seafarer is the Cape Point lighthouse. During the evening of 18th April 1911, the Portuguese liner *Lusitania* was bound from Lourenço Marques to Cape Town with 800 people aboard including 100 crew. She had sighted the Cape Point light, but then it became obscured by the fog until just before midnight when it cleared to allow the captain to realise that he was much closer to the point than he had estimated. He put the helm hard over to port to head out to sea, but a few minutes later the ship came to an abrupt halt and with such force that the fore mast went over the side. The ship had run onto Bellows Rock, but although the bow was crumpled, there was no immediate danger of sinking. A minor panic ensued, but 475 indentured labourers, who were amongst the passengers and on their way to work in the cocoa fields of São Tomé, on being reassured that there was no danger, wrapped themselves in their blankets and awaited events. The ship's boats were launched, and everyone except about thirty of the crew and the Africans departed, two of the boats landing in Buffels Bay where one was overturned and three people were drowned.

In the meantime the alarm had been raised. An Admiralty tug, the *Scotsman*, was the first vessel on the scene accompanied by a naval cutter, and these were joined by HMS *Forte* once she had raised steam in Simon's Town. The *Scotsman* arrived at 3 a.m. but a thick mist concealed the *Lusitania* although she was still burning all her lights. An hour later it cleared sufficiently to allow the tug to get alongside the stricken ship and take off the remaining passengers and crew. The *Lusitania* slipped off the rock and sank the next morning. Her loss, however tragic, brought a major benefit to mariners: the new lighthouse, built lower down at a height of 286 feet, was opened in April 1914.

The eastern edge of the Cape Peninsula runs almost due north and borders False Bay which is roughly square in shape. Each side is nearly seventeen miles, and it encloses an area of 319 square nautical miles. The coast on the east and west sides of the bay is rocky and steep-to, but at the northern edge are the low-lying Cape sand flats that extend to Table Bay, only some twelve miles distant. The bay offers good shelter to shipping from all but southerly winds, and has a number of small ports and bays dotted around its perimeter, the most important being Simon's Town, the main base for the South African Navy. It is open to the south between

Cape Point and Cape Hangklip which lies sixteen and a half miles to the east.

The first mention of False Bay is in Vasco da Gama's report, which states that 'Alongside this Cape of Good Hope there lies to the south a very large bay.' Bartolomeu Dias certainly missed it on his outward voyage, and the log from his homeward voyage has not survived although he must have seen such an important landmark. Saldanha gained an overall view of False Bay when he climbed Table Mountain in 1503 to try and establish his position. He noted that he 'saw the end of the Cape and the sea beyond it on the eastern side, where it formed a deep bay, into which, between two ridges of high rocks, now called the Picos Fragosos, a large river [Lourens] emptied itself, which from the volume of its waters seemed to have followed on its course from a long distance'. Unless the topography has changed, had Saldanha explored the bay he would have discovered that no large river exists, but he headed straight for the East after leaving Table Bay.

If any of the early ships did sail into the bay, they neglected to report the fact, but navigation at the time was still a hit-or-miss affair when close to land, and one extra bay sighted on a long voyage was probably not deemed worthy of attention, especially as it was so close to Table Bay which the Portuguese usually avoided after 1510. Perestrelo refers to it briefly in his *roteiro* of 1756, but his account is based upon hearsay as a storm prevented him from exploring it.

> The mouth is five leagues across. From the western side two large rocks are seen which appear to be islets. Within I observed some openings, apparently the course of a river that the chartmakers depict as very large and flowing from some open lakes at the source of the Nile and as watering a great part of the interior country. But this I doubt as no one has either seen it or given an early description of it. This open bay is entirely enclosed by a high and steep rocky shore, and terminates in a point of the same kind [Cape Hangklip].

This is a reasonably precise description, so either Perestrelo was able to take a good long look at the bay, or the Portuguese information which he quoted was quite correct.

An Englishman, John Davis, gives an account in his pilotage notes written in 1615:

> Cape Falso hath a latitude thirtie foure degrees thirtie minutes and is distant from the Cape of Good Hope nine leagues [about seventeen miles short], East South-East. Betweene these two Capes there is a deepe Bay, and before it there is a rocke even with the water [Bellows];

> but it lyeth neere the Cape of Good Hope. In this Bay is the great river called Rio Dolce [Lourens] that runneth farre up into the land. There is good refreshing, as the Hollanders report, for they have beene there with their ships.

The significance of this is that Davis, who was usually accurate, is convinced that the Dutch had used False Bay before 1615, and yet, as far as is known, there is no record of them sailing into the bay until after van Riebeeck had started the settlement at Cape Town.

It was inevitable that once the Dutch founded a settlement at Table Bay, they would commence some exploration of the land nearby. However, van Riebeeck had his hands full for the first few months ashore, building the fort and planting his vegetable garden. On 7th May 1654 two Hottentots arrived at the fort and announced that they had sighted two ships in False Bay, and van Riebeeck, assuming them to be foreign, sent a small party of soldiers to investigate. Two days later the party returned and reported seeing nothing. A year later another small group was sent out under a Corporal Muller. This time the purpose was exploration, and they marched across the Cape Flats and climbed the Hottentots Holland Mountains to the east. False Bay does not feature largely in the record of the expedition, which was concentrated upon the whereabouts of the Hottentots, and the availability of grazing. If it seems strange to us today that these early settlers took such little interest in the land around them, it has to be remembered that every man was required to help create the settlement and to be prepared to defend it if necessary. An edict existed at this time which forbade any of the settlers from straying more than three hours' walk from the fort.

As the settlement became more firmly established, men did start to wander further afield, and False Bay features in the early plan of Commissioner Rijkoff van Goens to protect the Company's cattle from theft by the Hottentots by building a canal across the Cape Flats. Van Riebeeck led a surveying party in February 1656, to examine the possibilities, but came to the conclusion that it was not a feasible proposition. Van Goens was not convinced, and on his next visit in March 1657, he demanded to see the area for himself. A plan was made to travel to Hout Bay on foot and there to join a small sloop which would take them on to reconnoitre False Bay. Unfortunately the sloop went to the wrong rendezvous, and the party, having explored Constantia Nek, returned to Cape Town. Two years later, during the Hottentot War of 1659, a party of Dutch soldiers pursued the Hottentots into the Cape Mountains, and fought a minor skirmish near Fish Hoek, but although they must have marched along the side of False Bay, they had other things on their minds at the time.

The Dutch East Indiaman *Orangien* is the first recorded ship to anchor in

False Bay, but apart from knowing that it was in the southern part, the exact anchorage is unknown. In September 1662, when on her way out to the East, she was driven past Cape Point by a storm, but managed to sail into the bay and anchor. She had eight of her crew dead, and 150 ill from scurvy, and sent a party across to Cape Town to seek assistance. On their way they met an official and some soldiers who were coming to investigate the rumour of a ship at anchor. Help was given to the *Orangien* to enable her to sail round to Table Bay, where she landed her sick, and replaced them with men landed from other ships who had convalesced after their illnesses. Nine years were to pass before the next ship called, but this time the *Ysselsteijn* which was also heading Eastwards reported so favourably concerning the anchorage and shelter he had found, that instructions were sent to the Cape for the Governor to take possession of the *Ysselsteijn*'s harbour and make a survey of the whole bay. The Dutch had become anxious in case one of their rivals might decide to establish their own provision station very close to Table Bay.

A Lieutenant Breitenbach was dispatched to make a proper survey of Hottentots Holland and False Bay in December 1671. His report on the former led to its subsequent colonisation. On the subject of the *Ysselsteijn*'s bay he said:

> In the summer the wind blows wide mouthed into this bay. On the south side of the aforementioned Ysselsteijn's Bay, is a mountain division between this and another but much roomier bay, and though ships may lie there protected from the winds during the times aforementioned, it nevertheless appears safer for them to choose this bay to avoid the peril of a certain blind rock lying right in the middle of the bay.

This is somewhat confusing, but it would appear that the southern of the two bays is Simon's Bay, as the blind rock could well be Noah's Ark, and the mountain division Elsie's Peak, in which case the *Ysselsteijn*'s bay was almost certainly Fish Hoek.

A year later, when the Dutch were at war with Britain and France, a Sergeant and twelve soldiers were sent to establish a post near the bay in Hottentots Holland, on the banks of the Lourens River. In January 1673 the *Goudvinck*, a hooker, was sent round to be in constant readiness to sail and warn the homecoming Dutch fleet if the Cape settlement was attacked. A hooker was rather similar to a ketch, but square-rigged on her main mast, so that she resembled a brigantine with a small mizzen. It was a type which was very popular with the Dutch at the time as a fishing vessel, but quite capable of longer journeys, and the Dutch East India Company used them for carrying small and less important cargoes. The captain was instructed to set up a signal post, and then, instead of idly waiting at anchor, he was to undertake a detailed examination of False Bay. His labours were interrupted after a month when his crew came across the survivors of another hooker, *De Grundel*, which had gone on the rocks towards Cape Hangklip, whilst returning from Batavia. Another vessel, the *Bruydegom*, was sent to recover any goods that might have been washed ashore from the wreck. Their shore party walked down the coast from Vissers Bay (Gordon's Bay) towards Cape Hangklip, discovering the camp site of the survivors, some wreckage but no signs of any cargo. They did come across evidence that the Freeburghers had been at work burning lime, so it seems that although there were no official outposts on the south-eastern side of the bay, some of the more adventurous spirits within the colony were already filtering into the hinterland.

When the threat of attack was removed, the *Goudvinck* was withdrawn, but the Cape settlement was beginning to expand across the Cape Flats, and when Governor Bax arrived from Batavia to take over as Commander of the settlement in 1676, he landed at Hottentots Holland to avoid a hard beat round Cape Point. Although he ordered the withdrawal of the small garrison there in 1678, owing to the loss of 100 sheep to lions and wolves, he managed to persuade two burghers to live in the area. By this time a cattle station had also been established in the vicinity of Muizenberg, and fishing boats from Table Bay were regular visitors.

When Governor Bax retired in 1679, he was replaced by one of the Cape's most energetic Commanders, Simon van der Stel. One of van der Stel's early actions affecting False Bay was to give his son Willem a monopoly of the fishing and shooting along the coast. This was not unnaturally challenged by the Freeburghers, and the Company Commissioners ordered it to be withdrawn, but in return the Freeburghers had to pay the Company for a fishing licence. Van der Stel had been in office nearly eight years before he found the time to explore the bay for himself, no doubt to assess its value and usefulness. He departed on 9th November 1687 to make his own survey, spending the rest of the month on the operation. He took a small galiot, the *Noordt*, which joined him at Ysselsteijn Bay on the 17th. A galiot was a small single-masted fore and aft rigged craft with a bluff bow and leeboards, which became very popular at about this time in the coasting trade of Holland and north Germany. Like most Dutch craft, she was originally designed for shallow water, and would have been ideal for exploration as she could approach close inshore. Van der Stel and his party reconnoitred right around the bay, and passed a day on Seal Island, which they described as being so packed with seals and seabirds that they could not put their feet down without treading on one or the other.

The three weeks spent exploring False Bay must have been both an exciting and rewarding experience for the party. They were treading new ground, and could never be sure what might lie around the next corner. Animals and fish provided a pleasant distraction, and the Commander caught a number of fish that were unfamiliar to European eyes. In due course van der Stel produced a useful chart and sailing instructions for False Bay, which he christened Simon's Bay after himself.

Poor access from Table Bay was the reason why no further effort was made to use the anchorages in False Bay, but the heavy storms of 1692, 1696 and 1697, during which six valuable ships were blown ashore in Cape Town, caused the visiting Commissioner to inspect the bay once more with Willem van der Stel, by then the Commander of the Station, who had taken over from his father in 1699. The Commissioner was not impressed as although the bay offered shelter, he could not see how to supply the water and provisions from local sources that the Company's ships required. Van der Stel disagreed, although it would have been a brave Commander who argued with a Commissioner, and he later established for himself a large farm called Vergelegen in Hottentots Holland. In due course the ownership of this farm led to conflict within the settlement as once again the Freeburghers complained of the unfair competition from a person in a privileged position to control prices.

Some fishermen were operating from Kalk Bay during the time of Simon van der Stel, and later, after his retirement, he built a fishing cottage at Fish Hoek. This is not to be confused with Gordon's Bay, which was also called Fish Hoek for a time. Both are still small fishing ports, but the Government banned fishing in False Bay for a large part of the year in 1979, and the weather conditions beyond the bay are usually too dangerous for the small craft that make up most of the fleet.

Despite the Company's decision not to develop False Bay, a retired soldier, Antoni Visser, obtained a lease on some land around Simon's Bay in 1724 for a rental of twelve rix-dollars (a rix-dollar equals 2½ guilders) and a tenth of his produce. Obviously he felt that the bay had a future, because he built a large two-storeyed house sometime during his occupation, which is shown on a map dated 1740. This house, later bought by the British Navy in April 1814 for 130,000 guilders, is the Admiral's House, or, as it is better known, Admiralty House, and still in use as a residence by the Commander-in-Chief of the South African Navy's Western Fleet today.

The disastrous storms which struck Table Bay in 1722 and 1728 caused the Dutch East India Company to reopen their files and investigate alternative anchorages. Surveys and reports were made again on Saldanha and False Bays, but neither proved encouraging, and it was not until after another great storm on 21st May 1737, when a further eight Indiamen were wrecked in Table Bay, that instructions were issued that Simon's Bay was to be used as a temporary winter anchorage by all the Company's ships until a long mole had been completed at Cape Town. In 1743 additional orders were given to build a warehouse and hospital at Simon's Bay, and to station a small troop of soldiers at the site. Another storehouse for vegetables was to be erected at Kalk Bay, and between April and September, the winter season and time when the storms were most likely to damage shipping in Table Bay, boats were to be detached from Cape Town to assist with the loading and provisioning of ships in Simon's Bay.

Prior to these developments, the bay had come into use on a very casual and infrequent basis, but occasionally causing the Governor considerable concern. In 1725 a strange ship was sighted at anchor and was identified as the *Great Alexander* carrying twenty-six guns. Some of her crew deserted and claimed that she was a pirate, but she sailed before she could be apprehended. Nevertheless, the presence of a powerful ship so close to the settlement and the vital Indian trade, and yet safe from any action by the Company unless a warship happened to be in the area, posed a serious problem for the Governor. In 1737 a Company ship, the *Pallas*, anchored in Simon's Bay with most of her crew sick with scurvy, and this time, arrangements were made for the crew to be treated at Simon's Bay, away from Table Bay for the first time. After 1744, the hospital existed for this purpose, and a small settlement began to develop around it and the warehouse. When another storm in Table Bay destroyed a part of the new mole in 1747, the instructions to captains to use False Bay in the winter months were made permanent, and a small battery was built to protect Simon's Bay. A village was developing, extending the settlement of the Cape from the Cape Flats at Muizenberg, through the little fishing village at Fish Hoek to Simon's Town.

Trade had grown to the point that in 1768 the building of a wooden wharf was justified at Simon's Town, and passengers no longer had to be carried through the water from the boats to the beach on the back of a seaman or slave. However, communication with Cape Town was largely by small sailing ships. Waggons were expensive as the road was poor along the shore, and near Fish Hoek lay a patch of dangerous quicksand which trapped an English officer in 1774. He was saved only by flinging himself off his horse which disappeared into the sand. If supplies were brought from Cape Town by land they were transferred generally to boats at Kalk Bay and rowed to Simon's Bay to avoid this difficulty.

The Swedish botanist Anders Sparrman, who was employed by the Resident at Simon's Town in 1772 as a tutor to his children, wrote an account of his stay during that winter:

> I was now to reside in False Bay till the end of winter, which is called the bad season and is reckoned from 14th May until 14th August. It is not distinguished by any particular degree of cold for we had frequently at

this time the finest summer days. Once or twice there fell some hail but I never saw any snow. We had sometimes the most violent showers of rain, and that mostly for several days in continuation by which means the air was very sensibly cooled. We were not infrequently troubled with the north west wind and this is the reason why the Dutch ships at the time of year before mentioned have been ordered to run into False Bay ever since the year 1722 [actually 1742], when out of ten ships belonging to that nation lying there [Table Bay] eight were cast ashore and lost. This likewise has induced the Dutch Company to have ready at hand every necessary for their ships under the inspection of the Resident of False Bay. They have erected here extensive magazines which at the same time includes forges and baking houses, with house room for the workmen who do the whole duty of the guard and are commanded by a sergeant and two corporals. The slaughter house makes a distinct building by itself as do the Resident's house and the hospital. About the time of my departure from Africa they were building another large and handsome house for the accommodation of the Governor when he chooses to retire thither for his pleasure. Good fresh water is conveyed from the neighbouring hill to a quay where it is very convenient for use. A tradesman or two have got leave to build an Inn here in which however there is not always room and convenience sufficient to receive all such as after a long sea voyage are desirous of refreshing themselves on shore, the ships which land here being chiefly such as contain not much above twenty passengers. Board and lodging are paid here as at the Cape from one rix-dollar to one and a half a day. A tolerable good table is kept here usually and the attendance is none of the worst. A person who wishes to go post to the Cape, a distance of about sixteen miles, will find it comparatively dear enough. Three or four rix-dollars must be paid for a saddle horse and from twelve to sixteen for a waggon, which is for the most part inconvenient and usually drawn by three or four pairs of horses or else by the same number of oxen.

Excepting in winter, False Bay is seldom or never visited by any ships as the south-east wind which prevails at every other time of the year makes this bay in many respects inconvenient, blowing with such violence as to cover two hills there with a thick layer of drift sand all along from the strand up to their very tops. This ridge of sand is seen from afar from the mouth of the harbour and serves as a beacon for ships, for Simon's Bay which is the place where they are to anchor lies directly to the left or something more to the south.

The road between the Cape and False Bay is very heavy and tedious and even sometimes dangerous. At this latter place at the time that the south-east wind prevails, there is wont to be so high a tide that the sea even at its lowest ebb at some places rises up to the foot of the mountains

> which partly encompass this extensive harbour, so that one is obliged to travel for a long way below the shore, though the breakers as they are called or surf of the sea often rises above the nave of the wheels and even into the body of the waggon.

He goes on to say:

> Ships of various nations, English, French and particularly the Dutch East Indiamen, anchored this season in Simon's Bay. The principal officers and passengers of this nation lodge chiefly with the Resident; so that at meal times various European dialects, together with the languages used in commerce with the Indias, viz the Malay, and a very bad kind of Portuguese, were spoken all at one time . . . We often enjoyed the company of English ladies, some of whom even stayed out our elegant dessert of pipes and tobacco. Some of these ladies came from the East Indies on their return to Europe and some from England . . .

This description gives the impression of a busy, cosmopolitan port, during the southern hemisphere's winter at any rate. The officers and passengers had a break from the rather dreary routine aboard ship by enjoying the hospitality of the Dutch officials ashore and ships could expect to obtain the fresh provisions that were so essential on a long sea voyage. Since the average stay of a visiting ship was about a month, the Dutch officials must have been extremely courteous and patient as well, but one assumes that they managed to levy charges for their hospitality, which would have provided an excellent motive for patience. Many of the passengers would have been Company officials, no doubt expecting free lodging, others, particularly the English and French, found accommodation elsewhere in the growing town. The provision of rooms for visitors seems to have been almost as profitable an occupation as supplying victuals to the ships, and probably explains the large size of some of the early houses. Sparrman joined Captain Cook when he passed through the Cape on the *Resolution* late in 1772 on his second voyage to the Pacific.

Even though Simon's Bay was considered to be a safe haven during the winter, and increasingly attractive to ships, although it lacked the size and facilities of Cape Town, False Bay was not immune to the natural dangers that threatened a ship at the time. Until the 1770s, however, there had only been four known losses in False Bay, the *Grundel* in 1673, the *Ternate* in 1680, the *Sarpine* in 1691 and the *Hollandia* in 1720. In the next few years the numbers grew, an indication of the expansion in traffic as False Bay and in particular Simon's Town became more important. One of the most interesting of these wrecks, because it emphasises the hazards that faced seamen before reliable surveys and charts, was that of the British East Indiaman *Colebrooke* on 25th August 1778. The *Colebrooke* was in company with two other Indiamen, the *Gatton* and the *Royal Admiral*, and the warship *Asia*, when she struck the then uncharted Anvil Rock whilst rounding Cape Point. A strong north-westerly wind was blowing, and although badly holed, the *Colebrooke* managed to stay afloat long enough to be beached on the eastern shore of Kogel Bay. It is difficult to blame the captain of the *Colebrooke* for the damage to his ship. Anvil Rock lies about one and a quarter miles south-east of Cape Point, and now has a depth of thirteen feet over it, but earlier surveys put this at six feet, so it is possible that the rock was nearer the surface in the past. Its location is suggested only when there is a heavy swell at low water, and occasionally the sea can be observed breaking above it. Boats from the other ships were launched to take off the crew, but by nightfall a third remained on board. The weather moderated, and next morning the third officer was able to take one of the ship's boats with survivors to Simon's Bay, a row of ten hours. On 29th August another gale destroyed the ship before any serious salvage attempt could be made, and the small quantity of goods recovered raised £177 at an auction. For some years after this accident, Anvil Rock was known as Colebrooke Rock, and Kogel Bay as Colebrooke Bay.

Whittle Rock was discovered in the same way when HMS *Trident* hit it in 1796, whilst returning from a search for the Dutch Admiral Lucas. A subsequent survey conducted by Lieutenant Whittle from the brig *Euphrosyne* discovered the rock about six foot six inches below the surface and described it as being of small dimensions but extremely dangerous, since it was in the fairway coming into Simon's Bay. Buoys were laid to mark the rock, but they were washed away constantly, and the *Euphrates* was badly damaged when she struck it in 1810. Eventually the rock was marked properly in 1822 by a set of beacons erected ashore near Buffels Bay.

The largest group of individual wrecks in False Bay, no less than nineteen, occurred along the stretch of coast fronting Simon's Town to Muizenberg, mainly caused by ships' captains mistaking the Muizenberg Mountains for Elsie's Peak in poor visibility, and so running on too far to the north. Another cause was the reflection of the moon on the sandhills behind Simon's Bay, which could be misleading to seamen. Too late they realised their error, and if they were running before a south-easter, the beach at Muizenberg was the classic lee shore, and there was no time to wear the ship around before she struck. Ships at anchor near Simon's Bay were equally at risk if their anchor cables parted. The French frigate *Penelope* went ashore from this cause in October 1788, but her entire crew of 430 were able to reach the beach through the surf and were saved. After the completion of the Roman Rock Lighthouse off Simon's Bay in 1867, which gave mariners an accurate idea of their position as they sailed in towards the town, wrecks caused by a mistaken position ceased.

The French, who virtually occupied the Cape colony from 1781 until 1784, devoted their energies almost exclusively to building defences for Cape Town. So when the French revolutionary war began in 1792, the Dutch saw the necessity of strengthening the fortifications of Simon's Town as well to prepare against possible French attacks. Two batteries were built, the Boetselaar and the Zoutman, each mounting four 24-pounder guns, but with an extra four 8-pounders at the Boetselaar.

Holland fell to the French at the beginning of 1795, and when on 11th June 1795 nine strange warships sailed into Simon's Bay and anchored, it was feared that this was the French invasion fleet. The only Dutch warship in Simon's Town was the frigate *Middenblik*, and her captain rowed out to investigate. It was some time before he returned, and in his absence, the alarm was raised ashore, and Simon's Town reinforced. Eventually when the captain returned, he announced that the fleet was British, commanded by Vice-Admiral Sir George Elphinstone, and that it included 800 troops under General Craig. The British Admiral carried dispatches from the Prince of Orange, who had fled to England after the surrender of Holland, which ordered the Cape Governor to accept the protection of the British against the French.

The Governor was in a quandary. He had just received news of the establishment of a new Dutch Republic, and was unsure as to where his loyalties lay. He was personally an Orange supporter, but many of the burghers had republican sympathies. A council meeting called to discuss the problem, consisting largely of burghers, voted to keep out the British, and Sir George Elphinstone was informed of this decision. The British had hoped to occupy the Cape peacefully, and this answer gave them a military problem. The Dutch could raise 3,600 men, against whom, even by making soldiers of sailors, the British could muster about 1,500. If they ignored the difference in numbers, the men would have to be landed under cover from the guns of the fleet, and the fleet would be unwise to risk itself against well-established batteries in Table Bay. The two batteries in Simon's Town did not present a formidable obstacle, but then the men would have to march via an easily defended pass to Muizenberg, which was well protected by fortifications. A stalemate ensued, whilst the British awaited reinforcements from St. Helena, and the Dutch mobilised and improved their defences.

Matters came to a head when General Craig heard of a Dutch plan to burn Simon's Town. On 22nd July 1795, he landed 350 marines and 400 men of the 78th Regiment and occupied the town as his headquarters. Although he intended awaiting his reinforcements, events began to take charge. Small patrol actions occurred, and a number of Dutch deserters were interrogated, from which it was discovered that the Dutch were not well organised, and an attack on Muizenberg might succeed. On 7th August, covered by the guns of the fleet, Craig's force was augmented by 1,000 sailors and, accompanied by armed cutters, the small British army began to march along the coast. Three hours later Muizenberg was captured, with negligible loss. The colonel in charge of the defences, de Lille, overawed by the warships, had been taken by surprise, and his men withdrew, only a small gun battery putting up more than a token resistance. The Dutch suffered two wounded. On the 8th there was an attempt at a counter-attack, but this soon fizzled out, and on the 9th Craig received the first of his reinforcements in the form of 400 more troops. Craig was now confident he could hold Muizenberg, but he still needed more men if he was to attack and occupy Cape Town. The initiative lay with the defenders, but they made no moves until 2nd September, when they advanced to attack the British position. But they had waited too long. On the 3rd, a fleet of fourteen ships, bringing a further 3,000 troops, dropped anchor in Simon's Bay. The pendulum had swung in favour of the British, and two weeks later the Cape was theirs.

Once the Cape was in his hands, General Craig immediately set about improving the defences, both of Cape Town and Simon's Town, against an expected counter-attack from the Dutch. News travelled slowly, and the Dutch fleet consisting of three ships-of-the-line, under Admiral Lucas, did not arrive from Batavia until August 1796. The fleet by-passed Cape Town whose formidable batteries were in British hands, and sailed straight to Saldanha Bay, which was expected to be lightly defended, hoping to rendezvous with a squadron of French warships that were rumoured to be on their way to assist.

At this point Admiral Elphinstone had an unexpected piece of luck. In May, a small British whaler, the *Lord Hawkesbury*, had been captured by a French squadron in mid-Atlantic. The French put aboard a small prize crew, and took all but three of the English crew away as prisoners. These three, Morrow, Laing and a cabin boy, soon worked themselves into a position of trust with their captors, to the extent that they were employed in the crew. As the *Lord Hawkesbury* approached the Cape, on a course set south of Cape Point, Morrow was on the wheel, and very slowly edged the course round to the north. He managed to put the ship ashore off Zoetendals Vlei, and the French became the prisoners. From these men Elphinstone learned that the French squadron that Admiral Lucas was expecting had already sailed round the Cape towards Mauritius, and the British would have to face only the Dutch and not a combined fleet. When he returned to Simon's Town on 12th August, having sustained considerable damage in a storm, he knew already that Lucas was at Saldanha Bay and the strength of the Dutch fleet. Three days later Admiral Elphinstone led his hastily repaired fleet of eight ships-of-the-line to Saldanha Bay. At the same time General Craig marched overland with a force of 2,500 men, and arrived just before the fleet. Confronted by a superior fleet blocking his escape and a strong force ashore, Lucas, who found that he could not rely on his men, had little choice but to surrender. As was the custom of the time, the Dutch ships were added to the fleet, and the Dutch seamen press-ganged into the Royal Navy. Only the officers and cadets were returned to Holland, where Lucas died before he could face a court martial.

General Craig was appointed first British Governor of the Cape and his initial priority was to safeguard it against attacks. One of his first moves was to strengthen the defences of Muizenberg, which remained a garrison until 1827 when it was no longer thought to serve any useful defensive purpose. Muizenberg almost ceased to exist after this, but eventually re-established itself as a resort in which capacity it continues today. At Simon's Bay he added a 24-pounder to the Boetselaar Battery, and then built one of the earliest Martello towers nearby to bolster the defences.

The origins of this Martello tower lie in the Mediterranean, as it was built in 1795 before the line of similar towers was constructed along the south coast of England in 1804. It is believed that the idea came from Sir David Dundas, a friend of Craig's, who had commanded the British troops which captured the first Martello tower protecting San Fiorenzo Bay in Corsica in 1794. Dundas had been impressed by the manner in which a small party within the tower had been able to inflict heavy casualties before being overwhelmed. Dundas was subsequently in command of the defences along the south coast of England in 1804, and one of his subordinates was General Craig; there is a further coincidence that in command of the sea defences was Admiral Elphinstone, now Lord Keith.

The year 1797 was a bad one for the Royal Navy, as in April the crews of the fleet at Spithead mutinied, to be followed a month later by those at the Nore. Mutiny is like a revolution: it usually starts with reasonable grievances, in this case the lack of pay and poor food, but then the mutineers, drunk with power, start to increase their demands, and extremists take over. It has to be dealt with quickly before the mutineers gain confidence. The Spithead mutiny was resolved swiftly. The men's complaints were justified, and it was agreed that they would be put right, and no one was punished. The ringleaders of the Nore mutiny, however, were captured and hanged, because their grievances were the same as the former which had already been settled. On 22nd October 1797, the nine ships at anchor at Simon's Bay mutinied for the same reason, but said that they would fight under their officers if an enemy appeared. The admiral and captains were made prisoners aboard the flagship *Tremendous*, but released after five days when it was agreed that improvements would be effected.

The brief return to Dutch Government under the Batavian Republic between 1803 and 1806, hardly affected False Bay. Although Governor Janssens set up extra defences at Muizenberg and elsewhere in anticipation of a fresh British invasion, in fact these were never put to the test because the British landed north-west of Cape Town in January 1806. The only time that the batteries fired in anger was when a French frigate, the *Canonnier*, sailed into the bay on 30th April 1806, expecting to be received by her Dutch allies. She sent ashore a landing party which was captured by the British, but since the frigate was outside the range of the shore batteries, she was able to sail away without further loss.

In 1808, Lieutenant Golovnin of the Imperial Russian Navy ship, the *Diana*, was on a world survey and detained by the Royal Navy in Simon's Town, whilst they investigated the clearance given to him by the Admiralty in London; he wrote of Simon's Town:

> Simon's Town cannot be called a town, as it is just a village, containing public buildings, i.e. a small arsenal, military barracks, a hospital and not a single church. It has about 25 private dwellings lined up on the shores of a small bay, part of False Bay and named Simon's Bay. At the entrance to it, on both sides of the town, the Hollanders have built two small batteries for its defence: but for this purpose they are quite superfluous. There are hardly 100 permanent inhabitants . . .

One can perhaps sympathise with the Russian lieutenant. He was being detained when he wanted to get on with his work, and must have had a fairly jaundiced view of his surroundings. His notes concerning the weather, however, are those of a seaman:

> In Simon's Bay a strong south-easter usually commences in the morning, with strong squalls, which become stronger and more frequent every hour; and after midday a strong and constant wind begins to blow. Before this, clouds will appear around the peaks of the distant mountain of Simon's Bay, to the north near Muizenberg, and these gradually get thicker and descend to cover the whole mountain. If the wind lasts, light cloud will appear on the mountain on the very edge of False Bay to the north, floating on the peaks and getting thicker by and by; fragments from this cloud will be borne over to the west coast of False Bay and will begin to envelop the high eastern mountain of Simon's Bay; going over to its southern end they speed to the west and though the mountains around are clouded, over Simon's Bay itself there will be none and it will remain clear. If however, on the eastern mountain of Simon's Bay the clouds thicken and cover it completely they will break loose and speed along in terrific squalls. According to my observations, when the

> mountains of False Bay are covered with cloud it is necessary to slacken the ropes, lower the top-gallant masts and get ready for a storm.

Golovnin, who eventually became a Rear-Admiral, was planning to take his ship to sea and escape the moment an opportunity presented itself, and so he would naturally have made a study of the weather conditions to help him choose the right moment. He continued his voyage to become the first Russian to circumnavigate the world.

Although nearly all British warships used Simon's Town as their anchorage after the loss of HMS *Sceptre* in Table Bay in 1799, it was not until 1814 that the shore establishment followed, thus marking the start of a liaison with the town that has lasted, via the South African Navy, to the present day. The completion of a good road round Fish Hoek in 1815, using men of the 83rd Regiment who were passing through the Cape, gave Simon's Town good land communications at last. From this time on the town and harbour slowly became more and more dedicated to the military, and almost totally so after the building of a protected harbour in Cape Town during the 1860s made the need for an alternative winter anchorage less important for merchant ships. The years of peace following the Napoleonic Wars, although it led to the usual reduction in the strength of the fleet, did not entail the abandonment of the plans to create a naval base at Simon's Town, and it soon had all the facilities required to maintain and repair ships. Barracks, mast storage, sail lofts, rigging sheds, victualling sheds, magazines, a forge, hospital and church were built or adapted from existing buildings, and these had to be extended over the years as the demands of the Navy, and the size and complexity of ships, increased. Navigation aids were improved, and from 1845 the Roman Rock was marked by southern Africa's only lightship until this was replaced by a small manned lighthouse in 1861. A major expansion took place in the 1850s when steam and iron ships made their appearance, requiring larger forges and machine shops. Finally, in 1898 the whole port was ceded to the Admiralty, just in time for it to become a major inlet for British troops landing to fight the Boers. In the midst of this war, the foundation stones were laid for a new graving dock, large enough to take the biggest ships contemplated by the Navy, and this, and the new East Dockyard, were opened in 1910 and were able to provide the services necessary for the First World War.

From 1815 until 1957 the Royal Navy kept a Cape or South Atlantic squadron of warships permanently based at Simon's Town. From the Cape station, these ships undertook the supply and guard of the island of St. Helena where Napoleon Bonaparte was kept in captivity until his death in 1821. They patrolled the waters from Walvis Bay on the west to Inhambane on the east, carrying out the policing tasks that the Navy took upon itself during the near 100 years that the Pax Britannica was in force. These limits changed as the demands of the Home Government and a growing Empire increased. In 1857, the West Africa Station came under the Cape Station, to become independent again in 1903, but, at the same time, the Cape Station's limits were extended to the equator, just north of Mombasa on the east coast, and the Cunene River, about 17° 15′ south latitude on the west. During these years the Navy had the responsibility of putting an end to the slave trade, and many captured slavers were brought back to Simon's Town, to be sold, and the freed slaves kept ashore until they could be indentured to farmers. One of these captured ships, the *Rowvonia*, went ashore in the bay in 1850. When necessary, raiding parties were formed from the crews of the little gunboats to effect punitive expeditions against tribes who had attacked missionaries or traders as they tried to establish themselves over this vast part of the African continent. The ships would return to Simon's Town for repairs, and land the sick and wounded members of their companies at the local hospital.

During the Boer War Simon's Town became a camp for Boer prisoners, and many of Cronje's army, after their capture, sat out the war under guard on ships in the bay and in the hurriedly constructed tented camps ashore. Others were shipped to prisoner-of-war camps as far away as Bermuda. At the outbreak of hostilities a party of 350 marines and two guns were immediately dispatched from the flagship of the Cape Squadron, HMS *Doris*, to Stormberg, and men were sent to support other naval gun parties landed to back up the British army ashore. The threat of a European power interfering on the side of the Boers was always present in the mind of the Commander-in-Chief at the Cape, and a strong naval force was kept available, whilst smaller scout-type cruisers constantly patrolled the coastline from the base. In the event there was no naval action during the war, apart from the shelling of adventurous Boer commandos, but Simon's Town had played an important part in providing the support for the ships brought to the Cape waters by the war, in the same way that it gave invaluable assistance in the two great World Wars.

A familiar sight lying at her mooring in Simon's Bay during the two decades between the World Wars was the old 3,000-ton second-class cruiser HMS *Thames*, built in 1885, and converted into a depot ship in 1903. In 1920 she was purchased at Sheerness in England by a Mr T. B. Davis, and steamed to Simon's Town. She was re-christened the *General Botha* to serve as a training ship for young men who wished to become officers in the Royal or Merchant Navies. The initial crew for the outward voyage consisted of Captain Renouf, two deck officers, and twenty-four inexperienced cadets, and the normal complement of engineers, seamen and stewards. The ship, which had been designed for a speed of seventeen knots, could manage only six, and called into Plymouth to have her fifth boiler repaired. On the voyage down-Channel she was swept by a wave which stove in the planking over the gun openings, and flooded much of the accommodation. As the wave approached, the second mate said to the captain, 'You know, Captain, the lower drawer in my cabin chest is full of water.' The captain is said to have replied, 'Here comes a sea that will fill your bunk as well!' After returning to Plymouth again for repairs, the old ship finally reached Simon's Town after a voyage of thirty-eight days. The school was transferred ashore in 1942, and the ship reverted to her original name and was used as an accommodation ship until 13th May 1947 when, there being no further use for her, she was towed into the bay and scuttled.

On 2nd April 1957, 143 years of continuous occupation of the Simon's Town Naval Dockyard came to an end, when the key to the West Dockyard Gate was officially handed over to the South African Navy by the last British Superintendent, Captain H. E. Bone, CBE, DSO, DSC, RN. Under the 'Simon's Town' agreement, the Royal Navy could continue to use the dockyard in the event of hostilities in which Britain and South Africa were jointly involved, and the facility was available for Britain and her allies, even if South Africa was not implicated. A signal station for the Royal Navy remained to operate from the Silvermines until 1965 when Britain withdrew completely from South Africa. Since taking over the dockyard, the South African Navy has doubled its size and greatly improved its facilities, so that it can today provide berths for its entire fleet, and perform work as complex as the full overhauls of its three submarines, and its missile-equipped strike craft.

9

The Cape Coast – Cape Hangklip to Port Elizabeth

Perestrelo's account of the coastline between Cape Hangklip and Port Elizabeth does, in the main, hold good today. His latitudes are quite close, but since he had to gauge the longitude by dead-reckoning, it is not always accurate. In places, though, his instructions are confusing, perhaps because he describes the coast from Table Bay going east, when in fact he surveyed it from the opposite direction.

> From it [Cape Hangklip] towards the east is a small and shelterless bay, and beyond that is Cape False [Danger Point] which stands out as a great rock with a dark patch on it.

The English seaman Cavendish, sailing around the Cape twelve years after Perestrelo, describes Cape Falso:

> 11 of May 1588 wee espied land to beare west of us, which as we did imagine was the Cape Buena Esperenca. The 14 day we espied the land again which was the Cape called Cabo Falso which is short of the Cape de Buena Esperenca 40 or 50 leagues. This Cape is very easie to be knowen for there are right over it three very high hills and the highest standeth in the midst.

This description of Cabo Falso fits Danger Point, but Cavendish was very inaccurate in his estimation of the distance between Cape Point and False Cape, which indicates that he cannot have had a good chart, or the weather must have been poor. A league was 3.18 nautical miles, but usually taken to be three nautical miles for practical purposes, so he thought that the distance from Danger Point to Cape Point was at least 120 miles, whereas, as we know, it is only forty-four miles. He does go on to say that he ran into a stiff storm, and did not round Cape Point for another two days. This suggests that the storm was a westerly, and his ship must have been tacking against it. It is interesting to note that he thought he had managed

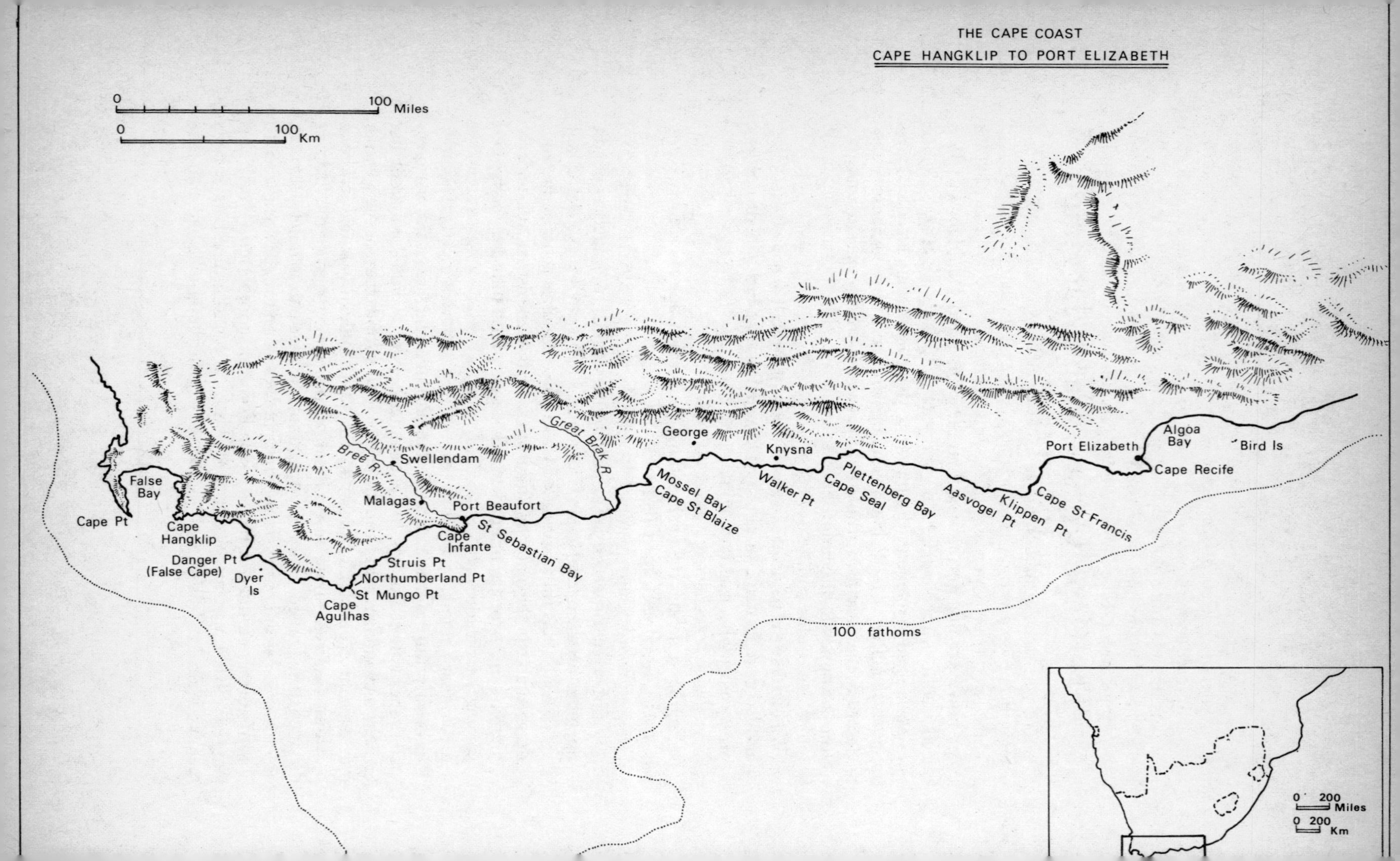
THE CAPE COAST
CAPE HANGKLIP TO PORT ELIZABETH
0
100 Miles
0
100 Km
Cape Pt
False Bay
Cape Hangklip
Danger Pt (False Cape)
Dyer Is
Cape Agulhas
St Mungo Pt
Northumberland Pt
Struis Pt
Cape Infante
St Sebastian Bay
Port Beaufort
Malagas
Swellendam
Breë R
Great Brak R
George
Mossel Bay
Cape St Blaize
Knysna
Walker Pt
Cape Seal
Plettenberg Bay
Aasvogel Pt
Klippen Pt
Cape St Francis
Port Elizabeth
Cape Recife
Algoa Bay
Bird Is
100 fathoms
0 200 Miles
0 200 Km

to sail 120 miles to windward, but in fact he may have sailed only about fifty. There are a number of possible explanations for this error, which would otherwise be surprising for so experienced a mariner. It could be that he suffered more leeway in the storm than he reckoned, but if he had been tacking, it is quite likely that he would have made long tacks, and this would have taken him well south where perhaps he picked up the east-going current. Like Perestrelo, without an exact method of determining longitude, and no land in view, he would not have realised that the current existed.

There was some confusion in the early years, as both Cape Point and Danger Point were known as Cabo Falso, since no doubt either cape could be considered false depending from which direction one approached. By 1507, however, the Portuguese were describing only Danger Point as Cabo Falso.

There is something delightfully logical in the habit of giving a point that can be mistaken for a more important headland, the title 'False'. With that one word the seaman is warned that the two headlands can be confused, and he knows that he should be extra cautious. The Portuguese made frequent use of this simple device, and other seamen obviously found it helpful because the name has continued down through the centuries. Cabo Falso also gave its name to the bay because it could be equally misleading since it was large enough for a navigator, particularly in bad weather and poor visibility, to believe it was the Atlantic.

Perestrelo describes the next section of coast as follows:

> Thence towards Cape Agulhas the land along the sea is low, and forms hillocks, some of which are peaked, others flat on top and long, with openings between them.
>
> Cape Agulhas is in a latitude of thirty-five degrees [actually 34° 50′]. Cape Infante [still so named] lies from it north-east by east, at a distance of fourteen leagues [fourteen leagues is 44½ miles, the actual distance is 49 miles]. Its mark of recognition is a bank of grey land which terminates in two sharp points, of which the one to the eastward is much the sharper [probably Northumberland and Struis Points]. The distance from one to the other is four leagues, almost east and west, and the coast between them is formed in round-topped ridges with a white spot, beyond which is a band of bushes. In the interior are high and large ranges of mountains, with six or seven breaks. To the westward of this Cape a little island, called Das Serras is placed on the charts but I doubt its existence. Although I passed there very close to the land, in truth it may be that with the fine and damp mist that was the forerunner of the storm from the west which I encountered that day, or through its being deep in the shadow of the land, I did not see it, and therefore I leave this question

> to be determined hereafter. From the eastern point of this cape in the same direction the coast turns to the north-north-east, making a bight, with low land along the coast, and having as its extremity a great rock. There is Cape Infante. From the sea these two capes can be seen, and not the low coast land between them, on which there is a great patch of sand, and in the interior there is a hillock like this [the drawing is missing].

The inhospitable coastline between False Bay and Cape Agulhas was undoubtedly one of the reasons why no small ports appeared to improve communications with the expanding farming settlements in the interior. However, in the latter part of the eighteenth century, the Dutch had extended their settlements along the south coast well beyond Cape Agulhas and had explored Mossel Bay and Plettenberg Bay, both of which were coming into usage as anchorages by small ships servicing the local communities. In other areas along the coast, vessels would occasionally anchor to load or discharge a cargo, but little shelter was available, and their stay would be very dependent upon the prevailing weather conditions.

The bay between Cape Hangklip and Danger Point is wide open to the south and west, and although some protection would be offered to an easterly, it would have been a foolhardy captain who dared to stay at anchor offshore in any strong wind. The only river of reasonable size, the Klein, has a bar at its entrance, which made it unsuitable as a port. A small harbour, now designated as a national monument, exists at Hermanus, near the mouth of the Klein River. A recently built breakwater provides some added protection from the waves but not the wind, and the depth precludes its use by anything but small craft. Fishing, which is the main maritime activity, is conducted from a new port which has been created nearby at Gansbaai.

Danger Point, the Cabo Falso of Perestrelo, twelve miles south of Gansbaai, is the infamous resting place of the troopship HMS *Birkenhead*. The ship was built in 1845 as a frigate, and was the Royal Navy's first iron steamer, but she spent her life as a trooper. She had sailed from Cork with reinforcements for the army in Kaffraria which was fighting the Xhosa tribesmen, and was due to land these troops at the Buffalo River. After a short stop at Simon's Town to take aboard coal and stores, she sailed on the calm evening of 25th February 1852 for Port Elizabeth. The ship was doing about eight knots when she struck a rock about a mile and a half south-west of Danger Point, which ripped out her bottom. Many of the men below were drowned, the others hurried on deck and attempts were made to launch the eight ship's boats. Only three could be lowered overside, and the women and children were put on board. At this point the order was given 'every man for himself', but realising that this would mean that the three boats would be swamped, the order was countermanded, and the men told to stand firm. Not one man moved. The fortitude of the young soldiers, many of them raw recruits, as the ship began to sink gave the sea one of its greatest traditions, that women and children are saved first. As the ship sank, some men tried to swim to the shore, but many were attacked by sharks. Others hung on to the rigging and were picked up the next day by the schooner *Lioness*. In all 454 souls out of a total of 630 perished. The subsequent enquiry found that the captain had been too confident of his distance offshore, and had been set much closer to the coast than he realised. Apart from the fatalities, the British Government also lost the quarter of a million pounds which was said to be on board.

Years later, in 1879, another troopship was lost in the same area, off Dyer Island. The *Clyde*, a 2,200-ton vessel, was on charter to the Admiralty, and the ship was loaded with 500 troops and large quantities of ammunition bound for the Zulu War. Fortunately the weather was calm, and everyone was transferred safely to the shore where a local farmer provided food.

The ship losses on this part of the coast are particularly heavy. This was due partly to the primitive navigation aids available until quite recently, but also to the variable currents, which frequently set unwary ships towards the shore and were difficult to predict. The Devitt and Moore steamer *Queen of the Thames* went aground close to Birkenhead Rock in 1871, although luckily with only a small loss of life, and ten years later the Union intermediate liner *Teuton* struck rocks in this area. Confidence in the ship's six watertight bulkheads caused the captain of the *Teuton* to delay giving the order to abandon ship, and she was turned back towards Simon's Town. Unfortunately the bulkheads could not stand the water pressure and they suddenly gave one after another in rapid succession. Deprived of her buoyancy the ship reared up into the air and quickly disappeared, dragging many of the passengers and crew down with her, and killing more as pieces of wreckage shot to the surface. Just thirty-six out of 272 on board at the time of the accident were saved.

Only thirty-seven miles beyond Danger Point lies Cape Agulhas, the southernmost point of the continent of Africa, and some eighty miles east-south-east of Cape Point. The name comes from the Portuguese word for a needle because the earliest navigators found that the needle of their compasses showed no magnetic variation at this point. Quite when this was realised is uncertain, as Pereira refers to the point as Ponta de São Brandam in 1506, but in 1514 João de Lisboa is calling it Cabo das Agulhas. Since the point is at the end of some fairly low-lying ground, and there are no obvious marks that represent needles close by, this explanation is a possibility. The coast to the east of Agulhas is low lying, and the two rocky points close by are named after the ships that were lost on them, the

St. Mungo in 1844, and the *Northumberland* in 1839. This section of the coast is still claiming victims. As recently as July 1974 a 59,000-ton bulk carrier, the *Oriental Pioneer*, went aground and later broke up off Northumberland Point.

About twenty-five miles north-east of Cape Agulhas lies the village of Arniston, formally called Waenhuiskrans (Waggon House Cliff). Close by on 30th May 1815 the British East Indiaman *Arniston* went ashore with very heavy loss of life. The *Arniston* had been requisitioned as a troop transport, and was part of a convoy dispersed by a storm near Cape Agulhas. On 29th May 1815 she sighted land which was wrongly estimated to be near Table Bay. She beat out to sea, but the next day breakers were sighted, and such was the strength of the wind that she was unable to make any headway to windward and three anchors were cut loose. Two parted almost immediately, and in an effort to save the 378 lives on board, the captain headed his vessel in towards the land, hoping to be able to beach her. She struck a reef thought to be about a mile and a half offshore, some twenty-five miles north-east of Cape Agulhas. The ship began to break up and only six men managed to get ashore alive. In 1982 members of the University of Cape Town's Archaeological Department located the site of the wreck about half a mile off the shore. Iron beams, such as were used in the construction of Indiamen, were found, along with fragments of porcelain, navigation instruments and cannon balls, some weighing 150 pounds. Part of the hull had been driven onto the beach and is occasionally exposed as the sand moves. The site has since been declared a national monument. A short distance away lies Rys Point, named after the rice cargo washed ashore from the *Victonshire* which stranded there in 1880.

Cape Infante is the next prominent point along the coast, some forty-eight miles north-east-by-east from Cape Agulhas. It was an important landmark for the Portuguese, as Perestrelo relates:

> Cape Infante is in latitude thirty-four degrees and a half [within two miles]. It lies in line with Cape Vacas [Vleespunt] to the eastward nearly east by north, the distance between them being fifteen leagues [five and a half miles more than actual]. Its mark of recognition is a high and circular mass of ground, flat on top, with a face to the sea which at a distance looks like an island, but is not one. It is situated between two rocks, which also look like islets, and it has near it two other rocks encircled with water. There is a lofty land which is seen from westward when passing Cape Agulhas. Anyone who is in a line north and south with it will see inland a flat range with some breaks in it making long mountains, and to the westward five or six round hills. Between this range and the cape there is a long flat topped mountain, not very high, which lies north and south. At this place, seven and eight leagues from

the shore, the bottom at sixty or eighty fathoms is fine sand. [This is confusing as at this distance today the depth is about 262 feet.]

Along this cape on the eastern side is a bay, to which I gave the name Saint Sebastian. It is some three leagues in extent, and is sheltered from the south-east round by the west nearly to the east-north-east. In it there are places eight and nine fathoms deep, but with a clean bottom and good holding ground for anchors. It is well provided with fish, and there is water in the valley the nearest to the cape of three that are seen here, although landing to obtain it is difficult in strong easterly winds, such as I had when I entered, owing to the rocky shore and the current, but with westerly winds it should be very smooth. Inside of this bay there is another, sheltered from all winds, which is about half a league in length, and large enough to contain any great fleet. I did not enter this bay with the boat, because the sea was breaking heavily between them with the east wind which was blowing, but from outside it appeared to me deep and clear. A river [the Breë] flows into it, which, according to what was told to me by those whom I sent to examine it by land, is as large as the Tagus in front of Santarem. The passage between these bays is about a quarter of a league wide, with some banks of sand on the eastern side and a sharp point of land on the western, where at low tide is seen a reef of rock that obstructs a portion of it, but sufficient space is left to give entrance to ships from one bay to the other, as I suppose that it is principally in the season of the west winds that they will need it to winter in. The waters from the mountains which run from the river of which I have spoken above [Breë] and from other rivulets then in existence should in that season open the whole channel that the east winds have blocked up with sand from the bottom and other parts of the bay and I might also have found an entrance if the sea had not broken so heavily, for close to the bar I found two fathoms and a half of water.

Anyone wishing to enter the first bay should not approach the point of the cape, although from it about a cannon shot distant is a shoal [Blinder Reef] upon which the sea does not break, but it can be known by the foaming there now and then, and between it and the land the water is so deep that any ship can pass. Shelter is to be had behind the other point that is seen beyond [St. Sebastian Point], because there is a reef which runs out a cross-bow shot, and helps to give protection by breaking the force of the waves. No small advantage for those who anchor in this bay and all the others on that part of the coast is the current that runs from the east, which, by setting outward, helps to support the ship in a way that there is much less strain on the cables, although the wind is from the east and strong.

I have treated of the entrance of this bay, as coming from the westward side, and thus I resolve to do of all the others, although I entered and departed from some of them on the eastern side and in the centres, and I found them for the most part deep and clean if they are approached with these winds, for reasons which I shall give farther on. Thence it is necessary to look for the entrances and shelter on this coast, which I thus describe, from the west towards the east, although I explored it from the opposite direction, so that all the tokens and marks of recognition may be more easily recognised by the pilot who approaches these ports, if he makes no mistake in his knowledge of them, because by these he will be assisted more than by the latitudes, on account of it being a locality where the course is east and west, or nearly so, and it is dangerous to depend solely on the sun, as a small error of the astrolabe produces incorrect distances. From this bay towards the east the land rises high and steep from the sea for a distance of five or six leagues, with white or reddish walls of rock [between Stilbaai and Ystervark Point] some of them high up from the shore, and others running along the coast. Beyond this the land is not so elevated; it has walls of rock of the same kind, but they are all white. The land becomes continually lower until Cape Vacas [Vleespunt] is reached, a league before coming to which is the river Fermoso or Dos Vaqueiros [River Gourits], that has on the eastern side a sharp point which runs farther out into the sea than the one on the west, with a small white patch along the water. Many currents run towards this river, although from outside it appears to be small for large boats, and as it was calm at times, they obliged me to come to an anchor.

The bay behind Cape Infante referred to here by Perestrelo is still called St. Sebastian Bay, and does indeed protect a small sheltered anchorage into which flows the river Breë. The Cape owes its name to one of Bartolomeu Dias's captains, João Infante, who went ashore when Dias anchored here in 1488. It was probably used by coastal sailing ships, and vessels seeking shelter, from the time of the Portuguese. In 1822 a small village a mile upstream from the mouth of the Breë River was christened Port Beaufort. A local trade was developed by a Swellendam company, Barry and Nephew, who sailed ships over the bar and twenty miles up river as far as Malgas, where they had a depot. In 1859 they built a 157-ton shallow-draught steam coaster on the Clyde, named the *Kadie*, and used her to improve the service with Cape Town. The little *Kadie*, the first steamer to cross the bar, worked hard for six years, but on her 241st crossing of the bar she stranded and became a total loss. All that remains today are her boilers. The *Kadie* was not replaced and Port Beaufort did not become a large port, although there was a brief renaissance between 1933 and 1939, when an ex-Admiralty tug was used for a local service. The port is now the home of fishing vessels and pleasure craft.

Between Cape Infante and Cape St. Blaize, seventy miles to the east, Perestrelo describes the coast as follows:

Cape Vacas [Flesh Point or Vleespunt] is in latitude thirty-four degrees and a third. Cape San Bras [Cape St. Blaize] lies north-east by east, at a distance of five leagues. Its mark of recognition running along the coast is a sharp point which ends in the sea in a mountain with some reefs at its base, which, until very close, one would take to be an islet, but it is not one. From it a league to the westward is the river Fermoso or Dos Vaqueiros, of which I have already treated. Between it and the cape are some large walls of rock, and the interior is a mountain divided at the top in a way that will be described in the chapter treating of the bay of San Bras [Mossel Bay]. In this locality seven or eight leagues at sea there are forty or fifty fathoms of water, and the closer to the coast it is deeper, but the whole bottom is of clean fine sand or mixed with small shells, and there is mud in some places.

Along this cape to the eastern side is the bay of Vacas [Cows], about a league in extent. It is a good port, sheltered from the south round by the west to the north-east. Anyone entering it must take care only to come to an anchor in eight or nine fathoms. In the beginning of the navigation to India ships touched there, and it was in this place that Joam de Queiros and almost all his people were killed in the year 1505 in the fleet of Pedro d'Anaya, because they went inland to take cattle by force. [Not so: d'Anaya was killed on another island named 'Das Vacas' in Delagoa Bay.] Close to the eastern part of this bay there are some shoals, and proceeding onward the coast runs northward with a narrow sandy beach along the sea until some reddish rocky walls are reached, and thence they become larger and larger to Cape San Bras.

Cape San Bras is in latitude a little short of thirty-four degrees and a quarter [actually 34° 11′]. Cape Talhado [Cape Seal] lies east by north, at a distance of eighteen leagues [seven miles short]. Its mark of recognition from the sea is a flat mountain which ends in two points distant five leagues from each other, and on the western side it is very low along the sea, terminating in the bay Das Vacas, of which I have already treated. The eastern point of Cape San Bras, which is formed by a great rock shaped above like a hat, and with reddish walls of rock at its base. There are some shoals and a rock surrounded with water. When this cape lies to the north-east there is upon it a flat piece of ground, with some white spots and others dark which look like ploughed lands, and when it lies to the west-north-west it appears like a round island. The mountains in the interior are high and serrated, but there are in them three peaks [Vreystant, Ruitersberg and Engelsberg] which make them easily distinguishable, one, of which mention has before been made, which is over and against Cape Vacas, although almost north-west of Cape San Bras, which looks like a pitched tent with high sides, and towards the north-east another still higher which has its top hanging over to the eastward, and between them are pointed mountains that I do not depicture here in order to avoid confusion.

Along this cape, on the eastern side, is the bay or watering place of San Bras, three leagues or more in extent. It is in places six and eight fathoms deep close to the shore, and the bottom is very clean. It is sheltered from south-east by east round by the west to the north-east. Inland from the point of the cape a cannon shot are two coves [Varkens Bay and Munro's Bay] and on the elevated ground between them are still standing to the height of five or six spans the walls of a hermitage [built by João da Nova in 1501] which at the time of the discovery of the sea route to India was built there and dedicated to the blessed Saint Bras. Near to it is the watering place on the shore of the sea. Deeper in the bay is an islet half a league from the mainland [Seal Island], and in the channel between I found five or six fathoms of water with a clean bottom. There are in it innumerable sea-wolves, some of which are of incredible size, and some birds as large as and shaped like geese which are called penguins. These have no feathers, but wings with which they make their way, and with only these stumps of wings covered with a very fine down they go under water in such a manner that with fish they feed themselves and their young that they rear in nests made of fish bones which they and the wolves bring there. From this islet to the north-west there are some banks of sand along the shore, and north of these is a little river [at Voorbaai]. Thence two leagues, near to the entrance of the bay, there is another low opening [Great Brak River], from which the coast rises along the sea in a high land, steep and flat on top, with some reddish ravines in it. Inland the country is formed in sharp peaks, as I have stated, among which are the three of which mention has been made. At this bay, upon the top of the point of the cape [St. Blaize], I left fixed a wooden cross, and fastened to it with brass wire a tube closed with cork and wax, within which was a document as follows: 'In praise of our Lord Jesus Christ and exaltation of his holy faith, and for the service and enlargement of the kingdoms and states of Dom Sebastian the most serene king of Portugal, Manuel de Mesquita Perestrelo, who by his command came to explore this coast, placed here this cross on the 7th day of January 1576.'

Mossel Bay provides the first real shelter from the westerlies after St. Sebastian Bay. It was the original Aguada São Bras of Bartolomeu Dias and Vasco da Gama, where both stopped to replenish their water casks. As has been mentioned previously, when Pedro d'Ataide sought shelter in the lee of Cape St. Blaize in 1501 on his homeward voyage he left a message in a shoe hung from a milkwood tree, so that any other ships following might know what had happened to him. The tree still exists, and is now a national monument. João da Nova found the message when he called into the bay the same year, and during his stay he erected a small stone chapel, the first European building in South Africa. The subsequent massacre of the Portuguese by the Hottentots in Table Bay, persuaded them to avoid southern Africa completely, and there are no records of further Portuguese calls after 1509.

The first Dutch fleet to sail to the East in 1594 under Cornelis de Houtman used the bay for shelter, but it was not until the fleet of Paulus van Caerden was returning from Bantam on 8th July 1601 that the bay received its modern name. Van Caerden says:

> On July 8th we anchored in a bay since the other ship *Hof van Holland* was very leaky, her outer sheathing having been for the most part torn away by the sea, in order to careen there and repair everything. I went ashore with 20 musketeers to speak with the people and get cattle, meeting seven men and a woman, who made signs that they would get cattle for us. We found it a lovely land, without many trees, but with deer and elephants. Apart from water we got little refreshment except mussels, and therefore gave it the name Mossel Bay.

Because of its protection from the westerlies, Mossel Bay was one of the anchorages to be visited regularly by the Dutch, and in 1788, the initial shipment of wheat took place from here to Batavia. This trade ceased five years later, and the anchorage reverted to being used only on occasions when a ship required shelter, or there was a small cargo to offload over the beach. With the growth of the coastal trade in the nineteenth century, a small rubble breakwater and timber jetty were fabricated in the 1850s, to provide protection from the easterlies for the boats that serviced the ships at anchor. Trade, which until the First World War included such exotic items as ostrich feathers, had improved sufficiently to justify the building of a more substantial structure in 1861. By 1899 the breakwater needed to be lengthened and the first slipway for small craft had been constructed. Ships for Mossel Bay still anchored off the port, and their cargo and passengers were brought ashore in lighters, a practice that continued until 1959, when a third quay was enlarged so that it was able to take coasters, although larger ships, and the mail steamers, had to anchor outside. The following year, in 1960, a multi-buoy mooring system was installed two miles out in the bay for the discharge of refined oil products, and this now provides the main cargo for the port. Coastal traffic continued after the last mail steamer, the *Southampton Castle*, had sailed, but in 1987 the remaining coastal visits were suspended. The port's main business today is servicing the oil exploration vessels that are searching the continental shelf for hydrocarbons, and acting as a home for more than twenty fishing trawlers.

Perestrelo describes the coast to the east:

> Proceeding thence towards the east, the coast forms a kind of open bay, with some banks of sand along the sea, and thence onward the land is not very high, flat on top and steep, with red banks of rock along the shore, which continue for six leagues from the watering place. It terminates in a right angle, with a rock close by surrounded with water, and along it runs a little river [Kaaimans River]. Thence towards the east the land is very low along the coast, with mostly white banks of rock, though a few are red. Close to it is an islet, which is not seen unless very near it. The coast then rises constantly until a point of white sand is reached, which, when it lies to the north, has three ridges with ravines between them, and the central ridge is the largest, and has its upper slope covered with bushes, which descend nearer to the shore than on the two others [Walker Point]. Half a league from these is a sharp point with round hillocks on it, that has in front a shoal which runs into the sea a cannon shot, and thus the coast continues for two leagues, at the end of which are two great rocks not far from each other, and between them is an opening or little bay [possibly Knysna], which may be four or five leagues from Cape Talhado [Cape Seal, about eighteen miles from Knysna].

The development of Knysna, a small port about forty-five miles along the coast from Cape St. Blaize is due to an Englishman, George Rex, who came out to the Cape as the Admiralty Marshal in 1797. When the Batavian Republic repossessed the Cape, Rex lost his job but decided to remain. He took his family eastwards and bought a farm at Melkhoutkraal, near Knysna Bay. A man of obvious energy, whose name constantly appears in the story of the development of the coast, it was rumoured that he was a natural son of George III. Knysna is on a bay which has a deep river twisting between mud banks, but at the entrance are two rocky headlands between which there is a sand bar. When the sea breaks over the bar, the entrance looks thoroughly unsafe for any vessel. This presented a twin problem in the days of sail, as not only could a vessel strike the sand if she happened to be caught at the bottom of a wave whilst crossing the bar, but the wind through headlands is notoriously fickle, and can change direction with little warning, a serious hazard in a narrow channel in a sailing ship that cannot be manoeuvred quickly. In 1817, the transport HMS *Emu* was caught aback by a sudden change of wind direction whilst in the entrance and struck the rock that still bears her name. The captain attempted to save the brig by running her onto the mud banks inside the heads, but the ship was too badly damaged to be saved. Her remains can still be seen on occasion at low water springs north of Fountain Point.

Despite the sailors' natural disinclination to hazard their ships, Rex was convinced that they could cross the bar without difficulty, and in 1817 arranged for the *Podargus* to cross the bar into the river, thereby commencing the first trade. A small wooden jetty was built, and sailings became regular. Knysna swiftly replaced Plettenberg Bay as the outlet for the timber from the Outeniqualand Forest, as it was closer to the trees and provided an easier access. The Rex family dominated the port and small town until the coming of the Norwegian Thesen family in 1870.

The modern growth of Knysna owes much to the Thesen family. Captain Hans Thesen was sailing his 117-ton schooner, *Albatros*, from Norway to start a new life in New Zealand when his ship was damaged by a storm off Cape Agulhas. He returned to Cape Town for repairs, and was offered a profitable charter to carry cargo to Knysna. Seeing the opportunities, Thesen bought land at Knysna, and moved his family there in 1870. He organised a regular service with the *Albatros* and after she was wrecked in March 1874, used the brig *Ambulant*.

Thesen kept to sail until 1895, when he bought his first steamer, *Agnar*, which was joined by others, and dominated the trade with Knysna until 1921, when his company was taken over by the Houston Line. He developed shipping, shipbuilding and whaling interests, and became the owner of large tracts of the local forest. Thesens still operate a boatyard at Knysna today. The port was deregistered in 1955, and since then has only occasionally been visited by shipping, most of the trade having been taken by the railways.

The next major landing is at Plettenberg Bay, which Perestrelo knew as St. Catherine's Bay.

> Cape Talhado [Cape Seal] is in latitude thirty-four degrees [34° 05′], and has Cape Baxas to the east at a distance of seven leagues. Its mark of recognition is a point not very high, and whether seen from the west or from the east it always appears to be an island, on account of the land between it and the coast being so low for the distance of a musket shot that it does not come in sight unless one is very close to it. Thus the cape has on its face a red ledge of rock, and there is a shoal running out from it in the sea a quarter of a league, west of which and near to it is an islet [Die Eiland, actually joined to the Robberg Peninsula]. The interior has nothing of which special mention can be made, as it consists of very high lands, except that towards the east-north-east at a distance of seven leagues there is one peak among others which when seen from three or four leagues at sea off this cape has the appearance of the straw sacks in

the fields of Santaram [Peak Formosa]. It is the highest mountain of all that coast.

Along this cape on the eastern side is a great bay, to which I gave the name Saint Catherine [Plettenberg Bay]. It is a good port from the westerly winds, sheltered from the south round by the west to the east-north-east. I did not enter it, because although I took in sail at its mouth, as it was too late to go in that day, hoping to do so on the next, the east wind increased so greatly during the following night that it took from me the power to do so, as when day dawned I had been driven by it far off: but by what I could judge from outside, it is deep and clean, with a capacity for containing any fleet. I remember an old and not untrustworthy man, who affirmed that he had lain at anchor in this bay in fifteen or sixteen fathoms, with a clean bottom, and that behind the western point there is a pond, where he took in fresh water; but I did not see more than I have stated. In this locality, in forty or fifty fathoms, all the bottom is of fine sand, not very reddish.

Plettenberg Bay is another indentation in the coastline that provides shelter from the westerlies, and is seventeen miles beyond Knysna. Bartolomeu Dias called the bay Baía das Alagoas (Bay of the Lagoons). In 1630 the carrack *São Gonçalo* started to leak severely as she approached the coast on her way home. Cargo was jettisoned to keep the ship afloat and she managed to anchor at Plettenberg Bay. Efforts to pump the hold dry failed because the pumps had become clogged with pepper, and three men were asphyxiated attempting to clear the blockage. Shortly afterwards a storm blew the ship ashore, drowning everyone on board, the only survivors being the 100 or so people who had been landed earlier. They decided to construct two small boats to sail to safety, rather than take the land route. During the eight months required to build these boats, a long time even in those days, they lived ashore, erecting makeshift buildings for shelter and even a church. The site of this camp has recently been identified where the Robberg Peninsula joins the mainland. They seem to have had no shortage of food, trading with the Hottentots for cattle, catching fish, and using the ship's stores that had been washed ashore. When the boats were completed, the survivors seem to have been sorry to go, and according to their descriptions, they found the countryside fruitful and attractive. One of the boats headed towards Table Bay, and its crew was rescued by a Portuguese ship on the way, but most of these sailors may have lost their lives when that ship was wrecked within sight of their home at the mouth of the Tagus River. The other boat sailed to Delagoa Bay, which the Portuguese considered to be the safer destination because it was visited regularly by their own ships.

After the *São Gonçalo* incident Plettenberg Bay was largely ignored apart from the Hottentots, for nearly 150 years. In the latter part of the eighteenth century, the Dutch herders began to move eastward beyond Swellendam, and in about 1763 started to settle to the south of the Outeniqua Mountains. The land was markedly different from the country they had left, being heavily wooded, and with a tangled undergrowth that made travelling difficult. Their reports of this wooded country reached Cape Town, which was always chronically short of timber, most of which was still being imported from Europe, and by 1772 a woodcutters' post had been established near George, on the Swart River. The same year a navigation beacon of stinkwood was erected on Beacon Island at the mouth of the Piesangs River. By 1778 the area had become sufficiently important to warrant a visit by the Governor, Joachim Ammema, Baron van Plettenberg, who changed the name given by Perestrelo to Plettenberg Bay. It is significant that the captain of his ship, the *Katwyk-aan-Rhyn*, did not have the bay on his charts, but described it as a fine bay, the first to the east of Mossel Bay. They found that a farmer, Cornelis Botha, was already living there.

The forests included yellow and stinkwood trees, both highly prized timbers, but it was not until 1788 that the first cargo of timber was shipped out aboard the *De Meermin* under the command of the Frenchman Captain François Duminy. Captain Duminy was a loyal servant of the Dutch East India Company. He had obtained his early training as an officer in the French Navy, rising quickly to the rank of captain. During the same month that he collected the first timber from the Outeniqualand Forest, he also provided assistance for the Dutch East Indiaman *Maria*, which was driven ashore in Plettenberg Bay when homeward bound, mainly because all but five of her crew were sick with scurvy. In 1793 it was Captain Duminy who erected markers and claimed possession of Angra Pequena (Lüderitz), Walvis Bay and Possession Island, for his Dutch masters.

In 1787 the Government spent the then considerable sum of £1,000 on a special timber shed at Plettenberg (the ruins still exist), in the expectation of obtaining large quantities of easily transported timber. Unfortunately these hopes were not realised. This was in part due to the difficulty of bringing the timber down to the bay, and also because of the bay's exposure to any easterly wind.

In 1797, Lieutenant McPherson Rice, of HMS *Trusty*, who had been sent to make a survey of the coast, reported:

> This place has not been frequented by any vessels but those sent by the Dutch Company for timber. There is no fishing carried out, tho in the months of July, August and part of September, the bay abounds in whales. There is good fishing with a Hook near the reef at Cape Seal and about the ledge of the landing place.

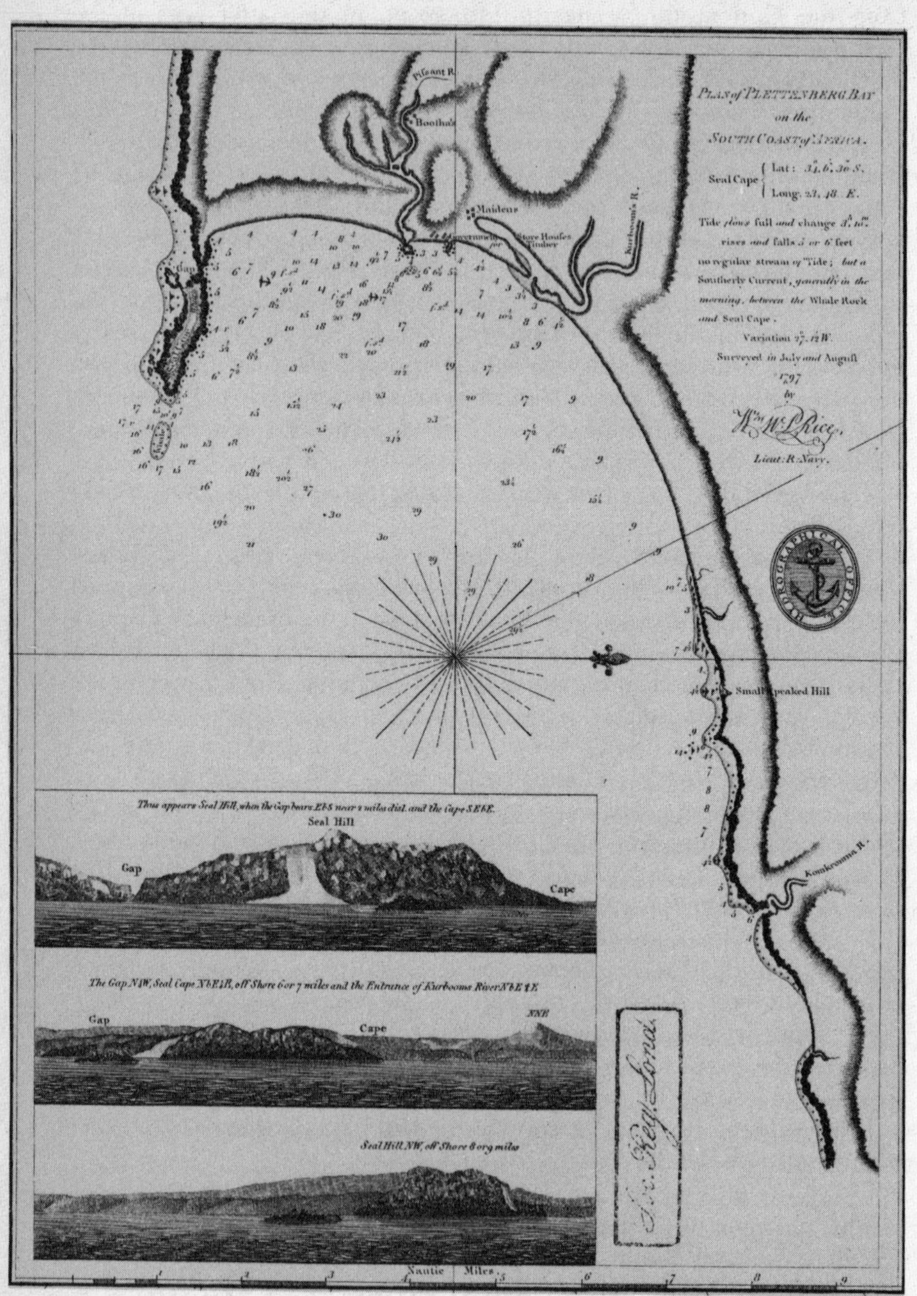

A chart of Plettenberg Bay by Lieut. McPherson Rice, RN, 1797.

> Fresh water for shipping is not convenient to be got as you have to roll the casks at least 350 yards over a heavy sand and then to raft them through a surf which generally breaks on the beach.

He makes reference to two stores belonging to the Government for receiving timber. In 1811, Captain Jones of the Royal Navy made a thorough report on the forests which he estimated to be much smaller than everyone had been given to understand, and emphasising the difficulties of extracting the good timber. He also warned again about the exposure to the easterly wind, pointing out that two small ships, the *Fanny* and *Flora*, had been wrecked in the bay in 1810. Plettenberg Bay might have been developed in a similar way to Mossel Bay, in the absence of any suitable alternative, but would have needed a large breakwater to give protection from the easterly winds. However, the opening of the sheltered harbour at Knysna, just seventeen miles to the west in 1817, gave the hinterland a much safer port. Apart from whaling, there was no requirement for another port so close by and Plettenberg Bay remained an anchorage that provided shelter from the westerlies and little more.

Whales were noted on the earliest visits to southern Africa, and many of the small ports around the coast were used as depots at one time or another. In the days before mineral oils, whales were a valuable source of oil for lighting and lubrication, and whalebone had any number of uses, not least in helping to support some of the more outlandish female fashions. Mention has already been made of the whale factory at Saldanha, but some small ports along the southern coast also supported whaling fleets and factories. In 1796 a Dutch company, the Southern Whale Fishery, went into business for a year, but finding it difficult to export their products, sold out to a British merchant, John Murray. Murray controlled the whale fisheries in Mossel, Plettenberg and Algoa Bays, and seems to have had some success, being credited with having caught between fifteen and thirty whales a season at Mossel Bay. In 1803, when the Batavian Republic took over again, three Dutchmen obtained a monopoly for whaling around the Cape, and Murray was forced to surrender all his equipment in exchange for twenty-three shares in the new Dutch company. The Dutchmen caught eleven whales in 1805, their first year of business. Whaling continued to be a small industry, operated along the coast by individuals such as John Sinclair and Cornelis Watson at Plettenberg, but the catches were not large. Watson died whilst at sea in 1899, after he had harpooned a whale from his oar-powered whaler. The whale towed the boat until long after nightfall, and then witnesses saw the boat's light extinguished. A right whale was washed ashore a week later at Cape Town with Watson's harpoon still embedded in its flesh.

In 1912 a Norwegian company announced that it was launching

operations with seven new steam whale-catchers, working from a base and factory in Knysna. Thesen and Company became the company's agent at Knysna. Huge boilers were erected on Beacon Island to render the whale blubber into oil, and catching began in the middle of 1913. Like so many other whaling enterprises, the Norwegians' had mixed luck. In 1914 a huge fire destroyed much of their Beacon Island base, and one of their catchers, the *Piesang*, was wrecked on the Knysna Bar. By 1916 the company had 16,000 barrels of oil stored in its tanks, but was experiencing great difficulties shipping the oil away, and financial problems forced it to close down in December that year. The tanks were sold to the Union Whaling Company, who had them towed round to Durban for their operations there. The Union Company was the last company to function as whalers in South Africa, and when they closed down in 1976 only the Russians and Japanese remained in a business that had become overtaken by cheaper man-made alternatives, and which was increasingly hard to justify on ecological grounds.

Perestrelo continues:

> Cape Baxas [probably Aasvogel Point in 34° 06′ south latitude] is in latitude thirty-four degrees. Fermosa Bay is to the east-north-east, at a distance of eight leagues. Its mark of recognition is a large black point rising steeply from the sea, and to anyone coming along the coast from the eastward it looks like an island. It has on its face a strip of white land which extends from the shore to the top, and there are some shoals around it which run into the sea half a league. On the eastern side is an open bay that has the appearance of being curved inward, but it is small and offers little shelter. It ends in that direction in another point of great sandbanks, but the better mark of recognition of this cape is the peak of which mention has before been made, which is almost due north of it, and to anyone four or five leagues at sea it looks low, and from it five leagues to the north-east are five very well formed domes with high sides upon the mountains. Thence the coast rises with some white and red walls of rock along the shore as far as a river which is four leagues from Point Delgada.

From Plettenberg Bay to Algoa Bay is a distance of 110 miles with no natural ports, and only one promontory, Cape St. Francis. Perestrelo named this Cape Serras, and the bay inside was called St. Francis Bay, only later did the cape become named after the bay. A number of rivers flow to the sea along this stretch of coastline, but apart from the Kromme and Gamtoos, none are navigable. The Kromme River can be navigated by small boats, and now houses a marina, and the Gamtoos changes its exit continuously as it chooses different places to break through the sand dunes in that area. The coast is made extremely dangerous for a navigator by the in-setting current, referred to by Perestrelo, which has caused a large number of casualties over the years.

Point Delgada [Klippen Point] is in latitude thirty-three degrees and rather over three-quarters [34° 11′]. It has Cape Serras [Cape St. Francis] to the east-north-east at a distance of twelve leagues. Its mark of recognition, coming from the west, is a very narrow point, and on that account I gave it this name. It ends in the sea in a small round hillock with some reefs near it, which until close by look like an islet but is not one. From it towards the mainland is a tract of sand very flat, without any verdure, which may have a length of a racecourse [this probably refers to the sand dunes inland of Klippen Point]. Four leagues before coming to the point is the river which I mentioned above, and between them is a bank of sand on the shore, which is larger in the middle than in the ends. Thence the coast becomes lower and lower, with some narrow tongues of white land running through the bush-covered soil, that look like roads, and they are in slanting direction, not up and down. This same point, to anyone running along the low coast to the eastward, has the appearance of two islets, but its clearest marks of recognition are the mountains of the interior, which appear from a great distance not only to be high and serrated with the peaks on them small and of about equal size, but to have among them one that resembles the rock of Cintra, which, besides being recognisable by its shape and height, may also be known by the five well-formed domes, of which mention has before been made, being three leagues to the westward of it. [This description would be more suitable to the coast between Cape St. Francis and Cape Recife.]

Along this point on the eastern side is Fermosa Bay [probably Slagbaai], which may be five leagues in extent. It is a good port for the west winds, sheltered towards the eastern side from the south to the north-east. The better mark of recognition in approaching it is, besides that of Point Delgada, the peak that I spoke of before as resembling the rock of Cintra. Anyone wishing to enter it should bring this peak to bear to the north, when he will be as far forward as the bay, and approaching Point Delgada to a distance of nearly a cross-bow shot, he must only take care to come to an anchor in nine or ten fathoms, where he will find clean sand. In from fifteen to twenty fathoms it is foul, and thence outwards it becomes clean again, the bottom, as the depth increases, consisting of fine sand, not very reddish. I entered this bay on the eastern side, running close along the coast, and I went out of it on the western side. Behind the anchorage place is a valley between higher lands, which all judged to be a lake, but I could not ascertain the certainty of this, because the wind blew so strong from the east that it was not regarded as prudent to send the boat away from the ship. Thence eastward stretches a sandy coast to Cape Serras [Cape St. Francis], four leagues before reaching which there is a river. [This river could be the Klipdrif or the Slang. As Perestrelo did not land, he could only note what was clearly observable from his ship.]

Cape Serras is in latitude thirty-three degrees and a half [34° 12′]. Cape Recife lies east-north-east at a distance of eight leagues. Its mark of recognition is a sharp point which ends in the sea in a small round hillock, with a shoal that runs out half a league. Four leagues before coming to it is the river of which I have just spoken, and between it and the cape is a bank of sand on the shore. Thence towards the point the land becomes lower, with some white tongues intersecting the bush-covered soil, that look like roads, so that this part presents the same appearance as Point Delgada. The only difference I found is that the sandbank is the same size throughout and not larger in the middle as the other is, and that towards the top of the bushy ground which runs from it towards the cape there are in places white spots such as are not seen at Point Delgada. On this account the better mark of recognition is the mountain of the interior, as all the ranges which are continuous from the Cape of Good Hope, and near to each other along the whole coast to this cape, terminate here, for which reason I gave it this name; and although at Cape Recife there are some peaks, they are isolated and separated from each other by a space of leagues. On the eastern side of this cape is a bay to which I gave the name of Saint Francis. It is a good port from the west winds, sheltered from the south round to the north-east. Its better mark of recognition is that of the mountains that terminate there, as I have already said, and in ending at the bay form three sharp peaks, of which that on the north is higher than the other two. Anyone who wishes to enter must bring these mountains to bear on the east, when he will be abreast of the bay, and approaching the point of the cape he must take care of the shoal of which mention has been made and anchor in fifteen or sixteen fathoms, where the bottom is clean. Within the cape, where there is a sandflat, he will find a good watering place. I did not enter this bay, as the wind was blowing strong from the east, and I had only two anchors, although I was for two days standing off and on in its mouth hoping that the weather would moderate, at the end of which I found myself at a distance from it. However, I take upon me to state what I have said as if I had seen it, because I speak the mouth of memory of Dioga Botelho Pereira, who lay here and in the bay of Saldanha [Table Bay] at anchor, and took in water, I think in the year 1539, when he came in the pinnace to this kingdom, with whom I was in close friendship, as he was my captain in the ship *Saint Benedict* the second time

> that I went to India, in the year 1549. And as his account agrees with all that I saw from the outside concerning the altitude, termination of the mountains, and sandflat, I believe that it is also correct as regards the anchorage and watering-place, which was all that remained for me to inspect. The appearances are as under. Proceeding thence, the land continues low along the sea with banks of sand, but constantly becomes higher until Cape Recife is reached.
>
> Cape Recife is in latitude thirty-three and a third. The Points of the Pillar lie almost east-north-east at a distance of fifteen leagues. Its mark of recognition is a large point with a flat shelf of rock, and some little islets around it; at a cross-bow shot from its end are some rocks on which the sea breaks. On the western side there is a flat bank of sand, and on the low coast some rocks that look like islets but are not. Between them and the cape there is a shoal near the land, and towards the interior runs an isolated high mountain covered with domes, but it is at a distance from the one at the bay of Saint Francis, nor is another to be seen to the eastward of it, because all the land thence towards the interior is formed in round-topped ridges and chains; and if there are any isolated mountains they are very different from these others.

The area around Cape Recife, which marks the southern point of Algoa Bay, has been the graveyard of many a ship, the first recorded wreck being of the Portuguese *Sacramento* in 1647 in Sardinie Bay. The *Sacramento* was a large ship for her time, and was on her maiden voyage, having been built at Bassein in India. She was accompanied by another large ship, the *Nossa Senhora de Atalaia*. Both were delayed in their departure from Goa by the need to await a shipment of guns, cast by the Bocarro family in Macao, probably the leading cannon makers in the East at the time, and did not arrive off the Cape until June, the middle of winter. On 12th June they met a great storm which separated the ships. The *Atalaia* headed into Algoa Bay, and went aground on the Rijbank. Having refloated herself she was driven north, and whilst attempting to reach Mozambique where repairs might be effected, she went ashore at Cintsa Bay. The *Sacramento*, a better found ship, continued her voyage, but whilst trying to tack close to land at night, she missed stays, and drifted onto rocks where she was quickly dashed to pieces. Only seventy-two out of a probable crew of over 400 survived, and these rested ashore for eleven days before setting out on 10th July on the long march to Delagoa Bay. In August they caught up with the survivors of the *Atalaia* and another ship, probably the *Santa Maria*, but few lived through the journey.

Some remains of the *Sacramento* must have still been visible in 1778, when Robert Jacob Gordon prepared a chart of the coast and showed a wreck at the site. He reported finding some shacks in the sand dunes, and skeletons, which he buried. He also found ebony, a carved ivory box, two rusty anchors and cannon. However, no one associated these with the *Sacramento*, whose final resting place remained a mystery until quite recently. Then in 1951 a bronze cannon was recovered close to the shore. The state of the gun made it unidentifiable, and it was thought that it might be from the Dutch corvette *Zeepard*, which had been wrecked in 1823. However, the place where this cannon was discovered was some two miles from the known site of the *Zeepard*, and tallied more accurately with Gordon's position. Two young South Africans, David Allan and Gerry van Niekerk, who had worked on the wreck of the *Meerstyn* in Saldanha Bay, took up the search in 1976, and within a short space of time found close to Gordon's site a large collection of bronze and iron cannon on the seabed. Forty of these were recovered in 1977, one of which was so well preserved that the crest of the city of Macao was clearly visible, which gave the investigators the conclusive evidence they needed to identify the ship as the *Sacramento*.

Two centuries after the wreck of the *Sacramento*, the first British steam-powered warship on the Cape station, HMS *Thunderbolt*, went aground on a reef off Cape Recife that still bears her name, but she was fortunate and was refloated, although she had to be beached in the bay for essential repairs. As recently as February 1976 the Greek-owned *Pati* hit Thunderbolt Reef, and broke up within a year, and in 1985 the bulk carrier *Kapodistrias* came ashore close by. At the end of the Second World War man added his hazards to the natural ones by dumping ammunition and mustard-gas cylinders in the sea fourteen miles south of Cape Recife. These have now been spread over a large area by the bottom currents, and are occasionally picked up by fishing boats, causing serious injury to the fishermen.

Algoa Bay was originally named Baía da Roca by Dias, but by the time Perestrelo wrote his report it had become known as Bahia da Lagoa, and subsequently Baía da Alagoa, from which its modern title stems.

> Along this cape on the eastern side is a great open unsheltered bay, which is called da Lagoa, although I had named it before the Bay of the Wolves [i.e. Seals] owing to the great number I found in it. It may have a mouth ten or twelve leagues across. Anyone who is in it will see in the interior the mountain that I have spoken of before, and south of it a peak with four or five hills. On the western side there are four islets which are called of the Cross, one of them larger than the three around it, where any ship can find shelter at all times, for the bottom is clean sand with twelve and thirteen fathoms of water. In the eastern side of the bay in the same latitude lie another two, that are called Chaos, because they are so flat that they cannot be seen farther off than two leagues. They lie along

the coast, and there is a shoal at a distance of half a league towards the south-west. The whole coast between these islets and those behind is of great banks of sand with patches of bushes, and towards the interior round-topped ridges of black ground with many small mountains. Thence towards the north-east there is a point east by north, which ends very low in the sea, with great sandflats along the shore between rows of black patches of bushes, at the termination of which is a mountain that is steep on the inland side and with an aperture in the middle. Half a league beyond is another, and in the valley between them there are some trees which look like pines and are the first that I saw along the sea from Cape Agulhas to that place. In the vicinity of these islets, seven and eight leagues from the coast, is a bank with thirty to thirty-five fathoms of water on it, and towards the shore it is deeper, at two and three leagues from it there being seventy and eighty fathoms, with a bottom of fine sand and in some places mud.

Algoa Bay, which faces south-east, and offers protection from the north round the south-west, was observed by Bartolomeu Dias in 1488, just before he turned for home. Its use was limited to short stops by vessels in need of refreshment or minor repairs for the next three centuries.

By 1754, the Trekboers had reached the bay, and were soon afterwards beginning to settle in the vicinity, thus coming into conflict for the land with the powerful Xhosa tribe, who were moving across the Great Fish River with their herds. Skirmishes became common, as was inevitable since both were competing for the same grazing land. During the first British occupation of the Cape in 1799, a small fort was built on the high ground on the north side of the River Bakens, and named Fort Frederick after the Duke of York. Designed for a garrison of 380 men, and armed with eight 12-pounder guns to protect the river approaches, this fort is one of the earliest British buildings in South Africa.

This outpost came to prominence in 1820, when it was decided to strengthen the eastern boundary of the Cape colony against the Xhosa tribe by establishing white farmers along the border. British immigration had begun soon after their second takeover in 1806 as the Government was quick to realise the advantages that would accrue from the introduction of colonists whose loyalty lay with it. About 5,000 settlers had arrived from England prior to 1820, when the total white population of the colony was approximately 45,000. In that year the English-speaking population was doubled by the arrival of 5,000 more settlers introduced to populate the Zuurveld area, subsequently named the Albany District, and provide a barrier of colonists along the Great Fish River, on the borders with the Xhosa. Many of these settlers were landed on the beach in Algoa Bay, near Fort Frederick, where the town of Port Elizabeth now stands, and were moved inland by ox waggons to start farms along the west side of the Great Fish River. Land communications at the time were dependent upon rough tracks and ox carts, and the connection between this border area and the centre of government and trade at Cape Town was slow and difficult. To improve communications, it was decided by Sir Rupert Donkin, who was the Acting Governor of the Cape in the absence of Lord Somerset, that a town should be built at Algoa Bay near the little establishment around the fort. He named the town Port Elizabeth after his late wife, and erected a pyramid in her memory overlooking the Indian Ocean, which is still standing. The town might have developed slowly, but many of the settlers, finding that the 100-acre lots of land they had been granted were either too small, or incapable of supporting agriculture, returned to Algoa Bay and swelled the numbers in the township. Those who remained in the Zuurveld were able long term to prosper by breeding sheep on larger farms by buying other lots of land, or land evacuated by the Boers who had left on the Great Trek. Wool shipments from about 1850 were one of the major reasons for the further expansion of Port Elizabeth, which by that time had become the colony's largest source of export income and was to remain so until the discovery of gold and diamonds.

In 1836 the first steam coaster arrived for service on the Cape coast and commenced operations between Cape Town and Port Elizabeth. The *Hope* was owned by the newly formed Cape of Good Hope Steam Navigation Company, which had the ship specially built at Greenock. A paddle-steamer, with two fifty-horsepower steam engines, she displaced 194 tons, and was able to carry a cargo of 115 tons plus thirty-eight passengers. Fares for the voyage varied from £7 10s. to £2, depending on whether the passenger chose to sleep in a communal cabin or on the deck. Unfortunately the *Hope* went ashore in thick fog on 10th March 1840, about ten miles west of Cape St. Francis, but all seventy-two persons aboard were saved. There was some delay in obtaining the insurance payment on the vessel, but a successor was ordered eventually. The *Phoenix* was a larger vessel of 405 tons, rigged as a brigantine but with a steam auxiliary engine. She measured 144 feet in length and could take thirty saloon passengers and fourteen in the cheaper fore-cabin. To this vessel must go the credit for establishing a regular steam coasting service between the Cape, Mossel Bay, Plettenberg Bay and Port Elizabeth between 1842 and 1852. Unfortunately the *Phoenix* never seems to have made money for the Cape of Good Hope Steam Navigation Company; her owners complained of rate cutting by the local trading schooners, and sold her to the Phoenix Steam Navigation Company in 1845 and retired from the business. For the next seven years she traded successfully, but with the arrival in 1852 of the *Sir Robert Peel*, a paddle-steamer of 233 tons, the first ship of the General Screw Steam Shipping Company, which inaugurated a service from the Cape to

Port Natal via the coast ports, she was no longer able to compete, and was sold to Australian interests.

Port Elizabeth quickly became the second most important port on the Cape coast, but no port facilities were started until 1840, when a jetty was built, but this was destroyed in a storm in 1843. In 1855 an attempt was made to construct a breakwater out into the bay to provide shelter for shipping. The area behind the breakwater quickly silted and became too shallow to use, and passengers and cargo continued to be landed onto lighters or small boats and run into the beach below the town. This could be a hazardous undertaking. Passengers were placed in a specially prepared basket, and then lifted by the derricks and swung overside into a small surfboat alongside. They then faced an often wet sail into the beach, where they were picked up and carried ashore piggy-back by porters. Cargo was often damaged or lost in the surf.

Demands by the people of the Eastern Province, and in particular Port Elizabeth, led to the Union Line extending its mail service from Cape Town in 1863. Until this time mail had taken ten days to reach the area from Cape Town after the arrival of the mail steamer from England, and the local people wanted a better service. In 1864 the first direct service from England to Port Elizabeth was inaugurated by the Diamond Line. Although the service was fast – their first ship, the *Eastern Province*, made the voyage from Falmouth in thirty-two and a half days – it soon ceased for financial reasons.

The landing situation was improved in 1881 when the north jetty was built, which provided shelter for small ships, tugs and lighters, and passengers were able to reach the shore in greater comfort and safety. The early services were run by the Messina Brothers, who had come to Algoa Bay in the 1860s from Cape Town and started work by carrying passengers and baggage ashore from the surfboats. They soon progressed to owning a boat to ferry people ashore, and when the north jetty was completed they purchased a launch and expanded their business. In a short time they were operating a tug and lighters, and dominated the lighterage of the port until 1922 when they were taken over by the Union–Castle Line. In 1873 the railway line reached Port Elizabeth and the town began to compete for the inland trade, particularly with the Orange Free State. Large ships continued to anchor out in the bay, however, and a number were wrecked as a result of strong easterlies. It was not until the completion of the Burton breakwater in 1933 that a sheltered port was created, the cruiser HMS *Dorsetshire*, flagship of the Africa Station, being the first ship to enter the new harbour which enclosed 127 hectares. The port is now South Africa's third in size, handling general cargo and ore.

Port Elizabeth's situation, at the south-east corner of the Cape and in a sheltered bay, means that it is an ideal port of refuge for ships that find themselves in difficulties along the eastern seaboard of the Cape. As recently as July 1987 the tug *Atlantic Ranger* put into port for a new towline, after she had broken her previous one and lost the barge she was towing. The captain reported winds gusting to 100 knots and seas of seventy feet, and the barge had to be recovered by the large salvage tug *Wolraad Woltemade*. In September a 96,000-ton tanker, the *Tassia*, being towed to the scrapyards, broke her towline, and after her tug had twice put into port for repairs, had to be taken on by another tug. As if this was not enough, on 27th December in mid-summer, the ill-fated ferry *Herald of Free Enterprise*, which had been salvaged after capsizing off Zeebrugge with heavy loss of life, together with the *Gaelic Ferry*, both on their way to eastern scrapyards, broke their towlines off Cape St. Francis in sixty knots of wind. Within two days the two abandoned vessels had drifted sixty miles apart, but both were recovered and taken to Port Elizabeth before continuing their journeys.

Towards the eastern end of Algoa Bay lies Bird Island, upon which the East Indiaman *Doddington* was wrecked on 17th July 1755. The twenty-three survivors of the total crew of 270 struggled ashore onto the island where they lived for the next seven months. The island is home for 30,000 gannets and a number of penguins, and was covered in guano, which must have made their living conditions appalling. To this day 500 tons or more of guano are recovered from the island each year. At the end of seven months the survivors had built themselves a small boat from pieces of wreckage washed ashore, which they christened the *Happy Deliverance*. They set sail in February 1756, and thirteen of the crew survived the voyage to Delagoa Bay where they arrived on 21st April the same year. Rumours that the *Doddington* was a treasure ship, and was carrying part of Robert Clive's wealth back to England abounded, but it was not until 1977 when the same team that had recovered the *Sacramento*'s guns began a search, that anything was found. The results of their search not only revealed the wreck, but tons of copper, guns, pieces-of-eight, and the ship's cargo. The sea had been persuaded to surrender another of its secrets.

10

The Cape Coast – Port Elizabeth to the Mozambican Border

Cape Padrone, which marks the north-eastern end of Algoa Bay, is the point at which the coast turns to the north-east in an almost straight line for 440 miles to Cape St. Lucia. The continental shelf is narrow throughout this distance, never more than twenty miles wide and frequently down to only five. The Agulhas Current flows south-westerly along the shelf at rates of up to five knots, and ships going northwards have to keep close inshore if they are to avoid this adverse set, and try to find the occasional counter-current. For the lumbering Indiamen of the seventeenth and eighteenth centuries, the passage northwards along the coast must have been a frustrating business when the wind came from the north-east. They would have to tack their way north, a long and laborious business, especially in ships that preferred to wear round as they had difficulty coming into the wind, and if they took long tacks out to sea they lost ground to the current. Until the nineteenth century there was no shelter on this coast, which became a graveyard for the East India traders of the Portuguese, Dutch and British. Eleven Indiamen are known to have gone aground in this area, but the full total may become higher as more evidence is uncovered. Surprisingly, all the wrecks took place on homeward voyages from the East, when the ships had the Agulhas Current aiding their progress. This would suggest that the major cause of shipwreck was faulty navigation, and although the outward voyage might be more difficult from a sailing point of view, it was the hazards from inaccurate charts and the inability to observe a longitude that provided the greatest danger.

Just four miles along the coast from Cape Padrone lie the Cannon Rocks, named after two iron cannons found there in the 1830s. The cannons were brought ashore in 1962, but to date no one has been able to identify their ship for certain although the *São João Batista* was wrecked in this vicinity. This site lies two miles south of Kwaaihoek, the place of Dias's *padrão* called St. Gregory. Perestrelo did not see the *padrão* on his voyage, but he describes the coastline quite well.

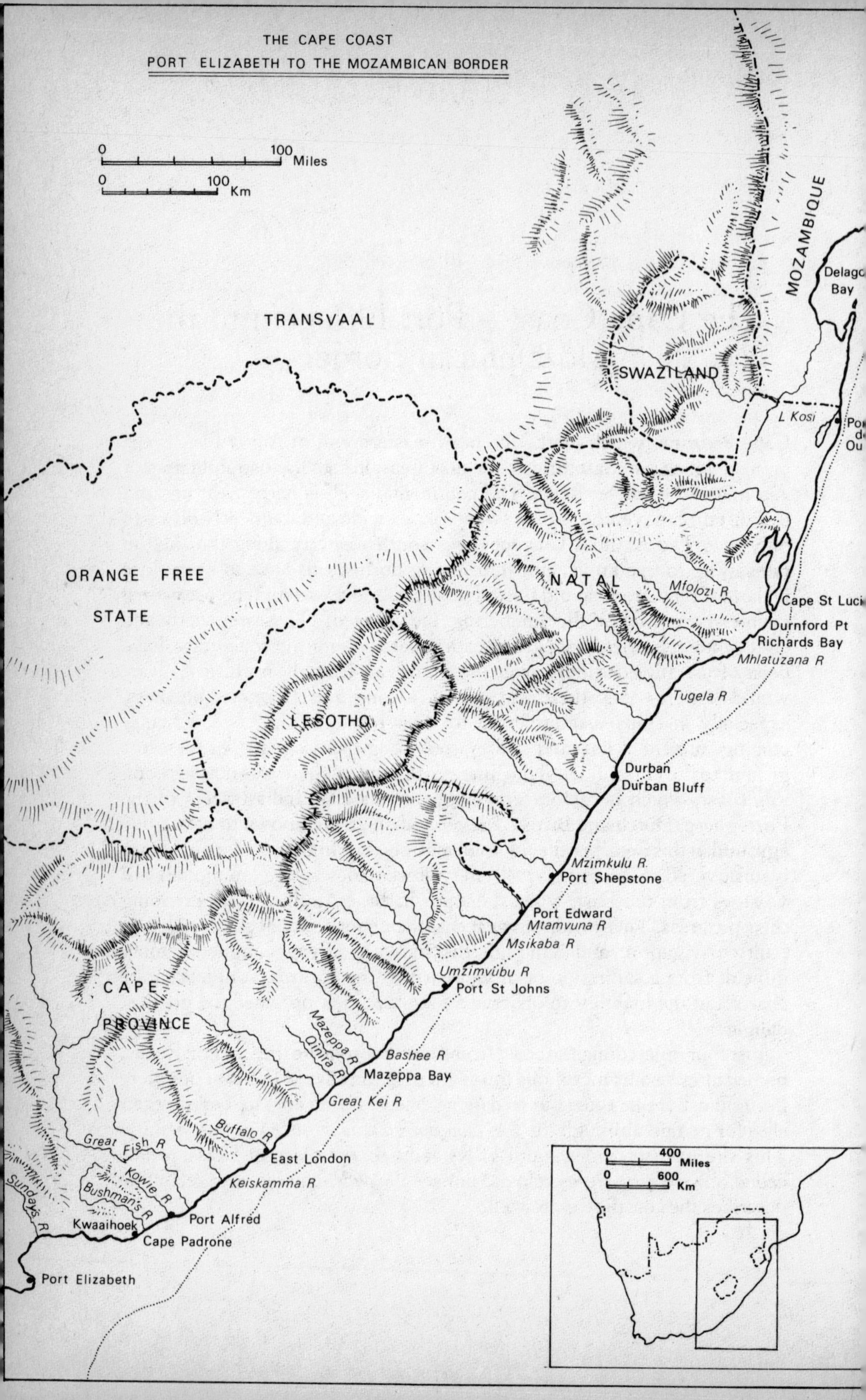
THE CAPE COAST
PORT ELIZABETH TO THE MOZAMBICAN BORDER
0
100 Miles
0
100 Km
TRANSVAAL
MOZAMBIQUE
Delago Bay
SWAZILAND
L Kosi
ORANGE FREE STATE
NATAL
Mfolozi R
Cape St Luci
Durnford Pt
Richards Bay
Mhlatuzana R
Tugela R
LESOTHO
Durban
Durban Bluff
Mzimkulu R.
Port Shepstone
Port Edward
Mtamvuna R
Msikaba R
Umzimvubu R
Port St Johns
CAPE PROVINCE
Mazeppa R
Qinira R
Bashee R
Mazeppa Bay
Great Kei R
Buffalo R
Great Fish R
East London
Kowie R
Bushman's R
Keiskamma R
Sundays R
Port Alfred
Kwaaihoek
Cape Padrone
Port Elizabeth
0
400 Miles
0
600 Km

> The Points of the Pillar [Dias's Cross] are four leagues east of the islets Chaos, in latitude thirty-three degrees. The first part of the Land of Natal lies north-east at a distance of twenty-five leagues. Its mark of recognition is two points of sand rising steeply from the sea, with a flat patch of bushes above, and close by is an islet shaped as under [drawing missing] which may be as large as a caravel. This is probably the place where the pillar called Saint Gregory stood, which Bartolomeu Dias set up when he was exploring that coast by order of the king Dom John the second, for it is stated that he left it fixed in an islet between the Chaos and the river Infante, in which locality there is no other, and therefore I gave it this name. A league from these points towards the north-east the coast forms another projection also covered with bushes, and beyond it in the round-topped ridges is a long and narrow strip of verdure different from the other around, which runs down from the top direct to the sea, where there are some shoals close to the land. Passing thence, a solitary large wide-spreading tree is seen upon the top of the ridges of the interior, and between it and the sea are some white patches. Towards the east the whole land along the coast consists of banks of sand, and towards the interior of round-topped ridges between green patches of meadow decked with trees that look like oaks. Eight leagues before reaching the river Infante [Msikaba River] some low openings are seen on the coast, and three leagues farther are some rocky banks, near which is the rock that is called Of the Fountains, which is a rock with a cleft in the middle, and it looks like an islet but is not one. All the land above is very green, with some trees scattered about.

Perestrelo gives the distance from Bird Island, one of the 'Islets Chaos', to Dias's *padrão* as four leagues, or twelve and a half miles, whereas it is in fact eighteen miles. Whatever the difference, the description was sufficiently accurate for Colonel R. J. Gordon to use it to find fragments of the original cross in 1778. The *padrão*, erected on 12th March 1488, was on a small ninety-five-foot-high headland called Kwaaihoek, and the remains were collected in 1938 and reassembled, and now lie in the entrance to the Cullen Library of the University of the Witwatersrand. A replica was erected at Kwaaihoek and the latest, made in Portugal, was put in position on 12th March 1988.

Between Port Elizabeth and Port Alfred a number of rivers empty into the Indian Ocean, the most notable being the Bushman's River, which is too shallow for anything but small craft. Port Alfred was christened Port Frances in 1825 by Lord Charles Somerset, but the name was changed in 1860 to Port Alfred in honour of the visit of Queen Victoria's second son. It lies at the mouth of the Kowie River, almost seventy miles from East London, and at the halfway point between Port Elizabeth and East

London. The Kowie River is navigable by small craft for seventeen miles from its entrance, but in those early days the entrance was restricted to small vessels on account of the shallow bar. One of the 1820 settlers, William Cock, who had been running small sailing ships up and down the coast, decided that if the course of the river could be altered so that the river flowed more directly to the sea, a natural scour would keep the entrance deep enough for larger ships. He obtained permission for his experiment from the Government, and is reputed to have spent £70,000 of his own money on the task. The existing entrance was blocked and a new one excavated using Hottentot labour. William Cock decided to purchase a steamship to improve the service between his new port and Cape Town, and in 1842 took delivery of a small paddle-ship, the *Sir John St. Aubyn*. On her first voyage she made the journey in five days, a considerable improvement on the previous service, but only five months later she grounded at the entrance to the Kowie River whilst towing the sailing vessel *Sophie* into the port, and became a total loss. The misfortune seems to have put paid to Cock's ambitious and adventurous plans.

The expansion of settlement in the interior brought the port a new lease of life, and in the late 1850s a new company was formed to develop Cock's project, with aid from the Government. A special tug, the *Volunteer*, arrived from England in 1861 to assist ships into the port, and a number of local coastal services were established, including those of Mr G. H. Payne, who used small sailing vessels until he bought the steamer *Ripple* in 1873. Between 1875 and 1889 the ships of the Union and Castle Lines made regular calls, but were obliged to anchor off the entrance. The arrival of the mail steamer was always a major social event in Port Alfred, with people coming into the town just for the occasion, and the ship provided free breakfasts and luncheons to those who came on board. As the railway system developed in the Eastern Province, it gave the hinterland served by Port Alfred a more efficient service, and the latter lost its trade to the larger ports of East London and Port Elizabeth. A number of plans were formulated to use the harbour, but nothing came of them, and today it is used mainly by pleasure craft. The entrance, which lies between two breakwaters, has a sand bar with depths of only three feet at low water, and dangerous breakers.

Fourteen miles to the north of Port Alfred lies the entrance of the Great Fish River, and the Keiskamma is ten miles beyond. Like most of the rivers along the coast, both have shallow entrances, and cannot be used by anything but small craft. The American ship *Hercules* is supposed to have gone ashore close to the Keiskamma River mouth in 1796, but the position has never been properly established. Some confusion was caused by the finding of guns on the beach in the vicinity, which were thought to have come from the *Hercules*, but more recent evidence suggests that these guns were discovered in 1783, before the *Hercules* was lost, and pottery found in the area is from an earlier time. If this is the case, the wreck near the Keiskamma is from another unknown Indiaman, and the site of the *Hercules* has yet to be found.

The earliest reports of the Buffalo River, twenty-six miles north of the Keiskamma, come from the Portuguese accounts, and later from Dutch survivors of the *Stavernisse*, which went ashore in 1686 about forty miles south of Durban. Nineteen of the crew were rescued by the *Centaurus* in 1687 from a point about seventeen miles north of the Buffalo River, which was known as the Eerste River by the Dutch at that time.

The site of the town of East London at the mouth of the Buffalo River was first claimed by Lieutenant Baillie, late of the Royal Navy and one of the 1820 settlers, in 1836 when he hoisted the Union Jack at Signal Hill. Baillie had persuaded Sir Benjamin D'Urban, then Governor of the Cape, that the river mouth might provide a more suitable landing point for supplies and troops for King Williams Town and Fort Beaufort during the Xhosa war, as it lay closer than Algoa Bay. Shortly afterwards a 142-ton brig, the *Knysna*, owned by John Rex, son of the founder of Knysna, was sent under the command of Captain John Findlay to survey the area. He named the anchorage Port Rex, and having conducted a reconnaissance lasting seven weeks, during which the *Knysna* rode out two gales, returned to Cape Town. The departure of Sir Benjamin D'Urban, and a reversal of British policy for the area, led to no further action taking place until the seventh frontier war ten years later, when the need for a port closer to the scene of action was recognised. A part of the 73rd Regiment was dispatched, and started work building a small outpost, Fort Glamorgan, on the west bank of the river entrance. On 14th January 1848, an area for two miles around the port was annexed to the Cape, and the name was changed to East London in 1848 by the Governor, Sir Harry Smith.

A small jetty had been constructed in 1847, and two years later a little township had formed. This town expanded rapidly after the decision to resettle German veterans of the Crimean War, who had fought in the British German Legion, in what was then known as British Kaffraria, now the areas of Griqualand East, Tembuland, Transkei and Pondoland, in order to stabilise the border with the Cape Colony. In all nearly 3,000 immigrants arrived in the area, but over 1,000 were sent to fight in India during the Indian Mutiny, and only 386 returned. As most of these immigrants were males, the Government sent out 1,600 females, mainly from Ireland, to provide wives and encourage the men to settle. In 1858 and 1859, a further 2,315 German immigrants, mainly families, were brought in from Hamburg under a Government contract, giving further growth to the town. The absorption of British Kaffraria into the Cape Colony in 1865 led to increasing competition with Port Elizabeth, and the year before, in 1864, the first Union Liner paid a call when the *Norman* anchored off the port. However, there was no regular service until 1876, mainly because the bar prevented large ships from entering the river which provided some shelter, and they had to anchor outside in the open roadstead. To take the cargo ashore, lighters were hauled out to buoys moored in the bay, and then warped alongside the anchored ships. The process was dangerous in a swell, and on average this system could only be worked about eighteen days in each month. Passengers were disembarked by the same uncomfortable methods used at Port Elizabeth until the introduction of the Castle Line's special tender *Dolphin* in 1883.

Although some improvements were made to the original stone jetty of 1847 and a lighthouse was built in 1856, the real development of the port began in 1872, when the breakwater was begun. A year later work started on the Queenstown railway, completed in 1874, which marks the beginning of modern communications with the interior. The railway was extended until 1892, when East London was finally connected to the main system, thus opening up the whole of the Orange Free State and the Transvaal as well as the Eastern Cape, to the port's facilities.

The breakwater of 1872 enhanced the shelter and made it safer for smaller ships, but it was not until 1886, when a steam dredger was delivered and began to remove the siltation at the river entrance caused by the Buffalo River, that most shipping could be guaranteed the safety of alongside berths within the port. The harbour required constant dredging and as the size of ships grew, the depth of water had to be increased. The 8,000-ton 'D'-class Union–Castle ships were unable to enter until 1914, and when the new *Arundel Castle* arrived in 1921, not only was she too large to enter, but the weather conditions made it impossible for her to discharge either cargo or passengers into lighters or tenders, and they had to be taken on to Port Elizabeth. However, work began on a turning basin in 1927, and by 1937 improvements to the port allowed the larger ships access on a regular basis. In October 1937 the *Warwick Castle* of 20,000 tons was the first of the very big ships to be docked alongside. The port was able to give alongside berths to all Cape shipping until the introduction of the even larger mail ships in 1959, when the turning basin had to be expanded. With 7,700 feet of alongside quay space, East London is the Republic's fourth largest port and serves the Eastern Cape, Transkei, Basutoland, and part of the Orange Free State. The port has a substantial dry dock, the Princess Elizabeth Graving Dock, opened in 1947 by Queen Elizabeth II before she came to the throne, which is capable of taking vessels over 600 feet in length.

Thirty-four miles north of East London lies the Great Kei River, the modern boundary between the Eastern Cape Province and the state of Transkei, the home of the Xhosa. The coast from here north to Durban is known as the wild coast, for its lack of shelter and the many wrecks that have taken place along its length. Even today, there are a number of modern vessels to be seen, seemingly intact, where they have been driven onto the shore by the waves. Going back in time, about five miles north of East London lies the Qinira River where Chinese porcelain has been found. This would indicate an East Indiaman, probably Portuguese, and the only vessel thought to have gone ashore in that area was the *Santa Maria de Deus* in 1643, possibly at Bonza Bay. The sole supporting evidence is that of the survivors' accounts from the *Nossa Senhora de Atalaia*, the consort of the *Sacramento*, which, having refloated herself from Algoa Bay, was found to be leaking so badly that she was run ashore, with about 200 of her crew managing to get to the beach. This crew encountered survivors from the *Santa Maria* who four years previously had walked some distance from the south, before deciding to settle. Some of the *Santa Maria*'s crew joined the new Portuguese party but others chose to remain and were no doubt absorbed into the Bantu tribes or died. The evidence points to the wreck of the *Santa Maria* being south of the position of the *Nossa Senhora de Atalaia* which went ashore in 1647 at Cintsa Bay, south of the mouth of the Great Kei River.

A complete report on the loss of the *Atalaia* was written by a passenger, Feyo, and is included because it graphically describes the typical conditions aboard a ship in difficulties at the time.

> We all took to the pumps, and found the water increased: and a great storm that rose next day contributed to this. We sailed with our fore storm sails, the sea running so high and the ship pitching so heavily that we expected her to part amidships every hour, the waves rising over the lantern and masts, so that the Fathers were obliged to relieve each other in the stern every hour and continue blessing the waves, for if they desisted for a moment we were overwhelmed. [This refers to the custom of priests blessing each wave as it approached the ship so that it would not cause damage.] The under pilot, who was at the helm, was almost drowned by a wave, and shouted for assistance, being alone, for we were all at the pumps. Our bodily strength was almost gone with the strain of working them, in which the religious and passengers never faltered. [. . .] At daybreak the large hatchway was opened, and the water was found to be above the ballast. Then barrels were diligently prepared to be filled with buckets; but it proved useless, for in less than two hours the water increased so much that with the pitching of the ship the barrels filled of themselves. Then the pipes in the hold and the bales of pepper gradually burst, so that the pumps ceased working altogether, being choked with pepper. [. . .]
>
> In this danger the ships prow sank as if she was broken backed, she

would not obey the helm as before, the water was already over the coamings of the lower hatches and the prow more than two spans deeper than the lower deck. We spent two days and two nights in this imminent peril without seeing land, and then we observed at daybreak the point of a ridge thickly wooded, which appeared to be the mouth of a river with a very long sandy beach, and a great bay where it seemed we could land with the boat dry shod.

It was determined in counsel that on account of the state of the ship we should run her on shore, throwing the artillery into the sea, but this was not done, being beyond our strength, and only two pieces were thrown overboard. With a favourable wind but a rough sea we unfurled the main topsail, which went to pieces as we hoisted it, and so did the fore topsail; and the spritsail was all torn, and the foresail had many seams open; then we tried the mainsail, and as we secured it with the tack, fixing a tack-tackle to assist it, it went to pieces.

At this time the Captain had already ordered the gunner, Francisco Teixeira, to put some powder and balls into a barrel, and to collect all the arms that he could and all the copper and bronze for the maintenance of the camp, as this is the current coin of Kaffraria, that we might trade for what was necessary. That night was spent at working at the buckets, and the Kaffirs were already on shore with great fires alight. The next day, the 3rd July, in the morning we set about preparing the boat to land some of the people should the sea permit. The wind rose, and raising the anchor we went ahead with foresail set, and cast anchor in the bay in seven fathoms. The master ordered the main halliards to be cut, and the yard lay across the middle of the deck, that being cut into pieces it might serve some to get ashore.

They were unable to land that day, and during the following night the ship grounded and damaged her rudder. The next day, however, they started to row people ashore, using a surf line attached to the ship to steady the boat through the waves. Others were being brought ashore when a Chinese member of the crew cut this line, and fifty people drowned. The boat was wrecked, and those left aboard the *Atalaia* were drowned when the ship eventually sank at her anchor. The survivors spent some time organising themselves for the walk to Mozambique, and then embarked on a journey that must have been as strange and terrifying as walking on the moon might be to a person today. The groups from all three Portuguese ships arrived at Delagoa Bay in one party, as the *Sacramento* crew had come across the others somewhere in northern Zululand. Only 124 Portuguese and thirty slaves were alive by this time, out of a probable total complement from the three ships of about 1,500 souls.

The *Atalaia* crew have left us with a mystery from their land journey during which they discovered the remnants of a boat on a beach. It has been suggested that this might have belonged to the *São Thomé* which sank in 1589, but this seems unlikely. The *Atalaia* survivors even thought that the party they encountered might be from this boat, until they realised they were from the *Sacramento*, and this would indicate they believed the boat to be fairly new. One would have expected the seamen amongst them to have known immediately whether the boat was wrecked recently or had been ashore a long time from its state and if, as is inferred, they thought the boat looked comparatively new, it must have come from some other unknown vessel.

A few miles north of the Great Kei River lies Mazeppa Bay, named after the coaster that used to land cargo through the surf in the 1930s. Five miles south, near the mouth of the Cebe River, is one of the possible wreck sites of the *São Alberto*, which went ashore in 1593, although Bell-Cross thinks that the porcelain near the Qinira River marks the correct position, whilst others would have the Hole-in-the-Wall, about forty miles further north again.

The loss of the *São Alberto* in 1593 was caused by the familiar problem, a leaking ship. However, this time Nuno Velho Pereira, the Captain Major of the homeward fleet, was on board, and was made of sterner stuff than most captains. He personally went down into the hold to fill casks with bilge water to help pump the ship and encourage the others to keep at the work, and when the ship closed the land, he had matchlocks and other useful items placed where they could be easily recovered. The account talks of the rudder striking the bottom in eight and a half fathoms and being ripped away, and the ship grounding in eight fathoms; since this would mean that the ship had a hold depth of at least forty-eight feet, the figure is an obvious exaggeration! The ship struck the coast somewhere south of Mazeppa Bay, and broke up. Some of those aboard panicked and threw themselves into the sea, but others, led by the captain, stayed aboard the separated poop and forecastle and eventually drifted ashore. Of the total crew of 347 on board, 285 reached the beach in safety. The captain had studied the experiences of the survivors from previous ships, and instead of taking the usual route along the coast which had cost so many lives, he chose to go inland. Whether it was his better control and discipline, or his route was safer, the result was that only eight Portuguese died on the journey to Delagoa Bay, and many of the ninety-five slaves who failed to arrive had deserted during the march to join the local tribes. Few groups of shipwrecked crews came through their ordeal in such good order, which says a great deal for the wise and firm leadership of Nuno Velho Pereira. He returned home aboard the *Cinco Chagas* the following year, and led the defence of the ship against a squadron of English ships under the Earl of Cumberland in the Azores. One of only thirteen survivors of the fight, he and the captain were taken to England and released a year later after paying a ransom.

Port St. Johns lies at the mouth of the Umzimvubu River, eighty-six miles up the coast from the Great Kei River and 130 miles south of Durban. Although it is the only port in the Transkei, it hardly deserves the title, as a shallow bar effectively blocks the entrance and the bay has silted. The name possibly comes from the appropriate saint's day on which the Portuguese first sighted the port, but another theory is that it came from the galleon *São João*, as it was originally thought that she had been wrecked here. The *Nossa Senhora de Belem* came ashore at the mouth of the river in 1635, and met survivors of the *São Alberto* and *São João*. The captain beached the ship when his pumps became clogged with pepper and he was unable to stop a leak. The survivors made a stockade within which they lived in small huts for seven months whilst they built two small boats, rather than face the rigours of a march. They had no shortage of provisions, bartering iron fastenings from their wreck with the local Bantu for food. Both the small boats tried to head west, and one succeeded in reaching Angola, having not dared to stop at the Cape because of the danger from the Dutch. The other boat was driven back by the westerly winds and turned north-east and landed in Mozambique.

The first ship known to have entered the Umzimvubu River over the bar was the schooner *Rosebud* in 1846, and for a while Port St. Johns was known as Rosebud Bay. The territory was a part of Pondoland until 1878, when HMS *Active* crossed the bar and the port was ceded to Britain. In 1884 the port and the area around it were annexed to the Cape Colony. Coasting vessels called from time to time, but the last occasion the bar was crossed was by the *Border* in 1944. Plans have appeared from time to time to reopen it, but as the silt increases, they become less likely to be attempted.

Perestrelo describes the next part of the coast with feeling, since he had had the misfortune to be shipwrecked there in 1554. He begins with the river Infante, but this should not be confused with Dias's river of the same name, as Perestrelo used the names that were in use at his time, nearly 100 years later.

> The river Infante is in latitude thirty-two degrees and a half [Perestrelo could mean the Msikaba River at 32° 19′, but he might be referring to the Buffalo River]. Its mark of recognition is its being high and rocky in the interior, with both its banks steep, and thus it enters the sea. Above, between it and a bushy patch, there are some large trees. The bar is deep, but not sufficiently so for passing ships to cross it. It runs from north-west to south-east. On the south-eastern side there is a reef or rock from which some shoals project into the sea a cross-bow shot. It was there that we ran aground with the ship *Saint Benedict* [*São Bento*] in

> the year 1554, in which ship came Fernam Alvares Cabral as commodore of the fleet. On the north-eastern side the shore is sandy, and the interior consists of mountains with forests. Eight leagues beyond this river is another too small for ships to enter, which is called Saint Christopher, and it also enters the sea between high rocks. Near to it are three islets close to the shore, two of them peaked and connected with each other, the third flat and at a distance. In this locality, four and five leagues from the land, there are not more than forty to fifty fathoms of water with a bottom of coarse red sand and in some places rock.
>
> The first point of the Land of Natal is in latitude thirty-two degrees. The last point is to the north-east inclined to the north, at a distance of forty-five leagues. Its mark of recognition is a great rocky point, and anyone being four or five leagues at sea will observe a grove of large trees in the interior, and when this lies to the north-east, above it three small mountains are visible. Thence a league towards the north-east is another forest which runs down to the sea, and above it a bare ridge and three other mountains larger than those behind. All this land which is called Natal is high, and has patches of sand along the sea. Most of the shore is rocky, and there are reefs. It has no ports. There are in it some rivers, but none capable of receiving large ships. All the sea is deep and clean, only there is a little islet very near the coast. The interior consists of green ridges and many patches of forest, between which there are also in some places wild olive trees, and in the valleys and low lands watercress, water parsley, and other herbs of this country. The appearance of the land for the greater part is high and fruitful, and thus it is well peopled and contains a great variety of animals tame and wild. After this manner the whole coast continues to the last point, which is in latitude thirty degrees.

There are four recorded wrecks, all of which took place before 1782, on the next fifty miles of coastline. A fifth vessel, the Portuguese *São Espirito*, was lost somewhere on the Natal coastline in 1608, but the exact position is currently unknown. The Portuguese used the term Natal to describe the coast well to the south of the present Natal Province, and although survivors reached Mozambique in a boat, their descriptions are not clear. The British East Indiaman *Grosvenor* went ashore south of the Msikaba River in 1782, the Portuguese *São Bento* was wrecked at the mouth of the same river in 1554, and the Dutch Indiaman *Bennebroek* somewhere in the same vicinity. Only recently has the site of the earliest of these wrecks, the Portuguese *São João*, been established just to the north of Port Edward from the remains of pottery and a cannon found there.

The *São João* was homeward bound from India in 1552, but her voyage had been delayed, and it was not until May that she reached South African waters. She ran into the almost inevitable bad weather at this time of year, and soon lost her sails and mainmast and had her rudder damaged. Knowing that they could not possibly round the Cape, the ship turned back and headed towards the coast, leaking severely. The condition of the ship deteriorated rapidly during this time, and the crew was eventually forced to cut away the foremast to try and reduce the leaking. The ocean-going ships of the period were not very manoeuvrable at the best of times, and their high superstructures aft meant that they tended to turn into the wind when no sails were set. Without the foremast, the ship would have swung into the wind, and there would have been no method left to the crew to turn her off wind again. When they cut away this mast, the crew must have realised that the ship was leaking too badly to reach Mozambique and there was no hope of saving the cargo. The best that they could hope for was to reach land before the ship sank under them and try to save as many of the crew and passengers as possible. In this state she drifted towards land, which was sighted on 8th June. Attempts to reach the shore were frustrated when both the ship's boats were overturned, and the ship drifted onto the rocks. Accounts of the wreck state that nearly 500 people managed to struggle ashore through the surf, and then, after a few days during which they bartered some of their ironwork for a cow with the local Bantu peoples, they set off in a column for Delagoa Bay. Only twenty-two survived the march, the others dying from starvation or in skirmishes with the natives. These lucky survivors were eventually picked up by another Portuguese ship that had stopped to trade for ivory, and they passed down the first accounts of the country and its people.

The survivors of the *São Bento* wrecked in 1554 took the same route. The *São Bento* hit a small rocky islet near the entrance to the Msikaba River and cannons and pieces of Chinese porcelain have been found in the vicinity. On their way north they reported passing the remains of a wreck, almost certainly the *São João*. Only twenty-four of the crew out of the 320 who had managed to struggle ashore arrived at Delagoa Bay, the rest having died or decided to join native settlements. On their long march, which took sixty-nine days, they met people from other wrecks living contentedly with the Bantu peoples, who could not be persuaded to leave. Unfortunately, there is no record of which ships these 'colonists' had come from, and only three ships are known to have been wrecked up to this time, one to the west of Mossel Bay in 1504, the *São João de Biscainho* in 1551 which disappeared, and the *São Jeronimo* in 1552. The mystery of these people has yet to be solved.

The Mtamvuna River, forty-six miles north of Port St. Johns, marks the northern boundary of the Transkei, and nowadays ribbon development extends from the river along the coast to Durban. In the middle of this area, twenty-four miles from the border, lies Port Shepstone, at the mouth of the

Mzimkulu River. The port operated for just twenty-one years from 1880, when the first coaster crossed the bar, until 1901, when the railway link with Durban was completed. Some fishing boats still function, but fine weather is essential for crossing the bar. The remainder of the coast as far as Durban has no ports as such, and somewhere along it in 1686 the Dutch Indiaman *Stavernisse* went ashore. The only position given was latitude 30° 28′ south, which coincides with Ifafa Beach, but there is no way of knowing if this is accurate.

The next major navigational mark for the Portuguese was Point Pescaria, which is not clearly identifiable from Perestrelo's text.

> Point Pescaria lies north by east, at a distance of twelve leagues. Its [i.e. the last Point of Natal] mark of recognition is a point not very large which on the western side has some walls of rock and banks of sand on the coast, and anyone passing it must keep to the east-north-east or west-south-west, because this Land of Natal has three points, to wit, the two already mentioned and another almost in the middle, the coast between these capes forming open bays. Point Pescaria is in Latitude twenty-nine degrees and a third.

If Perestrelo is right in his latitude, and he subsequently states that the point is fifteen leagues, or forty-six miles, south by west of Point St. Lucia, then Point Pescaria lies somewhere in the vicinity of the River Tugela. We do not know if he took an actual observation to obtain the latitude, or whether he based this position on his dead-reckoning. However, his other description indicates that the point is south of Durban, or that Point Pescaria is Durban Bluff itself. The explanation could be that since Perestrelo was sailing from the north, he experienced a considerable set from the Agulhas Current which he did not notice when calculating his dead-reckoning. Therefore his distances from Cape St. Lucia underestimate the true distance by as much as a half. In this case, Point Pescaria would be in the vicinity of the Bluff.

The Bluff is one of the most conspicuous points on the Natal coast and lies just to the south of the entrance to Durban Harbour. Its name indicates that the Portuguese found good fishing there, but this is not uncommon off the points on the coast, where the fish, including very large and quite edible barracuda, are frequently caught from a vessel trolling at between five and seven knots.

Durban Harbour, or Natal Bay as it used to be called, is a large sheltered lagoon, about eight square miles in area. Originally it was shallow and swampy, with mangroves growing around its shores, and was impassable to all but small ships until a channel was dredged through the bar in 1892.

Nowadays the bay is surrounded by the quays and industry of South Africa's largest port, and little remains of the lagoon shore.

The first recorded Europeans to live on the bay for any length of time were a group from the British East Indiaman *Good Hope*, which was wrecked near by in May 1685, but survivors from other earlier vessels may also have lived here. In 1686 part of the *Stavernisse* crew were visited by two Englishmen, who were living in the bay with at least seven others from the *Good Hope* and a small British twenty-ton ketch, the *Bonaventura*, which had floated into the lagoon at St. Lucia in 1686. There is also a possibility that some of these men were from the *Johanna*, another British ship wrecked in 1683 near Delagoa. Nine of the Englishmen and eleven Dutchmen from the *Stavernisse* built a small boat in Natal Bay and sailed to Cape Town. We do not know how many remained behind, but seven of the crew of the small boat were from the *Johanna*, whereas when she grounded her crew was ten in number.

The Dutch East India Company ship *Noordt* called at Port Natal in 1689 during her search for the *Stavernisse* crew, and collected three more survivors who had made their way there overland. Whilst anchored, the captain of the *Noordt*, on instructions from Simon van der Stel, bought the Bay of Natal and a surrounding area of land from a local headman for a few trifles. It is unlikely that the headman realised what he was giving away, but, in any case, the Company did not follow up their purchase.

The Natal coastline was avoided when possible by Europeans until the 1820s on account of its lack of shelter and the mixed reports on the attitude of the local natives to shipwrecked crews. In 1822 Captain Owen, RN, made a survey of the coast from Delagoa Bay southwards and reported favourably on the country. As a result, in 1824 a small party of English and Boers, with some Hottentot servants, led by James King and Francis Farewell, arrived at Port Natal to establish an agricultural community. The Boers soon moved out, but the others remained, having come to an arrangement with the Zulu king, Shaka, whereby they were granted all the land around Port Natal. These people organised themselves as small traders in ivory, sending their produce back to the Cape in coastal trading ships. Their hold on their base was tenuous, and dependent upon the good will of the Zulu kings, but the settlement grew with new European arrivals and refugees from the cruelties of Shaka and Dingane, so that by 1835 there were thirty Europeans and 2,500 Africans living around the base. In the same year the name of the settlement was changed from Port Natal to D'Urban, in honour of the Governor of the Cape.

The year 1837 saw the arrival of the first Voortrekkers, many of whom hoped to stay and use Durban as their access to the outside world. The death of Piet Retief and the Zulu attacks on Europeans led to the burning of the small settlement, the people only escaping with their lives because they were able to flee aboard the *Comet* which was anchored in the harbour. The arrival of 100 troops stabilised the situation and two weeks later the Battle of Blood River, in which a small party of Boers soundly defeated a Zulu army of over 5,000, put a temporary end to the Zulu menace and the settlement became safe to inhabit again. Shortly afterwards the Voortrekkers made their own enclave near the British village at Congella.

They were soon established and proclaimed their independence of the Cape as the Natal Republic with Durban as its seaport. However, their activities against the local tribespeople caused concern to the British Government in the Cape as it threatened the Cape's eastern frontier. No doubt the British were also worried that the Boers might become allied with an unfriendly foreign power and thus menace the whole Cape Colony, and so were not at all enthusiastic about the Boers having a deepwater port. To obtain control, 250 troops were sent to Durban in 1842 under Captain T. C. Smith. They were quickly besieged by a large force of Boers in the small fort and British shipping in the bay was captured. Reinforcements took some time to arrive, but eventually part of the 27th Regiment was taken from Port Elizabeth by the coastal schooner *Conch*, whose captain had crossed the bar before. The captain, William Bell, who was later to become Port Captain at Durban, found that many of his crew reported sick once they discovered where they were going, but the offer of thirty-six lashes apiece quickly restored their health! After awaiting favourable weather to cross the bar, during which the frigate *Southampton* arrived with elements of the 25th Regiment, the entrance was forced, and the troops landed. The troops under Colonel Josias Cloete quickly reversed the situation, and the Boers soon voted to accept British rule. Natal became a detached district of the Cape Colony in 1845.

Soon most of the Voortrekkers left Natal for the Republics in the Orange Free State and the Transvaal, and some 5,000 British settlers came out to replace them between 1849 and 1851. Just as the arrival of the 1820 settlers gave the impetus to the development of Port Elizabeth, so these new immigrants gave Durban the population necessary for its growth. Its situation, as the sole port between East London and Delagoa Bay, made it the only outlet for Natal, and well placed to handle trade from both the Boer Republics.

Usually ocean-going ships visiting Durban had to anchor off the harbour entrance on account of the bar of shallow water. Small ships could cross, but it was a hazardous undertaking as the depth could be as little as four feet at low water, and most preferred to risk the anchorage even though it was dangerous in onshore winds. The *Phoenix* had visited Durban in 1850 but the first steamship to cross the bar was the General Screw Steam Navigation Company's vessel *Sir Robert Peel*, on 15th August 1852, captained by John Boxer, later captain of the Union Line's *Celt*. In

1854 two sister ships of 500 tons were built for the trade, the *Natal* and the *Cape of Good Hope*, but were withdrawn from the service at the end of the year when the General Screw Steam Navigation Company went out of business. The *Cape of Good Hope* was purchased later by the Calcutta and Burmah Steam Navigation Company, the forerunner of the British India Steam Navigation Company, and was the first vessel they put into service.

Steamer services became less reliable for a few years after the demise of the General Screw Steam Navigation Company, until John T. Rennie brought out the *Madagascar* and *Waldensian* in 1857. These two vessels received a mail contract to collect mail from the Union Line steamers in Cape Town and carry it to Durban, thus re-establishing the regular sea connection with Cape Town. Unfortunately neither lasted very long, the *Madagascar* being wrecked off the Beka River in 1858, and the *Waldensian* near Struis Point in 1862. Another vessel that commenced a service to Durban at this time was the small steamer *Zulu* owned by Lamport and Holt. After the loss of the *Waldensian* the Union Line decided to enter the coastal trade with what they termed their 'Intercolonial service' connecting Cape Town with the ports along the coast as far as Delagoa Bay. A special shallow-draught steamer, the *Anglian*, designed to cross the Durban bar, was built in 1864, and the company's original five mail ships were transferred to the service at the same time. Not surprisingly, the Union Line was awarded the Natal mail contract in 1865.

Durban's growing importance in the 1860s can be judged by the number of shipping companies that were offering direct services from England. John T. Rennie had begun direct trade in 1858, and was soon followed by the White Cross Line, owned by two former ship's captains, Messrs Bullard and King. The White Cross Line changed its name to Bullard and King in 1869. Both these companies relied on sailing vessels until 1879, when each introduced steamers, and their sailing ships were phased out of service. However, their steamers were built deliberately small enough to be able to cross the bar, and avoid the inconvenience and danger of transhipping, a factor that made both popular on the Britain–Natal service. In the early days of the port, ships generally berthed at Congella or the Point, the end of the spit of sand that extends southward from the centre of Durban town to the entrance to the harbour. In 1860 these two townships were connected by South Africa's first railway.

Landing cargo and passengers at Durban was a dangerous operation until the bar was effectively dredged. Until the arrival of the baskets, used elsewhere on the coast, passengers were battened below in lighters and hauled from the roadstead, across the bar, into the harbour. Occasionally the lighter would ground, and the poor unfortunate people below would be thrown about by the surf until it could be refloated. The passage through the surf became safer with the arrival of Southern Africa's first tug, the

Pioneer, in 1860. Eventually both the Union and the Castle Lines built special light-draught coasters to cross the bar, the former's *Union* arriving in 1879.

The expanding settlement in Natal was threatened twice in 1879 and 1880, firstly by the Zulus and secondly by the Boers. Reinforcements to fight the Zulus, which included Scottish soldiers, were rushed to Natal. It was said that when the Zulus heard that soldiers wearing kilts had landed at Durban, they assumed that they had killed so many men at Isandhlwana, that the British had had to resort to sending their women to fight for them! The strengthened British army inflicted a crushing defeat on the Zulus, led by Cetewayo, at the Battle of Ulundi on 4th July 1879.

Within months of the removal of the Zulu threat, the Republican Party in the Transvaal, led by Paul Kruger, rebelled. Small parties of British troops, which had been stationed over the veld, could not be consolidated before the Boers attacked. After a bitter battle at Majuba Hill, a peace treaty was signed on 22nd March 1880, which led to the independence of the Transvaal five months later. The short war, the First Boer War, had been a remarkable success for the untrained Boer army against disciplined troops, but was regarded as a betrayal by most British and loyalists in the Cape and Natal, who had wanted the defeat at Majuba revenged by General Roberts and 10,000 troops who were on their way to South Africa, before concluding any treaty.

The regular direct mail steamers from England did not start calling at Durban until 1887, when the Union Line extended its terminal from East London. Not to be outdone, Currie's Castle Line followed the next year, but neither company's mail ships were able to cross the bar, and had to anchor off, a very uncomfortable business as the ships rolled unceasingly in the Indian Ocean swell. It was obvious that the development of the port was conditional upon providing access for deep-laden ships. When Harry Escombe became Chairman of the Harbour Commissioners in 1880, he made this his first priority. An attempt had been made in the 1850s to build a breakwater from the Bluff, but this had failed, largely because of lack of funds. This time a long breakwater was constructed 2,000 feet out to sea from the Bluff, and another from the Point. Dredging between the breakwaters commenced and slowly the depth of the entrance channel increased. By 1892, the intermediate mail ship *Dunrobin Castle* of 2,820 tons and drawing 17′ 2″ was able to enter, and the problem was considered solved finally in 1904 – when the *Armadale Castle*, at 12,975 tons, one of the largest ships in the world at the time, successfully entered the harbour and berthed alongside a quay. Since that date, the harbour and entrance have expanded so that they could take greater-sized vessels as they were built, but the entrance to the port can still be extremely dangerous in high seas.

Durban developed in area and importance as its links with the hinterland were improved with the building of the railways, particularly the connection with Johannesburg in 1896, but it was threatened again in 1899 by the outbreak of the Second Boer War, which caused very considerable concern for the safety of the port and the whole of Natal. The initial Boer advance against the thinly spread British troops might easily have captured Durban if the Boers had not been distracted by the defence of Ladysmith. Reinforcements were rushed to Natal including HMS *Powerful*, which landed her guns and mounted them on hurriedly constructed gun carriages, which, manned by sailors, were sent to help in the battle for Ladysmith. Shortly afterwards Captain Percy Scott in HMS *Terrible* arrived and set up twenty-eight guns drawn from a total of five warships to protect the approaches to the town. The gravity of the situation can be grasped when it is realised that both the *Terrible* and *Powerful*, which had arrived at full speed from England and China respectively, were amongst the most powerful cruisers afloat at the time. They displaced 14,200 tons, the tonnage of a contemporary battleship, and could run at an average of twenty knots almost indefinitely. Their heaviest armament was the 9.2-inch gun, but it was their smaller 4.7-inch guns that were in use at Ladysmith, although some of their 6-inch guns were landed for later operations.

Well before the Boer Wars, Natal had been developing its own products, the most important of which was sugar, grown using imported Indian labour. The two World Wars drew heavily on these products and upon Durban's port services. Durban has the advantage of having a very narrow entrance which made it easy to seal against submarine attacks. It was used extensively by troopships taking the Cape route round to reinforce the Allied armies in Egypt and India, and few of those soldiers will forget the 'Lady in white' who used to sing to the ships as they sailed away.

Until the 1960s there were still shipping links with India and other places on the east African coast, and a number of small coasting companies served the coast from the port, including African Coasters, Rennies, Smiths Coasters and Durban Lines. Only Unicorn Shipping still operates. This is an amalgamation of some of the smaller companies with African Coasters, which has a fleet of modern ships, including container and Roll-On/Roll-Off vessels. Durban today has six miles of quays, including specialised container berths, refrigerated berths for fruit, and grain and sugar terminals. The sugar silos are capable of storing half a million tons at a time. Apart from being South Africa's largest and busiest port, it also has an expanding naval base, Southern Africa's largest graving dock with an extreme length of 1,194 feet, and the major part of its shipbuilding industry.

To the north of Durban, the coast largely comprises rock cliffs interspersed with sandy beaches, cut in places by rivers, none of which are navigable. Port Durnford, at the mouth of the Mhlatuzana River, seventy-seven miles up the coast, was named after Colonel A. W. Durnford, RE, who was killed at Isandhlwana. It featured again at the end of the Zulu War when the Zulu chief, Cetewayo, was taken from Port Durnford to Simon's Town by the steamer *Natal.* The Portuguese ship *São Jeronimo* may have come ashore close to the river mouth in 1552, where survivors of other wrecks saw the remains of a great ship. However, there is no evidence, and she could easily have been one of the others that disappeared on the *Carreira da India*, such as the *São João de Biscainho* which vanished in 1551. The Mhlatuzana River mouth did not lend itself to development and Port Durnford has never been more than an open anchorage. It is hardly used at all now, the river has silted up, and just six miles to the north lies the new port of Richards Bay which has ample scope for expansion to handle any foreseeable increase in local trade.

In the 1960s, the need for another deep-water port on the Natal coast was recognised, and the site chosen was Richards Bay, named after Commodore Sir F. W. Richards, RN, who was involved in a survey of the coast, and landed troops there for the Zulu War in 1879. The lagoon inside the sand dunes along the coast is formed by the Umhlatuzi and Nsezi Rivers and has a water area of 3,050 hectares. Work commenced in 1972, with dredging operations, the building of two large breakwaters either side of the entrance, and the construction of a berm which effectively seals off the southern third of the lagoon. This has been designated a nature reserve. Originally designed to handle bulk cargoes, Richards Bay is now the largest coal terminal in the world, and is capable of taking ships of up to 165,000 tons.

Twenty-two miles north of Richards Bay lies Cape St. Lucia, the point at which the coast turns north for Delagoa Bay. Perestrelo's description is quite recognisable.

> Point Saint Lucia lies north by east [of Point Pescaria] at a distance of fifteen leagues. Its mark of recognition is a point not very high, with small rocky ledges, and in the interior there is another larger one behind that on the coast, with many white patches. From it towards the north-east the coast forms banks of rock. Between this point and that of Saint Lucia there is a small open bay, having little shelter.
>
> Point Saint Lucia is in the latitude twenty-eight degrees and a half. The land of Fumos lies to the north-east inclined to east at a distance of thirty leagues. It has no mark of recognition of which mention can be made, except a low point covered with bushes, that runs down to the shore, which by anyone running past it is seen to project farther into the sea than the adjoining land. Between it and the point of the Land of Fumos are the rivers of Saint Lucia and the Banks of Gold, in the locality of which there is a bank a league from the coast with not more than fourteen and fifteen fathoms of water on it, the bottom being of large

> gravel and broken shells, and farther seaward of the black sand with some shellfish among seaweed. The river contains much water, as it is connected with a lake which it makes inland, with three others of good size, and with some swamps which continue for several leagues. The bar is not very deep, and runs almost east and west. On the south-western side there are some shoals, which extend into the sea a cannon shot. The coast is low, and the shore consists entirely of sand banks.

Seven miles beyond St. Lucia lies the Mfolozi River, and the entrance to a wildlife park in a series of lagoons known collectively as Lake St. Lucia. These lakes have at times held both hippopotamus and sharks together, and although a tree-planting programme threatened this unique ecosystem because of the trees' requirements for water, the problem was recognised, and hopefully the park will survive. The river mouth is now shallow, and takes little but small ski-boats, but it must have been deeper in 1686 when the twenty-ton ketch *Bonaventura* went ashore inside the river mouth. The crew had landed whilst they waited for high water to refloat their vessel, and whilst they were away, the rising tide freed the ship and carried her into the river where she grounded again. This time she would not be refloated, and the crew had to abandon her and make their way to Port Natal.

From the Mfolozi River the coast is low-lying sand and rock points ninety-seven miles to Ponta do Ouro, the international boundary between the Republic of South Africa and Mozambique. Somewhere along this coast the survivors of the *São Thomé* came ashore in a boat in 1589. The ship herself sank off the coast, and a full report of the loss was made by Diogo do Couto, the official record keeper in Goa. The problem was the not unusual one of lack of maintenance, in this case too little attention being paid to the caulking between the hull strakes or planks. The ship started to leak when close to the island of Diego Rodriguez. The flapping of the sails against the foremast created sufficient vibration to shake out some of the caulking near the fore chains, the place where the shrouds supporting the mast are made fast to the ship's hull. This was successfully repaired. However, a few days later when the ship was in the latitude of the south of the island of São Lourenço (Madagascar), and estimated to be 300 miles from the African coast, a much more serious leak developed near the stern post. Cargo was removed to examine the situation, and it was found that the water was coming in fast enough to push away a man's hand, and even lead tingles which had been nailed over the seam were forced away from the timbers. The hole was stuffed with anything suitable and the leaking reduced.

The voyage was continued until the wind turned west-south-westerly on 11th March, and the ship's head was set to the north. The rolling before a following sea loosened the caulking again, and everyone on board was put to the pumps, whilst the course was altered towards the land, which was sighted on the 16th. Immediately the ship's boat was hauled out and launched, and over 100 people placed on board. Much to the disgust of those left behind, who had expected it to remain close by so that if the ship sank it could guide rafts to land, the boat pulled away. However, it was overloaded, and the officers were asked to choose six people to be pushed overside to lighten the load. The unfortunate victims were thrown into the sea and disappeared. The boat found that it could make little headway, and drifted back to the ship, hoping to return some of the people. On the ship meantime, the main deck was now awash and discipline had broken down. Everyone was far too busy praying or wailing to construct rafts. Since the boat could not offload any of its crew to the ship, further Portuguese and slaves were thrown into the sea. As the boat started to row towards land again, the ship gave a lurch and disappeared beneath the waves. The ninety-eight people who eventually landed burned their boat to obtain iron for barter with the natives but few lived through the march to Sofala. The survivors took thirteen days to reach Delagoa Bay, which indicates that their landing site was close to Hully Point.

It is fitting to end with a wreck, since it is an apt reminder of the dangers faced on the Cape coast by so many mariners over the centuries. The Portuguese discovered the way round the Cape right at the beginning of the era of long-distance trading voyages and it became the dominant point on voyages between the North Atlantic nations and the East, and possibly the wealthiest of all sea routes. Yet for more than half this span of time the coastline was largely unexplored, and although other areas have suffered greater shipping casualties, none were as remote, and few have achieved so much respect from seamen.

Selected Bibliography

Allen, G. & D., *The Guns of Sacramento*, Robin Garton, London, 1978

Axelson, E., *Dias and his Successors*, Saayman & Weber, Cape Town, 1988

The Portuguese in South-East Africa, 1488–1600, Struik, Cape Town, 1973

The Portuguese in South-East Africa, 1600–1700, Witwatersrand University Press, Johannesburg, 1960

Bell, Wm., *Entrance of the 'Conch' at Port Natal*, Adams & Co, Durban, 1869. Reprinted G. Christison, Pietermaritzburg, 1988

Bennett, J. A., *The Divided Circle*, Phaidon, Oxford, 1987

Blake, G., *B.I. Centenary*, Collins, London, 1956

Boorstein, D. J., *The Discoverers*, Random House, New York, 1983

Boxer, C. R., *The Tragic History of the Sea*, Hakluyt Society/C.U.P., Cambridge, 1959

The Dutch Seaborne Empire, Hutchinson, London, 1969

From Lisbon to Goa 1500–1750, Variorum Reprints, London, 1984

Brock, B. B. & B. G., *Historical Simon's Town*, A. A. Balkema, Cape Town, 1976

Burman, J., *The Bay of Storms*, Human & Rousseau, Cape Town, 1976

The False Bay Story, Human & Rousseau, Cape Town, 1977

Strange Shipwrecks of the Southern Seas, Struik, Cape Town, 1968

Burman, J. & Levin, S., *Saldanha Bay Story*, Human & Rousseau, Cape Town, 1974

Clarke, J. D., *The Pre-History of Southern Africa*, Penguin, London, 1959

Costa, F. da, *Roteiro da Africa do Sul (Manuel de Mesquita Perestrelo)*, Lisboa Agencia Geral das Colonias, Lisbon, 1939

Davenport, T. R. H., *South Africa*, Macmillan, London, 1977

Davidson, B., *Africa in History*, Granada, London, 1974

Davis, M. & M., *A Victorian Shipowner*, Cayzer Irvine & Company, London

Fairbridge, D., *A History of South Africa*, O.U.P., London, 1918

Green, L., *Harbours of Memory*, Howard Timmins, Cape Town, 1982

Hall, M., *The Changing Past*, David Phillip, Claremont, Cape, 1987

Herodotus, *Histories*

Howarth, D. & S., *The Story of P & O*, Weidenfeld & Nicholson, London, 1986

Africa Pilot, vols II & III, Hydrographic Dept, The Admiralty, Taunton

South African Sailing Directions, Hydrographic Office, South African Navy, Silvermines

Kimble, G. H. T., *Esmeraldo de Situ Orbis (Duarte Pacheco Pereira)*, Hakluyt Society, London, 1937

Kirby, P. R., *The True Story of the Wreck of the 'Grosvenor'*, O.U.P., 1960
Ley, C. D., *Portuguese Voyages 1488–1680*, J. M. Dent & Sons, London, 1947
Lubbock, B., *The China Clippers*, Brown, Son & Ferguson, Glasgow, 1973
Lubke, R. A., Gess, F. W., & Bruton, M. N., *Field Guide to the Eastern Cape Coast*, Wildlife Society of South-Africa, Grahamstown, 1988
Maggs, T., *Great Galleon 'São João'*, Natal Museum, 26 (1), Pietermaritzburg, 1984
Mitchell, W. H., & Sawyer, L. A., *The Cape Run*, Terence Dalton, Lavenham, Suffolk, 1984
Motley, J. L., *The Rise of the Dutch Republic*, Swan Sonnenschein, London, 1894
Murray, M., *Ships and South Africa*, O.U.P., London, 1933
Union Castle Chronicle 1853–1953, Longman, London
Pack, S. W. C., *Anson's Voyage round the World*, Penguin, London, 1947
Parry, J. H., *The Discovery of South America*, Paul Elek, London, 1979
Payne, E. J., *Voyages of Elizabethan Seamen*, O.U.P., London, 1907
Picard, W. W. J., *Masters of the Castle*, Struik, Cape Town, 1972
Raven-Hart, R., *Before van Riebeeck*, Struik, Cape Town, 1967
Ravenstein, E. G. A., *Journal of the First Voyages of Vasco da Gama*, Hakluyt Society, London, 1898
'The Voyages of Diogo Cão and Bartholomeu Dias, 1482–88', *The Geographical Journal*, London, 1900
Solomon, V. E., *The South African Shipping Question*, Historical Publication Society, Wynberg, Cape, 1982
Storrar, P., *Portrait of Plettenberg Bay*, Centaur, Johannesburg, 1983
Drama at Ponta Delgada, Lowry, Johannesburg, 1988
Sutton, J., *Lords of the East*, Conway Maritime Press, London, 1981
Taylor, J., *Ellerman's – A Wealth of Shipping*, Wilton House Gentry, London, 1976
Theal, M. G., *History of South Africa*, Swan Sonnenschein, London, 1897–1904
Villiers, S. De, *Robben Island*, Struik, Cape Town, 1971
Wexham, B., *Shipwrecks of the Western Cape*, Howard Timmins, Cape Town
Whiting Spilhaus, M., *The First South Africans*, Juta, Cape Town, 1949
Willcox, A. R., *Shipwreck and Survival on the South-East Coast of Africa*, Drakensberg Publications, Natal, 1984
Wilson, M. & Thompson, L., *A History of South Africa to 1870*, David Phillip, Cape Town, 1982
Woollard, C. L. A., *The Last of the Cape Horners*, Arthur H. Stockwell Ltd, Ilfracombe, Devon, 1967

INDEX

Index